Romans:
Made Easy for the Layman

Harold F. Hunter, Th.D.

Trinity Academic Press

Trinity Academic Press

World Wide Web: Trinitysem.edu
Email:Contact@trinitysem.edu

©1990 by Harold F. Hunter. Edited for 2015 publication by Braxton Hunter

All rights reserved. No part of this publication may be reproduced, stored in a retrieval system, or transmitted in any form or by any means – electronic, mechanical, photocopy, recording, or any other – except for brief quotations in printed reviews, without the prior permission of the author.

All Scripture quotations taken from the King James Version of the Bible.

ISBN-13: 978-0692565964 (Trinity Academic Press)
ISBN-10: 0692565965

Printed in the United States of America

*For my wonderful grandchildren,
Ollie, Millie, Jolie, and Jaclyn Isabelle*

Table of Contents

THE RIGHTEOUSNESS OF GOD	1
THE MORAL, RELIGIOUS SINNER	29
JUSTIFICATION INTRODUCED	43
JUSTIFICATION CONTINUED	57
JUSTIFICATION CONTINUED	73
SANCTIFICATION INTRODUCED	87
UNION WITH CHRIST	105
DELIVERANCE AND ASSURANCE	119
THE SOVEREIGNTY OF GOD	145
GOD'S PLAN FOR RIGHTEOUSNESS	161
THE BLINDNESS OF ISRAEL	171
THE PERFECT WILL OF GOD	187
THE CHRISTIAN AND CIVIL GOVERNMENT	201
CONSECRATION INTRODUCED	209
CONSECRATION CONTINUED	221
PAUL'S BENEDICTION	235

Chapter One

The Righteousness Of God

It has been a joy for me to have the gracious privilege of studying God's Word rather diligently for a quarter of a century. Each page has never failed to yield an abundant harvest of sweet spiritual fruits for delicious contemplation. I have marched down the judicial corridors of the five books of law (Genesis, Exodus, Leviticus, Numbers, Deuteronomy); I have been led into exciting adventures in the books of history (I and II Samuel, I and II Kings, I and II Chronicles, Ezra, Nehemiah, Esther); I have lolled in the lush meadows of the books of poetry (Job, Psalms, Proverbs, Ecclesiastes, Song of Solomon); I have listened with rapt attention to the oratory of the major prophets (Isaiah, Jeremiah, Lamentations, Ezekiel, Daniel); I have winced upon hearing the straight talk and warnings of the minor prophets (Hosea, Joel, Amos, Obadiah, Jonah, Micah, Nahum, Habakkuk, Zephaniah, Haggai, Zechariah, Malachi); I have walked with Jesus down the dusty paths of Galilee with the writers of the four gospels (Matthew, Mark, Luke, John); I have sailed away on the first missionary journeys in the New Testament's book of history Acts); I have gone to the classroom of Paul for his lectures on church policy and doctrine (Romans, I and II Corinthians, Galatians, Ephesians, Philippians, Colossians, I and II Thessalonians, I and II Timothy, Titus, Philemon); I have watched with keen interest the reaction of the Lord to the attempts of recently-saved Jews to combine grace and works in His letter to them (Hebrews); I have been convicted by teachings about personal responsibility (James); I have been comforted by lessons on God's concern for the suffering as we near the end of the age (I and II Peter); I have been madeaware of Satan's seductive attempts to steal my victory (I, II, and III John); I have been chillingly informed of the threat of false teachers (Jude); I have been swept away on the wings of glorious anticipation as I look for the Lord's return (Revelation)! But of all these masterpieces from the world's greatest library, I am convinced that the Book of Romans stands tallest in practical and eternal value because in it are given essays on the five major Christian doctrines which are:

(1) Condemnation;
(2) Justification;
(3) Sanctification;
(4) Glorification;
(5) Consecration.

No other Bible book spells these fundamental doctrines in such orderly, yet succinct, fashion. All of these doctrines together comprise the gospel of God; and really, that is indeed the theme of the entire book. Not only is the gospel the theme, but it is also the subject of the key verse in the book: "For I am not ashamed of the gospel of Christ: for it is the power of God unto salvation to everyone that believeth; to the Jew first, and also to the Greek" (Romans 1:16). Before we move to our verse-by-verse exposition of the book, I think it would be good for you to understand the major divisions of Romans as based upon the five doctrines. Also, I will include a thumbnail description of each of these vital Christian teachings.

The doctrine of condemnation is discussed by Paul in Romans 1:18-3:20. This doctrine is God's statement that all mankind is guilty before Him and is totally depraved—to wit, that man can do absolutely nothing to save himself. Condemnation is the result of the work of man in Adam by which the entire human family was infected by the sin nature.

The doctrine of justification is laid before us in Romans 3:21-5:21. This doctrine is God's statement that man need not stay under the sentence of condemnation. It maintains that man may be saved so thoroughly from the penalty of sin that even the taint of sin is removed from his life so that he is viewed by God as absolutely righteous. Justification is the work of Jesus Christ who died at Calvary that we might have life in Him.

The doctrine of sanctification is outlined in Romans 6:1- 8:39. This doctrine is God's statement that the man who is saved is destined to become exactly like the Lord Jesus Christ. Sanctification is the work of the Holy Spirit who day by day is correcting and encouraging the saint as he works through this world from salvation to heaven.

The doctrine of glorification is presented in Romans 9:1- 11:36. This doctrine is God's statement that He is sovereign, working His will for both the nation of Israel and the household of faith. Glorification is the work of God the Father as He brings to successful conclusion His divine plan for the ages.

The doctrine of consecration is shared in Romans 12:1- 15:33. This doctrine is God's statement that the man who is saved is expected to live a life of self-control and holiness before the Lord. Consecration is the work of man as he removes his own human restraints from his life in order that God may have complete control.

The first seven verses of chapter one reveal for us Paul's estimation of himself. These verses constitute the introduction to the Book of Romans:
1 Paul, a servant of Jesus Christ, called to be an apostle, separated unto the gospel of God.
2 (Which he had promised afore by his prophets in the holy scriptures,)
3 Concerning his Son Jesus Christ our Lord, which was made of the seed of David according to the flesh;
4 And declared to be the Son of God with power, according to the spirit of holiness, by the resurrection from the dead:
5 By whom we have received grace and apostleship, for obedience to the faith among all nations, for his name:
6 Among whom are ye also the called of Jesus Christ:
7 To all that be in Rome, beloved of God, called to be saints: Grace to you and peace from God our Father, and the Lord Jesus Christ.

Paul begins by identifying himself as a "servant of Jesus Christ." The word, "servant," comes from the Greek word, "doulas," which carries the meaning of bondage. Paul perceives himself as being bound to Christ. The desires of Christ are to be his own desires; the goals of Christ are to be his own goals. This statement applies to every follower of Jesus. We are His! He owns us! We have no personal rights! We are a bond servant to Him! "What? know ye not that your body is the temple of the Holy Ghost which is in you, which ye have of God, and ye are not your own? For ye are bought with a price: therefore glorify God in your body, and in your spirit, which are God's" (I Corinthians 6:19-20). Anytime you hear some person say that he "knows his rights," mark him well. Either he is not saved or he has a very poor understanding of his servant relationship to Christ. If that man was ever saved, his rights were, at that point in time, given over to the Lord Jesus Christ. Therefore, he no longer has any rights; they all belong to Jesus! Second, Paul affirms in verse one that he was called. Serving Jesus Christ is not a choice one makes as he might in the consideration of an entrance into a business or a profession. Many times the Bible makes reference to a divine call in relation to salvation and service. We are told in I Corinthians 1:20 to ". . . abide in the same calling." In Philippians 3:14, we are exhorted to press toward the mark of the " . . . prize of the high calling." In II Thessalonians1:11, we are to walk " . . . worthy of this calling." In II Timothy 1:9, we are advised that God " . . . called us with a holy calling." In Hebrews 3:1, we are made". . . partakers of the heavenly calling." In II Peter 1:10, we are warned to " . ..make your calling and election sure."

Dear reader, have you been called of God to salvation? Can you recall an actual time and place when you responded to that call? No issue in life is more important!

Third, Paul presents himself as " . . . an apostle." This title may apply in a very broad sense to anyone who is directed by the Holy Spirit into some specific task. It simply means, in its original definition, "one who is on a divine mission." You may never have noticed that "apostle" also is one of the many titles for Christ: "Wherefore, holy brethren, partakers of the heavenly calling, consider the Apostle and High Priest of our profession, Christ Jesus" (Hebrews 3:1).In the broad definition of the term, therefore, all of us who are saved may also be "apostles"—we are "on a divine mission" to glorify God before an unbelieving world.

In the stricter sense, the term more directly applies to those who had physically seen the Lord. We know this to be the case because of the requirement of apostleship laid out by Peter as the twelve were choosing a replacement for Judas, who had betrayed the Lord and subsequently hanged himself: "Wherefore of these men which have companied with us all the time that the Lord Jesus went in and out among us, beginning from the baptism of john, unto that same day that he was taken up from us, must one be ordained to be a witness with us of his resurrection. And they appointed two, Joseph called Barsabbas, who was surnamed Justus, and Matthias . . . and they gave forth their lots; and the lot fell upon Matthias; and he was numbered with the eleven apostles" (Act 1:21-23; 26). In these verses, the clear qualifications of apostleship are outlined. We have modern churches who designate certain people in their memberships as apostles. Their support verse for this practice is Ephesians 4:11: "And he gave some, apostles; and some, prophets; and some, evangelists; and some, pastors and teachers." Please read carefully! He did not give "all" churches; the Lord gave "some" churches. Not all churches were to receive all of the positions named in this verse. In fact, only the first church could, and did, have within its ranks of spiritual leadership each of the positions listed in Ephesians 4:11. If we are to believe the qualifications for being an apostle set forth by Peter before the selection of Matthias, which we must, then it is evident that the position of apostle in the church exists no more. We have no one now living who walked with Christ or met him personally while the Lord was here on earth.

Paul called himself an apostle. How could this be? We have no record of his being with Christ during the three years of our Lord's ministry. Nonetheless, Paul is identified as an apostle, and the reason is given in I Corinthians 15:8-9: "And last of all he was seen of me also as of one born out of due time. For I am the least of the apostles that I am not meet to be called an apostle, because I persecuted the church of God." From these verses, we now understand Paul's designation as an apostle. He was a witness to the fact that Christ had been literally, physically, raised from the dead.

Does this mean that with Matthias, Paul, and Judas there were thirteen apostles in all? Possibly, but I think not. It is my conviction that Paul was God's choice to fill the vacancy caused by Judas' death, instead of Matthias. Somehow, it does not seem in harmony with the unique nature of the call of the other apostles that Matthias should be chosen by the casting of lots. It is also interesting that after his selection, we hear no more of Matthias while we hear much of Paul and his ministry. Matthias, in my estimation, was man's hasty choice; Paul was God's deliberate choice.

A fourth thing we learn of Paul in Romans 1:1 is that he was …separated unto the gospel of God." No other matter beat in the heart of Paul with such intensity as did the glorious news of salvation that had just recently been made possible for all mankind through the death, burial, and resurrection of Jesus. The theme of his life and the theme of this book is the gospel of God.

This gospel, according to Paul in verse two, had long been anticipated and promised by the prophets of the Old Testament era. This is an amazing Bible fact! The very gospel of Jesus Christ was preached as early as Abel, the son of Adam and Eve. That remarkable truth is shared in the following verses: That the blood of ALL THEPROPHETS, which was shed from the foundation of the world, may be required of this generation; from the blood of Abel unto the blood of Zacharias. . . " (Luke 11:50, 5l).Please note that Abel is listed as a prophet. Now continue in Acts 10:43: "To him give all the prophets witness, that through his name whosoever believeth in him shall receive remission of sins." What an extraordinary discovery! All the prophets, beginning with Abel who was slain by Cain, preached the same fundamental message of salvation that is proclaimed by multitudes of faithful preachers today! Paul recognized that there had been many before him who had steadfastly looked toward the coming of Jesus into the world as a mediator between the unholiness of man and the holiness of God.

Paul continues his discussion of the prophets' witness by speaking of " . . . Jesus Christ our Lord, which was made of the seed of David according to the flesh." The authoritative stamp of Christ's messiahship is made by the apostle as he relates Jesus to David. Why is this so important? The covenant made to David ("the Davidic Covenant") is one of the most important contractual statements between God and man. It is found in II Samuel 7:8-17 and promises David four blessings:
A "house": a continuing family on earth;
(2) A "throne": an authority of royalty;
(3) A "kingdom": an unending place of rule;
A perpetual time": an eternal throne.

The fulfillment of this promise is in Jesus who will one day sit on the throne of David in the Millennial Kingdom. An objection is often raised by the suggestion that since Israel rejected Jesus as her messiah, this covenant with David was made null and void. We must remember that there are two kinds of divine covenants in the Scriptures. We have the bilateral which is dependent upon the faithfulness of both parties, and we have the unilateral which is dependent upon the faithfulness of only one party. The covenant with David was unilateral. God made the covenant as a promise to David, and that promise was made unconditionally. As long as there is time in God's universe, this covenant will be binding upon the Lord.

The Davidic Covenant's greater completion will be in the Lord Jesus, as mentioned already. Read the words of Gabriel, the angel, as he announced the soon-occurring birth of Jesus: "And, behold, thou shalt conceive in thy womb, and bring forth a son, and shalt call his name Jesus. He shall be great, and shall be called the Son of the Highest: and the Lord God shall give unto him the throne of his father David: and he shall reign over the house of Jacob forever; and of his kingdom there shall be no end" (Luke l':3l- 33). Not only do these verses confirm God's plan for Jesus as heir to the throne of David, but we have other substantiating verses of Christ's relationship to that ancient king of Israel. In the first chapter of Matthew is recorded the family tree of Jesus through Joseph, the Lord's earthly foster father, and this genealogy runs back to David through Solomon: "And Jesse begat David the king; and David the king begat Solomon of her that had been the wife of Urias" (Luke 1:6).

The family tree of Jesus through his mother Mary is recorded in Luke 3 and runs back to David through his son, Nathan: "Which was the son of Melea, which was the son of Menan, which was the son of Mattatha, which was the son of Nathan, which was the son of David"(Luke 3:31). In both genealogies of Jesus, we see his ancestry having its origin in David. Paul is right on target in Romans 1:2 in his description of our Lord's earthly ties to the royal house of Israel.

But not only is Jesus the Messiah because of earthly relationships, he is the Messiah because of the declaration by God that Jesus is His son and the fact that that declaration was authenticated by His bodily resurrection from the dead. Many men have died; many have died for the sins of others as would-be "messiahs" and martyrs. Only one was able to die for the sins of others and be subsequently resurrected from the dead, and His name is Jesus.

Verse five shares not only the purpose of the Book of Romans, but the purpose of Paul's salvation as well. That purpose is ". . . obedience to the faith among all nations, for his name." The evangelistic scope of Paul's ministry was an unlimited one. He was to take the glorious news of free salvation through the atoning death of Christ to all the nations of the world. His commission makes clear that God's dealings with mankind are to be confined no longer to the people of Israel. It is an open gospel with a worldwide audience. We, who are non-Jews, ought to thank God every day of our lives that Paul faithfully discharged this difficult assignment from the Lord.

Verses six and seven share the people of the book even as verse five gave us the purpose of the book. Two groups are to be the privileged recipients of this letter, one indirectly and the other directly. Indirectly, all of us who are "...the called . . ." are to benefit from this epistle. Second, and directly, he has written this essay on church doctrines to the beloved saints in Rome. "Beloved" is a stronger word than "loved." It denotes a very special affection from the Lord. Undoubtedly, these were called such because God was so aware of their devotion and faithfulness in spite of the rigors of their trials at the hands of the cruel Caesars.

Even more important is that they are called "saints." You will note that the words "to be" are in italics in verse seven, and you will remember that italicized words in the Scriptures are words that were not in the original manuscripts but were added later by the translators for easier reading. Sometimes, I think, the added words cloud the meaning more than clarifying it. Such is the case here. These Christians in Rome were not "called to be saints"; they were "called saints."

This word, "saints," always refers to a saved person set apart in salvation by the Lord. It never is to used for some special believer who is given sainthood by some religious leader because of some extraordinary deed. If you are saved, you are a saint. You have been set apart by the Lord. The word, "saint," has its origin in the word, "sanctified," which literally means, "set apart." So, a saint is a "set apart one." Even in the Greek you are able to see the similarities in the two words. "Saint" is "hagios" and "sanctified" is "hagiazo."

Paul's Desire To Go To Rome

8 First, I thank my God through Jesus Christ for you all, that your faith is spoken of throughout the whole world.
9 For God is my witness, whom I serve with my spirit in the gospel of his Son that without ceasing I make mention of you always in my prayers;
10 Making request, if by any means now at length I might have a prosperous journey by the will of God to come unto you.
11 For I long to see you, that I may impart unto you some spiritual gift, to the end ye may be established;
12 That is, that I may be comforted together with you by the mutual faith both of you and me.
13 Now I would not have you ignorant, brethren, that oftentimes I purposed to come unto you (but was let hitherto, that I might have some fruit among you also, even as among other Gentiles.
14 I am debtor both to the Greeks, and to the Barbarians; both to the wise, and to the unwise.
15 So, as much as in me is, I am ready to preach the gospel to you that are in Rome also.

In these verses, we are able to catch the heartbeat of the Apostle Paul. He was driven with a desire to arrive in Rome in order that he might have joyful fellowship with the church located there. These verses may be outlined in a fashion that will describe for us the character of this godly man. Paul was:
(1) Selfless (verse 8);
(2) Spiritual (verse 9);
(3) Steadfast (verse 9);
(4) Surrendered (verse 10);
(5) Specific (verse 10-ll);
(6) Sincere (verse 12-13);
Sacrificial (verse 14-15).

Paul was a selfless man. Note the phrase in verse eight, "... I thank my God through Christ for you all..." That speaks of a generous heart of love, expressing gratitude to the ones to whom this letter is sent, rather than heaping praise to himself. Also, note that "... your faith is spoken of throughout the whole world." What a statement! Consider it in the light of the fact that these words were penned by the man who did more for the cause of Christ than any person who has ever lived! And it is this remarkable man who, in these verses, is found applauding the Roman believers.

Would it not be a grand thing to be in the position of sincere faithfulness from which we could hear similar accolades being passed toward us from such a warrior as Paul? If someone came to the street where you live, and asked for a person of great Christian faith, would your name immediately come to your neighbors' minds? The full beauty of our faith is best viewed against the backdrop of adversity instead of the draperies of prosperity. These saints in Rome lived in the daily awareness that death or imprisonment could come at any moment. They were forced to worship in the catacombs which were underground rooms and passageways outside the city of Rome. Their joyous life of triumph in spite of trouble brought glad words of commendation from the lips of the Apostle Paul.

Not only was he a selfless man, Paul was also a spiritual man according to verse nine: " . . . whom I serve with my spirit in the gospel . . . " There is a marked difference between the soul of man and the spirit of man. "Soul" comes from the Greek word, "psuche," from which we get words like "psychiatrist" and psychology"; Soul, therefore, pertains to matters of man's mind and emotions. "Spirit" is a different word in the Greek; it is "pneuma," from which we get words like "pneumonia" or "pneumatic." These words denote air or wind or breath. The spirit of man is that deep, inner presence of God within the individual's life. Paul did not serve God with his soul; that is, his mind and emotions. Paul served God with his spirit, that special divine and holy unction of spirit.

It is so sad that much of the work that is done in God's name is motivated by the carnal desires of ego in a man's mind. Applause, compliments and financial gain have become the unspiritual goals of many of those who lead in modern religious movements—both inside the church and out. So-called work for God has been bought, bartered, bribed, and built as monuments to man's pride and ability, rather than out of a sincere love for Jesus. In the twentieth chapter of John, our Lord gave only one reason as acceptable for service when He said to Peter, "If you love me, feed my sheep."

He did not say, "If you love feeding sheep, feed my sheep." He did not say, "If you love sheep, feed my sheep." He said, "If you love me, feed my sheep."

Often we hear Bible teachers in a church's Sunday School exclaim, "I want to teach because I just love those little children." That may be a good reason, but that is "loving the sheep" and is not approved by God. Someone else says, "I want to teach because I just love to teach the Word of God." On the surface, that seems noble, but it is only "loving to feed." How good it is when we hear someone say, "I want to teach because I just love the Lord." That is the motivation for service that our God honors! It is spiritual! It is real!

Third, Paul was steadfast. His was not a faith of "fits and starts." It saddens me to watch believers with tremendous ability as they steadily lose interest in their service to God. Finally, they are no longer seen at the house of God and scarcely ever mention His name to others. Other saints do not depart from active service in a continuous, downward slide, but instead, they are sporadic. Neither of these two sad conditions is to be desired.

We need steadfast people! The church lacks that special breed of believer who is aggressively moving forward and upward at all times, never pausing and never retreating. Paul was that kind of man. Verse nine says that " . . . without ceasing I make mention of you always in my prayers."

Fourth, he was surrendered. Verse ten declares his spirit of obedience by simply sharing, " . . . if by any means now at length I might have a prosperous journey by the will of God to come unto you." Paul lived right in the center of God's perfect will for his life. Nothing that our Lord could request of him was considered by Paul as too difficult. The phrase, " . . ., by any means . . . ," indicates the extreme to which Paul would push himself to follow God.

Fifth, Paul was specific. His was not a mission with no goal, neither was it a mission of several goals. This faithful apostle concentrated his work into special areas with specific objectives. Verse eleven tells us " . . . that I may impart unto you some spiritual gift, to the end ye may be established . . . " Most of the prayers, of most of the saints that I know, are very general with no particular direction. How much better to pray for God to answer our petitions in very definite and described ways.

Sixth, Paul was sincere, as clearly evidenced in verses twelve and thirteen. The word, "sincere," is truly an appropriate word to describe the character of Paul, It comes from the Latin words, "senna cera," which mean, "without wax." In ancient times in Rome, furniture builders would smooth over flaws in their woodcraft shops with clear wax. Inside the dark rooms of their workshops, such wax-covered flaws could not be detected by the eye or felt by the touch. To the dismay of the buyer, when he took his newly-purchased item into the bright sunlight, he found the hidden blemishes. To counter the questions of suspicious buyers, quality craftsmen developed the use of little tags that they attached to their products. These tags bore the words, senna cera," in other words, "without wax." In essence, these words told the buyer that what he saw in the dark was what he would see in the sunlight.

The unselfish Apostle Paul, with a sincere heart, shared the simple truth that he needed the Roman saints' ministry to him as much as they needed his ministry to them— ... that I may be comforted together with you by the mutual faith both of you and me." Add those words to those of the following verse, "Now I would not have you ignorant, brethren, that often-times I purposed to come unto you . . ._
The loving, compassionate Paul wanted the readers of this letter to know that his care for them was unfeigned. His integrity and sincerity was of priceless value to him.

In verses fourteen and fifteen, we witness the sacrificial aspect of Paul's nature. Many intend to share the gospel, but they are unwilling to go beyond their self-determined limits of personal convenience. Paul says, however, "I am debtor both to the Greeks, and to the barbarians; both to the wise and to the unwise. So, as much as in me is, I am ready to preach the gospel . . . " Two things that are expressed here are worthy of serious contemplation. Why did Paul consider himself a debtor? And why was he willing to give all that he possessed within his very being for the advancement of the gospel?

To understand his reason for making these statements, we must first place ourselves in Paul's position. Here was a man who persecuted the early church. Had it not been for his spectacular encounter with Christ on the road to Damascus, his doom might well have been sealed. Paul was clearly aware of that fact. Equally was he aware that he was blessed by that vision of Christ, as no man had ever been before, and as no man would ever be again. Those two things being true, Paul considered himself as a truly fortunate man. Since he was unaware of any other man having a similar "Damascus road" experience, Paul was possessed with a spirit of urgency and of obligation to take this gospel message that had transformed his life to those not as fortunate as he.

His first two groups toward whom he felt a spiritual debt were the Greeks and Barbarians. The Greeks represented the highly-educated, cultivated peoples of the world; the Barbarians represented the uneducated, unmannered, uncouth peoples of the world. The gospel is for both of these groups.

His second two groups toward whom he felt a spiritual debt were the wise and the unwise. A person may be very knowledgeable with all the advantages of formal education but remain very unwise. Wisdom has to do with what one knows about God. In this context, I believe Paul sensed his mission was to God's chosen people, the Jews, and to the unwise Gentiles of the world, bereft of the blessings of God that had for centuries been confined to the borders of Israel. The gospel is for both.

Verse fifteen challenges all of us with Paul's confident assertion, "I am ready . . ." Oh, how badly the cause of Christ needs men and women who are ready to do whatever is expected of them by the Lord. Paul had made adequate preparation. He was ready! Dear Reader, are you ready? Can you say with Paul that you are precisely where you need to be in order to be in step with God's own divine timing? How sad it is to be just one-half step behind the place where God would intend for you to be at that particular time in your life.

The Key Verse In Romans

This unique book is actually an orderly discussion by Paul of the five major Christian doctrines. Each of these doctrines (condemnation, justification, sanctification, glorification, consecration), has its origin and power in the message of the gospel of Jesus Christ. Therefore, the place of the gospel in the believer's life is presented in Roman 1:16. Verse 17 follows that key verse of the book with a brief definition of the gospel:

16 For I am not ashamed of the gospel of Christ: for it is the power of God unto salvation to everyone that believeth; to the Jew first, and also to the Greek.
17 For therein is the righteousness of God revealed from faith to faith: as it is written, the just shall live by faith.

To fully appreciate Paul's ardor for the gospel, please note the three times he uses the phrase, "I am," in verses fourteen, fifteen, and sixteen:
"I AM a debtor" (v.14);
"I AM ready" (v.15);
"I AM not ashamed" (v. 16).

The first "I am" indicates Paul's commitment to the winning of the unsaved. But why should he consider himself a debtor? To answer that question, we need only to consider the grace and love of the Lord Jesus Christ who so unselfishly died that any of us might be saved. Salvation is so wonderful because it means for us that eternal condemnation to hell has been abolished but eternity in heaven has been gained! That being the case, every saved person should be so grateful that he cannot conceive of himself ever failing to do everything possible in the bringing of lost people to the Lord; and in so doing, at least partially repay Jesus for His matchless love. Such was the attitude of Paul. Intense gratitude drove him to the masses of the spiritually blind.

The second "I am" in verse fifteen declares Paul's readiness. The indebtedness in the heart of Paul was translated into personal involvement. It is one thing to identify needs; it is another thing to purpose with a holy resolve to do something about them. Paul knew that the entire world needed the gospel and he did not wait for someone else to take the good news to the four corners of the earth. Oh no! This dear man of God was ready to preach! Thank God for men who, through the ages of church history, have flung themselves with reckless abandon into the work of God!

The third "I am" in verse sixteen is a statement of Paul's boldness concerning the gospel message. He was not ashamed! There was no hesitancy, no timidity, in his presentation of the gospel's life-changing truths.

To examine these key verses (w. 16-17) of the Book of Romans, let us analyze the gospel according to its:
(1) Person;
(2) Purpose;
(3) Power;
(4) Plan.

The Person of The Gospel

This is Christ's gospel: "For I am not ashamed of the gospel of Christ . . ."(v.16). This was a particularly important statement by Paul to the Romans because of the prevailing attitude in Rome that many gods were worthy of worship. However, any gospel that does not embrace the substitutionary life and death of Jesus is not really the gospel. The Biblical definition of the gospel is found in I Corinthians 15: l-4: Moreover, brethren, I declare unto you the gospel which I preached unto you, which also ye have received, and wherein ye stand; By which also ye are saved, if ye keep in memory what I preached unto you, unless ye have believed in vain. For I delivered unto you first of all that which I also received, how Christ died for our sins according to the scripture; and that he was buried, and that he rose again the third day according to the scriptures." Please note that twice in this passage, the phrase, "according to the scriptures," is used. The gospel, the true gospel, is a gospel that conforms in detail to the Scriptures. Any so-called gospel that deviates at all from the words of the Bible is not the gospel of our Lord. Every religious teaching should be measured with the straight-edge of the Scriptures. That is the reason that Paul warns: "I marvel that ye are so soon removed from him that called you into the race of Christ unto another gospel, which is not another; but there are some that trouble you, and would pervert the gospel of Christ. But though we, or an angel from heaven, preach any other gospel unto you than that which we have preached unto you, let him be accursed. As we said before, so say I now again, if any man preach any other gospel unto you than that ye have received, let him be accursed" (I Corinthians 1:6-9).

Dear Reader, your controversy will be with those who pollute the pure gospel of Christ with deceptive lies of hell. Most believers readily recognize out-and-out teachings of false religion. Buddhism, Shintoism, Satanism, secular humanism, and atheism present no challenge to the believer's discernment. They are easily identified as false. Without a good working knowledge of the Word of God, however, a believer can be trapped by cultists who comfortably speak of Jesus but very cunningly include apparently insignificant unscriptural statements about the Son of God. When this happens, the Jesus they proclaim is not the Jesus of the Bible! Does that seem strange? Read Paul's words about "another Jesus" in II Corinthians 11:2-4: "For I am jealous over you with godly jealousy: for I have espoused you to one husband, that I may present you as a chaste virgin to Christ. But I fear, lest by any means, as the serpent beguiled Eve through his subtlety, so your minds should be corrupted from the simplicity that is in Christ. For if he that cometh preacheth another Jesus, whom we have not preached, or if ye receive another spirit, which we have not received, or another gospel, which ye have not accepted, ye might well bear with him."

Not only do these verses tell us that there are false Christs, but there are also false spirits (imitators of the Holy Spirit) and false gospels. Dear Reader, listen carefully! If a man is wrong about Jesus, it does not matter what he is right about! At the very heart of genuine Christianity is the person of Jesus Christ! Without the Christ of the Bible, there is no Christianity! Little wonder, then, that we have the warning of John:

"For many deceivers are entered into the world, who confess not that Jesus Christ is come in the flesh. This is a deceiver and an antichrist. Look to yourselves, that we lose not those things which we have wrought, but that we receive a full reward. Whosoever trangresseth, and abideth not in the doctrine of Christ, hath not God. He that abideth in the doctrine of Christ, he hath both the Father and the Son. If there come any unto you, and bring not this doctrine, receive him not into your house, neither bid him God speed: For he that biddeth him God speed is partaker of his evil deeds" (II John 7-11).

The Power of the Gospel

We have seen the person of the gospel. Let us now turn our attention to the power of the gospel. Verse sixteen says that". . . it is the power of God."

The word used for "power" in this verse is the Greek word, "dunamis," from which we get our word, "dynamite." The gospel is the explosive power of God. It is not just explosive power; it is God's explosive power! Therefore, we can now understand that the gospel is the explosive power of a being who has omnipotence as one of His divine attributes! Omnipotence is "all-power," or the "ability to do anything." Paul says that the gospel is "the explosive ability to do anything and is the special characteristic of God.

And, Dear Reader, the gospel has all of that power indeed! Hardened sinners with cruel countenances become as tender and sweet as new-born babes under the power of the gospel. Wicked men with perverse intentions start working toward noble and decent goals. Women with soiled reputations who have flung their virtues into the gutters of this world find themselves suddenly pure as they plunge into the "fountain filled with blood drawn from Immanuel's veins."

Be well-assured, God has no power outside the gospel! That is such an important statement, I feel that I must say it again for emphasis. God has no power outside of the gospel! No man can by-pass Calvary to the throne of God. The channel through which the energy of heaven flows begins at the old rugged cross.

The Purpose of the Gospel

Now that we understand a little of the gospel's person and power, let us look at its purpose. It can be readily recognized in two words found in verse sixteen, ". . . unto salvation." We must be very careful that we never make the gospel's primary objective anything other than personal salvation. Someone may disagree by asserting that the gospel is God's demonstration of His love for the human race. Indeed, it is an expression of His love, but He could have found other less dramatic ways to show us how much He loves us. Others suggest that the gospel is God's first example of genuine humanitarianism and social action. True, the highest form of caring was exemplified on the cross when Jesus died, for "greater love hath no man than this, that a man lay down his life for his friends." But God could have found other less costly ways to show us how to love one another. The one supreme thing that was accomplished at Calvary that could not have been done in any other way was the payment of the sin debt that separated man from God.

Never be misled! Many wonderful manifestations of the Father's grace became ours to enjoy because of Christ's death, but far beyond them all is the inexpressible joy of knowing that on that dread day, Jesus purchased our salvation.

In a world being pulled into communities of chaos, it is comforting to know that God has prepared a way for the individual inhabitant of planet earth to be secure regardless of the particular geographic spot on which he may dwell. Since man has no control over his entrance into the world and very little over his exit, it would do him well to contemplate the only thing that is uniquely his to do that can yield eternal benefits. He can be saved! With the exception of salvation, man is the product of others in terms of the kind of clothes he wears, the kind of food he eats, the kind of house he chooses for a residence, and the places he goes. But salvation cuts across all socio-economic, racial, cultural, and national boundaries. The primary purpose of the gospel is uniquely individual in the salvation it affords a person.

The Plan of the Gospel

The fourth characteristic of the gospel given in verse sixteen is its plan. It is "... to everyone that believeth." This particular characteristic will be the subject of detailed scrutiny in succeeding chapters of this study. At this point, it is only sufficient that we understand that this verse clearly sets forth an individual's belief of the full measure of the genuine gospel as the sole requirement for salvation. We are not saved by belief plus anything else or belief minus anything else. We are saved by believing, by trusting, by exercising our faith.

This simple plan is equally provided for all mankind. Is it not a mark of God's grace that He did not develop one plan for salvation for one nation and another plan for another culture? Had that been the case, our world would have become a mish-mash of faith conflicts that would have surpassed in severity the multitude of holy wars that this world has already suffered through the centuries. But God chose only one plan by which all men may be saved.

The universal nature of the gospel is declared in verse sixteen in its application "... to the Jew first, and also to the Greek." Certainly these two groups did not constitute all the various groups of Paul's world, but their importance lies in the fact that the Jew represents those who are very religious while the Greek represents those who are very intellectual. Paul's suggestion is simply that if the gospel is good for the Jew and the Greek, it is definitely good for every man.

But the glory of this miraculous plan of salvation is that it is not for mental assent alone; it literally transforms the believer's lifestyle. Note verse seventeen:
17 For in it is the righteousness of God revealed from faith to faith; as it is written, the just shall live by faith.

The word, "righteousness," will appear again and again in our study. As used here, it means literally, "the kind of right living and thinking and speaking which has God as its source." The Jews well-understood an external form of righteousness that did not always match what was in the heart. God's righteousness, however, begins at the time of that man's salvation. Finally, that righteousness is expressed outwardly by the things its possessor says, thinks, and does.

The phrase, "from faith to faith," speaks of an experience that is unique to the Christian faith. Ours is a religion that is characterized by an exercise of heart faith that brings a man into a right vertical relationship with God. After this union with God is completed by faith, the new saint can look toward a right horizontal relationship with his fellow man, thereby revealing the righteousness of his heart.

The Doctrine of Condemnation

With verse eighteen we are introduced to the first of the five major doctrines, and we will continue our study of condemnation until we reach Romans 3:20. So, we begin:
18 For the wrath of God is revealed from heaven against all ungodliness and unrighteousness of men, who hold the truth in unrighteousness.

Make no mistake! God's anger is firmly set against sin! He will not overlook any form of iniquity! There are two Greek words in the New Testament for wrath. "Orge," the word used here in Romans 1:18, should be distinguished from "thumos," which indicates a "sudden, emotional outburst." Orge, however, is less sudden than thumos and is much longer lasting. Also, orge is more active in its outward expression than thumos. Thumos may arise quickly because of an emotional response such as revenge, but itsubsides as quickly as it arises. Orge, on the other hand, is the end result of a long series of flagrant insults and injuries until finally, like boiling water, there is a horrible destructive force unleashed that will not be cooled or calmed. The word for the wrath of God in this verse is "orge," the more awesome of the two Greek words.

What does this mean to man? Very simple, the worst possible expression of God's displeasure is not just directed at SOME of man's sins, but ALL of man's sins: ". . . the wrath of God is revealed from heaven against ALL ungodliness and unrighteousness of men." It is a sobering thought that our Lord is just as unhappy with the "white lies" of the middle class American church member as He is of the atheism of a non-believing Russian. God hates sin! His righteousness and holiness cannot allow sin to continue without judgment, regardless of the social position of the one committing that sin. If ever one-half of one sin goes unpunished by God, He will topple from His throne! God hates sin!

You will notice that these ungodly individuals "hold the truth in unrighteousness" (v.18). What is "the truth?" The foundational truth upon which all theology is built is "God is." Atheists arrogantly asset that "God is not." It is therefore a pitiful thing to behold stupid self-proclaimed intellectuals parade their pride and blasphemy against God in radio or television interviews. Little do they recognize that in spite of their protests and jeering mockery of the thrice-holy God of Israel, alleging that He does not even exist and that mankind is the product of purely evolutionary processes, God's wrath is getting ever nearer its boiling point even as they speak.

But what of those in foreign lands who have never heard the gospel of Jesus Christ? Are they included in this same group? Is there no hope for them? Paul quite clearly answers that question and shows that they are also under the sentence of condemnation and without excuse:

19 Because that which may be known of God is manifest in them; for God hath shewed it unto them.
20 For the invisible things of him from the creation of the world are clearly seen, being understood by the things that are made, even his eternal power and Godhead; so that they are without excuse.

No man will ever be able to stand in the eternity of hell and shake his puny fist in the face of God, and argue that he did not have a chance to be saved. Logically, if a man is somehow saved although he has never heard the gospel or is in some manner given a second opportunity to be saved in eternity, it would make better sense to seal off the nation in which that man lives and never send a missionary to tell him of Jesus. In fact, by that same logic, Jesus should have never commissioned the church to evangelize the world and preach the gospel to every creature (Matthew 28:19-20).

The truth of the matter is that all men everywhere need to be saved! That is the argument of Paul! To understand how God views the man who has never heard the gospel, let us begin by reading John 1:9: "That was the true Light, which lighteth every man that cometh into the world." When a person 1S born physically, God places a small divine light in his heart that will respond to a direct or an indirect touch by the true Light, Jesus Christ our Lord.

Even the. man in a pagan land, bereft of any communication at all about Jesus Christ, is indirectly touched by Him. In verse twenty, we see that the invisible things of God (i.e. His love, wrath, power, glory) can be understood by the things that have been made (i.e. sun, moon, stars, mountains). In other words, when a man looks at the wonders of creation, there will come a little bit of truth to the divine light placed within his heart at his birth. Even the Psalmist recognized this :

"The heavens declare the glory of God; and the firmament sheweth his handywork" (Psalms 19:1). If that man responds by earnestly desiring to know the identity of the God who made the mountains, the skies, and every other thing that exists, God is required by a covenant of His own making to reveal His plan of salvation to that man. "And ye shall seek me, and find me, when ye shall search for me with all your heart" (Jeremiah 29:13).

The way God chooses to reveal Himself to the man who is seeking Him is solely a decision for the Lord to make. But the Scriptures are clear that God will find a way!

One illustration should suffice to clarify this teaching. Many years ago, just before the turn of this century, a young Peruvian girl was taught to read and speak the English language by some industrialists who had established a colonial business in her homeland. One day, as she was starting for a long hike into the rugged mountains that surrounded her little village, she found a mail sack lying beside the trail. Picking it up, she decided to carry it with her and then find the one who had lost it when she returned from her walk. Alone in the wilds of that mountainous terrain, that young girl fell, injured herself, and was unable to get back to her home for help. Finally deciding that death was inevitable, she began looking at the high peaks of the mountains and the sky. The light in her heart began to flicker that perhaps there was a God above and beyond all the other gods she had been trained to worship. Wishing that she had had the opportunity to try to find Him, but realizing that she did not, she opened the mail sack. Inside was a copy of a London newspaper. This particular edition had a front- page weekly feature in which was printed the previous Sunday morning's sermon by Charles Haddon Spurgeon, pastor of Metropolitan Tabernacle. His message that she read was simply titled, "What Must I Do To Be Saved?" Immediately, after studying this great message, the girl bowed her head and asked the Lord Jesus Christ to come into her heart. Through a series of "coincidences," she was found and thereby lived to recount the events that led to her salvation. This is just one example of how God allowed Himself to be found by one who was seeking Him!

But what would have happened if this young lady had rejected that little flicker within her heart? After all, millions of people around the world choose to refuse the Spirit of God as He tenderly woos them. To answer that, we must first examine what these people do as an act of their own wills in rebellion:

21 Because that, when they knew God, they glorified him not as God, neither were thankful; but became vain in their imaginations, and their foolish heart wasdarkened.

22 Professing themselves to be wise, they became fools,
23 And changed the glory of the uncorruptible God into an image made like to corruptible man, and to birds, and fourfooted beasts, and creeping things.

Seven terrible things are done by these wicked ones as they reject God's offer of salvation.

THEY GLORIFY HIM NOT AS GOD (v. 21): One clear Bible principle is that the chief end of man is to glorify God. This is the age of secular humanism, a godless philosophy that is permeating our social institutions, particularly those of education and government. It simply teaches that the only God that exists is that inner drive within man's own consciousness, that there is no power outside of man's self. So, those people who accept secular humanism, arrogantly strut their disregard for even the existence of an Almighty God, much less their willingness to honor Him.

THEY ARE NOT THANKFUL (v. 21): Why be thankful? If a person does not accept the fact of God, and if he believes that all that he possesses has resulted from his own ingenuity and perseverance or else by sheer coincidence, there is no reason to be grateful.

(3) THEY ARE VAIN IN THEIR IMAGINATIONS (v. 21): If we eliminate God, we eliminate the source of all authority. The very codes of civil law have as their origin the Judeo-Christian ethic. Once the idea of God is destroyed, therefore, all social and moral restraints that were designed by God for the good of man are likewise destroyed. Then, the "liberated" man may do whatever he may choose or imagine to do without consideration of divine truth. Always that man, whoever he may be, will choose that which is of a downward, less uplifting, course.

(4) THEY ALLOW THEIR HEARTS TO DARKEN (v. 21): Do you remember the little light of divine truth that is placed in the heart of every man at his birth (John 1:9)? Finally, that light is extinguished through the ungodly man's continued refusal to respond to the Spirit's convicting power upon it. Once that happens, he not only will never be saved, he CAN NEVER be saved! One of the fundamental facts of salvation is that a man cannot be

saved at the time of his choosing; he must be saved when he is drawn by the Lord: "No man can come to me, except the Father which hath sent me draw him" (John 6:44). Is there an example in the Word of God of people losing the very ability to respond? Yes, there is! Jesus did many miracles among the people of Capernaum. They were good, morally upright people. But look at these awful words of doom that He was forced to pronounce upon them: While ye have light, believe in the light, that ye may be the children of light. These things spake Jesus, and departed, and did hide himself from them. But though he had done so many miracles before them, yet they believed not on him: That the saying of Esaias the prophet might be fulfilled, which he spake, Lord, who hath believed our report? And to whom hath the arm of the Lord been revealed? Therefore THEY COULD NOT BELIEVE, because that Esaias said again, He hath BLINDED THEIR EYES, and HARDENED THEIR HEARTS; THAT THEY SHOULD NOT SEE WITH THEIR EYES, NOR UNDERSTAND WITH THEIR HEART, AND BE CONVERTED, AND I SHOULD HEAL THEM" (John 12:36-40).

Did you note that these "good" people refused the light? That was their sin! Nowhere in these verses or the surrounding verses do we find any indication at all that the citizens of Capernaum were immoral or lawless. Their sin was the worst sin of all. It was a sin against light. Adultery or murder has never caused a man to go to hell, but to sin against the light of God's love and forgiveness can and will! Please note again verse 39 that states they "could not believe." It was no longer a matter of they "would not". They could not! They had lost the very ability to generate the necessary faith to be saved!

John 12:40 speaks of Jesus blinding their eyes and hardening their hearts. That is precisely the condition of the ungodly man who is the subject of our study in the first chapter of Romans. He chooses by the exercise of his will to continue to refuse God's work upon the light in his heart until that light gradually dims and goes completely out. Once that has taken place, he is a spiritually-dead, hopelessly lost, man. His thinking becomes so twisted that he no longer sees any moral absolutes and he enters a life of atheism.

THEY PROFESS TO BE WISE (v. 22): Now with a darkened heart they turn to the "light" of their own intellect. Do not find that strange! Satan, the great counterfeiter, tries to imitate that divine light of God that has just been extinguished in the lost man's heart. Satan's light is that of broadmindedness and unbridled intellectual curiosity: And no marvel; for Satan himself is transformed into an angel of light. Therefore it is no great thing if his ministers also be transformed as the ministers of righteousness; whose end shall be according to their works" (II Corinthians 11:14-15).

THEY BECOME FOOLS (v. 22). "Fool" does not mean whimsical, comical, or silly in its scriptural usage. In the Bible, "fool" is used for that man or woman who has lost all spiritual discernment and has, therefore, moved beyond the reach of God. Only the Almighty has the right to call a man a fool, and when He does, it is always with eternal disgust. By the exercise of his own will, the fool now receives exactly what he had previously wanted, no interference by God as he indulges in his sinful pleasures.

THEY MAKE THEIR OWN GODS (v. 23): Man must have something or someone to worship. He has an emptiness in his heart that was God-given at birth. If he chooses to align himself with the hell-bound multitudes of this world, he will nevertheless look for a "spiritual filler" on his way down. The praise he should have lavished upon Jesus will be poured out by him upon his business, family, or material objects. His gods may be recreation or sin. Other cultures may erect to themselves gods of stone or wood or of animals. But man will always have some kind of object to worship! His very nature demands it!

THE CONSEQUENCES OF A DARKENED HEART

24 Wherefore God also gave them up to uncleanness through the lusts of their own hearts, to dishonour their own bodies between themselves:
25 Who changed the truth of God into a lie, and worshipped and served the creature more than the Creator, who is blessed forever. Amen.
26 For this cause God gave them up unto vile affections: for even their women did change the natural use into that which is against nature:
27 And like wise also the men, leaving the natural use of the woman, burned in their lust one toward another; men with men working that which is unseemly, and
receiving in themselves that recompense of their error which was meet.

*28 And even as they did not like to retain God in their knowledge, God gave them over to a reprobate mind, to do those things which are not convenient.
29 Being filled with all unrighteousness, fornication, wickedness, covetousness, maliciousness; full of envy, murder, debate, deceit, malignity; whisperers,
30 Backbiters, haters of God, despiteful, proud, boasters, inventors of evil things, disobedient to parents,
31 Without understanding, covenant breakers, without natural affection, implacable, unmerciful:
32 Who knowing the judgement of God, that they which commit such things are worthy of death, not only do the same, but have pleasure in them that do them.*

It is vitally important that you underline one fact clearly in your own mind. These ungodly people cannot blame anyone but themselves for the impending judgement of the Almighty upon them because verse twenty-four says that God gives them up as a result of the "LUST OF THEIR OWN HEARTS." The dirtiness of their bodies began in the darkness of their hearts. Jesus warned the multitudes of the bad influence that a wicked heart can have on the actions of a man: "But those things which proceed out of the mouth come forth from the heart; and they defile the man. For out or the heart proceed evil thoughts, murders, adulteries, fornications, thefts, false witness, blasphemies" (Matthew 15:18-19).

Oh, how important is the heart of man! The depth of degradation and gutter living to which ungodly men can sink is graphically presented in the closing verses of this first chapter of Romans. No sane man should ever take lightly the dread declarations found in this passage. Worst of all is the fact that three times it is stated that God finally gives up on these deluded men. And, if you will note carefully, they are given up by the Lord in body, then soul, then spirit.

First, God gives up on these men in their bodies (v. 24). They choose " . . . to dishonor their bodies between themselves." Verse twenty-five says that they " . . . changed the truth of God for a lie," better translated, "the lie." What is the lie of all lies? Very simply, it is that "God is not." This lie is in contrast to the foundational truth upon which all theology is built, which is, "God is." But these ungodly atheists with darkened hearts, thoroughly convinced that "God is not," now begin worshipping the creature (creation) instead of the Creator.

Look around your community, especially on weekends. Sports of every sort abound. Churches struggle to maintain a handful of faithful folk in worship services while beaches, parks, and stadiums are filled to capacity. The increasing popularity of body-emphasis events like health spas and beauty contests testify to our society's inordinate concern with physical excellence at the expense of spiritual deterioration. When a man takes more delight in his physical welfare than his spiritual welfare, Satan has successfully completed phase one in the destruction of that man.

Second, God gives up on these men in their soul(v. 26). You must understand that the soul and spirit are entirely separate. "Soul," in the Greek, is "psuche," from which we get such English words as "psychiatry," or "psychology." On the other hand, "spirit," in the Greek is "pneuma," which literally means "wind, air," and from which we get such English words as "pneumonia," or "pneumatic."
The soul of man has to do with man's emotional desires and personality. Please note in verses twenty-six and twenty-seven, women are seen involving themselves in the ugly sexual sin of lesbianism and men entangle themselves in homosexuality. In these modern days, mainline denominations are appointing study committees to determine whether such sexual activities should be labeled as sin, or whether churches should open their doors to these "alternative sexual preferences." In this passage alone, God's attitude is categorically stated. It is found in verse 32:
"... *they who commit such things are worthy of death.*"

Regardless of the learned protestations of the liberal churchman, God says that homosexuality and lesbianism are sins and all who participate in such sin deserve to die. That should settle it!

Although verses twenty-six and twenty-seven are concerned primarily with the two aforementioned sins, we must not overlook that these ungodly have been given over to "... vile affections." Not every person so judged by the Lord will indulge themselves in homosexuality. However, all will manifest wicked, uncontrollable desires. An extreme drive for personal power or greed for material gain can become consuming passions that are as damning to the individual as the sins of sexual perversion.

The interesting aspect of it all is that such emotional aberrations cannot be altered. Should friends or relatives persuade the one given up by the Lord to seek psychiatric help, it will be to no avail. Once God has given him up in his emotions (soul), that man will never be whole again. Phase two in Satan's diabolical scheme to destroy the individual is now complete.

Third, God gives up the ungodly sinner in his most critical area — his spirit (v. 28). God gives them over to " . . . a reprobate mind." Such individuals are filled with " . . . all unrighteousness" (v.29). Can you imagine such evil control? God offers to fill man with His precious Holy Spirit which some men rudely refuse. When a man reaches this sad state, he is filled with the unholy spirit of hell! Being filled with "all" unrighteousness conveys the fact that there is no longer a single shred of that which is good that can be found in his life to recommend him to God. He is now under the total dominion of the devil.

Verses twenty-nine and thirty contain a list of the ugly sins that are common in the lives of those about whom God has declared, "I give up!" In body, soul, and spirit they have been rejected by God. Hellish in action, hellish in attitude, and hellish in authority, they have consigned themselves to hell.

So, chapter one comes to a dismal conclusion. Sad it would be if this passage contained all that needed to be said about those in this world who are under the sentence of condemnation; but infinitely worse is that these deceived workers of evil represent only a small segment of the total number who are right now condemned to hell without Jesus Christ! These others will be the subject of our study in chapter two.

Chapter Two

The Moral, Religious Sinner

Chapter one was a general overview of the entire Gentile world under the sentence of condemnation. I hope you were able to note that the judgments expressed in that chapter are not confined to a particular time period or set of circumstances; on the contrary, they are judgment principles that universally apply with certainty to all who are disobedient; none is exempted. Chapter two narrows the focus of these principles to the individual, making each person aware of his own responsibility before God.

We will begin our study of this chapter by examining the first nine verses. As you read this section, do so from the perspective of its theme, that to judge others is to judge yourself:

1 Therefore thou art inexcusable, O man, whosoever thou art that judgest: for wherein thou judgest another, thou condemnest thyself; for thou that judgest doest the same things.
2 But we are sure that the judgment of God is according to truth against them which commit such things.
3 And thinkest thou this, O man, that judgest them which do such things, and doest the same, that thou shalt escape the judgment of God?
4 Or despisest thou the riches of his goodness and forbearance and longsuffering; not knowing that the goodness of God leadeth thee to repentance?
5 But after thy hardness and impenitent heart treasurest up unto thyself wrath against the day of
wrath and revelation of the righteous judgment of God;
6 Who will render to every man according to his deeds:
7 To them who by patient continuance in well doing seek for glory and honour and immortality, eternal life:
8 But unto them that are contentious, and do not obey the truth, but obey unrighteousness, indignation and wrath,
9 Tribulation and anguish, upon every soul of man that doeth evil, of the Jew first, and also of the Gentile;

Verse one is directed toward our generation today just as much as it was to the believers of two thousand years ago. It has been a common weakness of man throughout all of recorded history to accuse and judge. But Paul says that we are "without excuse." This phrase is better translated to mean "without a reasonable defense." Simply put, there is absolutely no justification for a spirit of judgmentalism, which I consider to be the most prevalent negative attitude in the modern church.

However, the primary interpretation of this verse is in reference to the lost man who compares his outward moral uprightness with the ungodly deeds of the immoral man in chapter one and takes pride in himself that he is such a good person. What a mistake! If a lost man feels that he must resort to comparison, let him use the character of Jesus rather than stretching himself alongside some degenerate bum in the gutter of sin. Paul places all men under the sentence of condemnation; therefore, the moral sinner is just as condemned as the wicked sinner whom he is judging. The moral sinner's judgmentalism of the wicked sinner is as foolish as a man who is on death row for the murder of only one person pointing a finger of accusation at another man who is on death row as a mass murderer. One manifests a murderer's heart more than the other, but both have a murderer's heart. So it is with the moral sinner and the wicked sinner. Both are not sinners alike but both are alike sinners.

Verse two declares God's standard of judgment. He does not measure a man by the changing ethics of society. Nor does He assay a man's value by the estimation of others. Nor does He consider the reasoning of comparisons. God judges "according to truth."

Truth is a concrete reality. It may be that we are not always able to discern the truth, but that does not alter the fact of it. There are times that God's revealed truth in the Bible seems contradictory to a particular need that we have, but that does not grant us the luxury to disregard it and live as we please. For these reasons and the warning of this verse that the truth will be our judge, it behooves us to do everything that is within our power to rightly divide the Word of God and live by its precepts and teachings. Please note the word, "sure." Judgment by the truth of God is a certainty! There is no escaping it and no avoiding it. "Sure," as used here, is the strongest word that can be employed to express an established fact. This verse says that the foolish moral sinner is on a collision course with God at the judgment bar of absolute truth.

Verse three reiterates the solemn warning of the first verse. Do you see the word, "thinkest" In the original Greek, this word is actually, "reckonest." It is a bookkeeping term which means, "to figure up." Here is an interesting situation. The moral sinner is described in this verse as a spiritual accountant, figuring up his own salvation by determining that he is not a bad person. He concludes that he will not be summoned to the judgment bar of God. Many verses could be enumerated that refute this foolish notion, but suffice it to say that "every man's works shall be tried by fire" (I Corinthians 3:13).

Verse four is a blunt accusation of the moral sinner. He is so stupid that he thinks the goodness of God in his life is an endorsement by the Lord of the way that he is living his life. Living comfortably and with little pain, he sees no reason to change his pattern of living. Yet, the plain fact of the matter is that this verse categorically teaches that God's loving goodness toward us as individuals is to bring us to repentance, not to reinforce our personal satisfaction of our own self-styled relationship with God. Indeed, God's acts of wrath do not cause man to repent. Consider, for example, Revelation 9:20-21: "And the rest of the men which were not killed by these plagues yet repented not of the works of their hands, that they should not worship devils, and idols of gold, and silver, and brass, and stone, and of wood: which neither can see, nor hear, nor walk: neither repented they of their murders, nor of their sorceries, nor of their fornication, nor of their thefts." This explains why adversity and tragedy seldom bring people to Jesus Christ.

Verse five details the ultimate end of this self-righteous moral sinner. Each day that he lives in rejection of Jesus Christ as his Savior, his heart gets harder and he stores up more of God's ever-increasing wrath. The word "wrath" conveys the idea of a pot of water slowly approaching the boiling point. Of course, that awful point of divine fury will be reached at the Great White Throne judgment of the lost when all of the unsaved will be cast into the lake of fire.

Please note that his judgment will be according to the hardness of the inner man. Whatever good deeds may be done by the outward influences of this moral sinner, he will be judged harshly by the Lord because of his refusal to repent in his heart. His heart has "hardness;" it is "impenitent." As believers commanded to witness to all men, we must never be distracted in our efforts by the external ethics and behavior of any person, regardless of the high standards of those ethics. We must always be mindful of the desperate condition of a heart without Christ.

Verse six is a plain statement of the universal nature of the doctrine of condemnation. The word, "every," is important. By its usage here, we see that the entire population of earth is condemned. But not only do we see the lost condition of the masses, but we also are reminded that "every" indicates God's judgment of the individual.

Verses seven to ten divide all mankind into two groups. Verses seven and ten deal with the redeemed; verses eight and nine deal with the unsaved. Dear reader, in which group are you? Because you are reading this book, it is safe to assume that you are not one of the ungodly sinners of chapter one. However, is it possible that you are like the moral sinner of this chapter? Is it possible that while you are not a drunkard or sexually sinful person, you have never sincerely asked Jesus to be a personal savior to you? Let me implore you to join me and millions of others in the ranks of the saved.

First, let us look at the judgment of the saved in verses seven and ten. Although the believer's works have absolutely nothing to do with his salvation, they do determine his rewards. This is important to remember as you study the believer's judgment—salvation is a gift, but rewards are earned. God always pays fair wages. If you work little, you will be paid little by Him at the judgment bar; if you work much, you will be paid much. That is the reason Paul warns us in I Corinthians 3:10 to be careful how we build our lives: "According to the grace of God which is given unto me, as a wise master builder, I have laid the foundation, and another buildeth thereon. But let very man take heed how he buildeth thereupon." These are sobering words, food for serious meditation!

Verses eight and nine are addressed to the unbeliever. Regardless of

how noble he may outwardly appear to be, the Bible teaches that he is inwardly "contentious." Better translated, this means that he is "factious" or "feuding" with God. Can you imagine anything so horrendous as this? Alost man is at war with God! How absurdly horrible!
39

In verse eight it is said that the unsaved man "obeys not the truth." This "truth" is not a mere creed or philosophical tenet. The "truth" is the Lord Jesus Christ! John 14: 6declares in His own words: " I am the way, the truth, and the life." These contentious ones are those men in a lost state who are feuding against Christ. The sad result of such foolishness is "wrath, indignation, tribulation, anguish." "Wrath," as translated here from the original Greek, means, "the slowly increasing vengeance of God." The unsaved man faces wrath. He also faces "indignation," better translated as, "the pressure of distressing circumstances." There is more! He must deal with "tribulation," more accurately, "crushing periods of pain." Finally, anguish ,"becomes his inheritance. Anguish is "consuming terror.

Please note that verse nine teaches that no lost man is exempted from the aforementioned judgments of God. But these four manifestations of God s anger upon the wicked will pale alongside the ultimate Judgment of the lost at the Great White Throne Judgment. The place of honor that God originally gave the Jew in the House of Israel will give him no advantage over the Greek. Groups will not exist as the lost world stands before the Eternal Judge. 'Each person will stand upon his own, personal relationship with God.

Now we turn our attention to the next section of verses in chapter two:
11 For there is no respect of persons with God.
12 For as many as have sinned without law shall also perish without law: and as many as have sinned in the law shall be judged by the law;
13 (For not the hearers of the law are just before God, but the doers of the law shall be justified.
14 For when the Gentiles, which have not the law, do by nature the things contained in the law, these ,having not the law, are a law unto themselves. _
15 Which shew the work of the law written in their hearts, their conscience also bearing witness, and their thoughts the mean while accusing or else excusing

one another);
16 In the day when God shall judge the secrets of men by Jesus Christ according to my gospel.

Verse eleven uses the term "respect of persons." This phrase is made up of two words in the original Greek. The word for "persons" carries the idea of position or social rank. The word for respect suggests the reception of a person that is based on partiality. In other words, "respect of persons" actually means "to receive some one according to his place in society," or more literally ,"to receive a person according to the esteem given him by other men." I urge you to be aware that how others may view you will have no influence at all upon the Almighty in His judgment. He is not a respecter of persons.

Verse twelve reiterates the principle of universal condemnation. While some who are not Jewish may protest that they are "without the law" and should, therefore, be excused from judgment, the Scriptures teach that every man has been given the fundamentals of the law. The Jew, of course, has the written law. As indicated in verse fifteen, the Gentile has a law written in his heart. God has such a disdain for sin that He has placed within the bosom of everyman, even the most pagan man, an indisputable alarm that signals the wickedness of certain basic acts of sin. This alarm is commonly called "conscience." In this passage, Paul terms it as "law." This verse, verse twelve, is a clear statement of condemnation upon the Gentile "without the law" who violates the inner law of his conscience.

Verse thirteen does not grant the law the power to save, as some misinformed Bible teachers proclaim. "Doers of the law" is a phrase that strongly suggests a salvation plan base don works. Of course, that is contrary to the Scripture.

What does this mean? To answer this question, we must recognize that our judgment will ultimately come before Jesus Christ, as indicated in verse sixteen. Therefore, a "doer of the law" is one who rightly used the law as it was intended by God to be used; namely, to bring lost mankind to Christ for redemption. As we study the remaining verses of this chapter, we will be able to underline Paul's emphasis on this very crucial point. We will understand that it is possible to be a "doer of the law" who always obeys the smallest details of the law without being truly a "doer of the law" who is continually seeking the Lord Jesus Christ.

Verse fourteen is a declaration that there are many ethical and upright Gentiles who live outside the written law of the Jew but live as nobly, and in many instances more nobly than those who are Jewish. Yet, in spite of his moral goodness, he is seen by the Jew as a despised thing unless he has coupled his high moral standards with a desire to become a part of the Jewish faith and to display that desire by a submission to circumcision. To the Jew, circumcision is more important than any other command or stipulation of the law.

How important is it? Hyman E. Gold in, in his book, The Code of Jewish Law writes: "An infant who dies before circumcision, whether within the eight days or thereafter, must be circumcised at the grave, in order to remove the foreskin which is a disgrace to him, but no benedictions should be pronounced over this circumcision. He should be given a name to perpetuate his memory, and that mercy may be shown him from heaven to be included in the resurrection of the dead and that he may then have sufficient understanding to recognize his father and his mother. If he was buried without circumcision and they become aware of it immediately, when there is no likelihood that the body has already begun to decompose, the grave should be opened and the circumcision should be performed. But if they become aware of it only after some days, the grave should not be opened."

Verse fifteen, however, shows that although the Gentile may not perform such Jewish rites of the law as circumcision, he still has a law written in his heart. If that were not so, how can Joseph's rejection of the seductive plan of Potiphar's wife be explained? Joseph lived prior to the law. How do we account for Abraham's faithfulness to the principle of tithing, again pre-dating the law given to Moses at Sinai? This verse's importance is often not noted. Contrary to the beliefs of Judaism, the conscience is not a reflection of the law; the law is a reflection of man's conscience. The implication is rather clear. If a man spent sufficient time in meditation, he would find the same requirements of the law in his heart, even though he may never have read the law. God, in His love, simplified the process by pulling from man's heart and placing on tablets of stone the standards of outward holiness.

    Verse sixteen is an emphatic warning to all men. There is a definite day that has been appointed, during which Jesus will judge every man. Although we are tempted to disregard the commands of the law during this present Church Age since Calvary, let me remind you that God's standards of holiness have never changed. In I Peter 1:16 is this command, "Be ye holy; for I am holy." Jesus says in Luke 13:5, "Except ye repent, ye shall all likewise perish." Whatever the failings of the law may be, it did set up a line of separation in living for the people of God that attempted to divide them from the world.

    We now turn our attention to the religious sinner, the Jew. In chapter one, we saw that the immoral sinner is condemned. In this chapter, verses one to sixteen, we have seen that the moral sinner is likewise condemned. The remaining verses will show us that the religious sinner is also under the sentence of condemnation:

17 Behold, thou art called a Jew, and restest in the law, and makest thy boast of God,

18 And knowest his will, and approvest the things that are more excellent, being instructed out of the law;

19 And art confident that thou thyself art a guide of the blind, a light of them which are in darkness,

20 An instructor of the foolish, a teacher of babes, which hast the form of knowledge and of the truth in the law.

21 Thou therefore which teachest another, teachest thou not thyself? thou that preaches a man should not steal, dost thou steal? _

22 Thou that sayest a man should not commit adultery, dost thou commit adultery? thou that abhorrest idols, dost thou commit sacrilege?

23 Thou that makest thy boast of the law, through breaking the law dishonourest thou God?

24 For the name of God is blasphemed among the Gentiles through you, as it is written

25 For circumcision verily profiteth, if thou keep the law: but if thou be a breaker of the law, thy circumcision is made uncircumcision.

26 Therefore if the uncircumcision. keep the righteousness of the law, shall not his uncircumcision be counted for circumcision? _

27 And shall not uncircumcision which is by nature, if it fulfill the law, judge thee, who by the letter and circumcision dost transgress the law?
28 For he is not a Jew, which is one outwardly; neither is that circumcision, which is outward. in the flesh:
29 But he is a Jew, which is one inwardly; and circumcision is that of the heart, in the spirit, and not in the letter; whose praise is not of men, but of God.

Verse seventeen challenges the man who calls himself a Jew to live up to the highest commands of Judaism. at a man calls himself and how he lives what he calls himself may be poles apart. Wearing a cross does not make a person a Christian any more than living in a garage will make him an automobile. The basic problem of the Jew is his pride that he is a Jew. His conformity to the traditions of Judaism is of higher priority to him than his relationship to God. But is that so different from the man who is more proud of his position as a Baptist or a Methodist than he is of his relationship with God? While the Jew is bound to the commands of the law, there are those of the church who are shackled by the chains of denominationalism. What is going on in the room where the deacons meet is of greater concern to them than what is happening in the throne room of God.

Verse eighteen chides the Jew's perception of "excellent" things. God's application of the term, "excellent," does not always agree with man's use of the same term. The rabbis taught a man should not scratch his head because of a flea on the Sabbath; that would be hunting — which was not allowed. Does it make a man a better Jew if he refuses to scratch his head and drives himself into nervous agitation all day because of it? It does not. I challenge any Jew to show me such an insane requirement anywhere in the law. The view of the rabbis, as far as the Jew is concerned, is "excellent" and should be held in the same high regard as the written law.

But the Jew has kindred spirits in the modern church. Many a pastor has felt the sting of criticism by traditionalists who cry out their protests with, "We never did it that way before!" The procedures of the church have taken greater priority over the purpose of the church. It was to that sad condition that our Lord said, "Ye blind guides, which strain at a gnat, and swallow a camel" (Matthew 23:24).

Verse nineteen continues Paul's attack on the religious sinner. False confidence in oneself is terrible! They think of themselves as guides of others in matters of religion. They regard themselves as "lights." How foreign to the Scriptures! Psalm 119:105 says, "Thy word is a lamp unto my feet, and a light unto my path." Jesus says of these blind religious traditionalists, "And if the blind lead the blind, both shall fall into the ditch" (Matthew 15:14).

Unfortunately, the unsaved in darkness who make no pretense of religious faith may encounter these blind, false lights and be deceived about the true faith in God that brings salvation. After all, the religious sinner knows the language of God's people and appears to speak with authority. However, the poor lost sinner who follows him will not be brought to a living encounter with Christ, but instead, to dead orthodoxy. How sad!

Verse twenty tells us that the religious sinner is an "instructor of the foolish." "Instructor" is more accurately translated as, "corrector." The word, "babes," means, "simple or unwise; ignorant or uneducated." The religious sinner perceives himself as having the responsibility of teaching others the "right way." Obviously, education and training are important! But remember! We can train those who are right with God, but we cannot train them to be right with God.

The flaw in the instruction of the religious sinner is found in the phrase, " . . . form of knowledge and of truth." The word, "form," means "outer outline." All he knows of faith is what he has been able to learn from tradition. He has no understanding of real faith that is to be found outside the outline of the law's commands and the commentaries of the rabbi, or, in our day, the politics of the church.

Verse twenty-one serves as an indictment of the religious sinner. The Jews taught that stealing was a sin. The word, "teach," is very strong in the original language and actually means "commands." When Paul says that they steal after having told others not to steal, he is not accusing them of a violation of that eighth commandment alone. A fundamental scriptural principle is that to break one commandment of the law is to break all the commands of the law. Paul is saying to the Jew, "If you break the law of covetousness, which you view as a rather harmless sin, you make yourself at that moment a thief, an adulterer, a murderer." Therefore, as a violator of a "little" law, one becomes a violator of a "big" law, such as murder, which carries with it the ultimate penalty of death by stoning.

Verse twenty-two continues Paul's scolding of the Jew. The same application of stealing in verse twenty-one can be made here to the sin of adultery. It is interesting, however, to note the subject of idol worship. These Jews, religious sinners that they are, are commended by Paul because they "abhor" idols. The word, "abhor," literally means in the Greek, "to turn away from on account of the stench." After the 'Jews returned from captivity in Babylon, they never again have indulged in idol worship. One of the sins of idol worship is to put a higher value on a material object than is ordinarily attached to it because of its position as an object of worship. Paul is suggesting that to rob a temple of an idol is to recognize its monetary value and by that recognition put oneself in a type or form of idol worship. If the Jew truly "abhors" idol worship in the sense that we shared in the definition of the word, he will not have anything at all to do with the objects of idol worship, much less profit financially from them.

Verse twenty-three presents a puzzling dilemma for the Jew. On the one hand he glories in the law which was given exclusively to the Jewish nation by the Lord. On the other hand, he is found in violation of the law thereby bringing reproach upon the name of God. The Jew's glory of himself in relation to the law is seen in thirteen ways. He points toward himself with pride that he is:
(1) A man of praise;
(2) A man of thanksgiving;
(3) A man who trusts in the law;
(4) A man whose boast is God;
(5) A man who notes God's will;
(6) A man who approves the excellent things;
(7) A man who leads the spiritually blind;
(8) A man who is a light;
(9) A man who instructs the ignorant;
(10) A man who teaches babes;
(ll) A man who directs others;
(12) A man who preaches against sin;

(13) A man who glories in the law's commands.

As you read these thirteen qualities, you can readily recognize that this is indeed the kind of person that our Lord wishes all of us to be. However, as we have already studied in this chapter, the Jew is deceived into believing that he embodies all of these characteristics, when in actuality, he has none of them.

Verse twenty-four tells us how God's name is brought to ridicule by an unsaved world when we profess to be something that we are not. The Jews prospered under God's bountiful care as long as they obeyed Him. When that obedience was half-hearted, non-existent, or false, God had to judge them harshly before the eyes of the unbelieving Gentiles. These pagan Gentiles could not understand the principle of the chastisement of the Father upon His children. Therefore, they mocked Jehovah God as being a weak and ineffective God.

What a ministry could have been the Jews to enjoy if they had matched their walk with their talk! The world would have long ago embraced Israel's Jehovah. But because of the hypocrisy of the Jew, the Gentiles were totally unimpressed with God. As a result, any blasphemy of God's name among the Gentiles was a consequence of Israel's failure to live in holiness.

Verse twenty-five focuses its attention upon the heart. I have already described the value that the Jew places upon the ritual of circumcision. The Jew has never been fully convinced that there is no power in circumcision to make a person right with God. Does that seem strange? We have multitudes of Bible teachers who are falsely advising people that water baptism is essential to salvation. Nothing could be more untrue! Water baptism is essential because of salvation, not in order to obtain salvation. No ritual in the church is valid unless the heart of the participant is clear before God.

Paul is sharing here that circumcision becomes uncircumcision unless the Jew's heart is pure. Likewise, baptism is not baptism unless a person has been saved. It is only a dunking in water instead of a precious outward symbol of an inward change as the Lord intended. Verses twenty-six and twenty-seven should be studied as a couplet. The bottom line of Paul's discussion is that while scriptural rituals are important, they are not God's primary concern. His greatest desire for man is that He can have spiritual fellowship with him, made possible by the mediatoral office of the Lord Jesus Christ. Paul, in these verses, summarizes the fallacy of the Jew's unbalanced regard for circumcision. Paul asks, "If an uncircumcised person lives a faithful life and keeps all of the other requirements of the law, is he not as esteemed by the Lord as a circumcised person who fails in many of the other aspects? The conclusion is obvious. Circumcision is of secondary importance to the keeping of the law, just as baptism is of secondary importance to the repenting of sins, and the trusting of Jesus Christ for salvation. During the days of the Old Testament period, Israel was surrounded by many ungodly nations where circumcision was not practiced. It is Paul's contention that the Jews' uncircumcised hearts were more wicked than the pagans' uncircumcised bodies.

Verses twenty-eight and twenty-nine explicitly declare this fact. Circumcision of the flesh is a demonstration that satisfies men, but circumcision of the heart praises God. Can there be any question of the imperative need for us to live inward lives of holy separation before the Lord? I urge you, dear reader, to examine closely your faith to insure that it is not merely ceremonial. Be sure that your heart is right with God!

Chapter Three

Justification Introduced

To this point in our study, we have examined Paul's orderly declaration that all men are under the sentence of condemnation. In chapter one, we were confronted with the awful sinful condition of the wicked sinner who opposes everything that has any relationship to God. Chapter two brought us to the pitiful condition of the high ethical standards of the moral sinner who compared his lifestyle to that of the ungodly person in chapter one. By such judgment, he found himself to be superior. His own conclusion was that surely God would be impressed by his outward goodness, unlike that of that morally bankrupt sinner in the first chapter. Also, in chapter two, Paul led us into his analysis of the religious sinner. Now, in this third chapter, we come to the truth of God's Word that all men are condemned, and the first eight verses indicate that the greater our spiritual light, the greater our condemnation:

1 What advantage then hath the Jew? or what profit is there of circumcision?
2 Much every way: chiefly, because that unto them were committed the oracles of God.
3 For what if some did not believe? shall their unbelief make the faith of God without effect?
4 God forbid: yea, let God be true, but every man a liar; as it is written, That thou mightest be justified in thy sayings, and mightest overcome when thou art judged.
5 But if our unrighteousness commend the righteousness of God, what shall we say? Is God unrighteous who taketh vengeance? (I speak as a man)
6 God forbid: for then how shall God judge the world?
7 For if the truth of God hath more abounded through my lie unto his glory; why yet am I also judged as a sinner?
8 And not rather, (as we be slanderously reported, and as some affirm that we say,) Let do evil, that good may come? whose damnation is just.

Verse one comes directly to the point, but painfully so, for the Jew. Most of us in the church will readily accept the biblical fact that the Jews are God's chosen people through whom He is working His plan for the ages. Yet, if we believe Paul in chapter two, we are faced with the question of the value of being one of God's chosen if the Jew is as lost as the Gentile. Indeed, it would seem that there should be a greater advantage for the Jew because the word, "Jew," comes from the Hebrew word, "Yehudah," which means, "praise to Jehovah."

Verse two quickly introduces the answer to this query. Had it not been for the Jews, we would have none of the Bible today. We should be thankful to them. Every verse of the Scriptures, from the first verse of Genesis to the last verse of Revelation is ours because of the Jew. Even the writings in the Bible that had a Gentile author, like Luke, would never have come into existence had it not been for the witness of a converted Jew. .

The Word of God is alive! Even though the preponderance of Jews today reject the New Testament and are abysmally ignorant of the Old Testament, the Scriptures still promise their nation a great blessing during this world's end-time. To that end, if no other, they have an advantage over any other nation in the world.

Verse three draws a line of difference between the Jew as an individual and the Jew as a nation. I encourage you to recognize that difference; otherwise, much of the Bible will remain a hodge-podge of impossible prophecies. Please note. While the individual Jew is a part of God's chosen people, he is not exempted from the necessity of personal salvation.

Some teachers of the Bible suggest that to believe that God is going to bless Israel at the end of time is to believe that the Jew will get a second chance to be saved. That is utterly false. It is a "must" that you understand that the Abrahamic Covenant and the Davidic Covenant were both promises of blessings to the nation of Israel, and not to the individual Jew.

The individual Jew that is convicted by the Holy Spirit but rejects salvation will be lost. If he accepts Christ, he will be saved. There is no second chance for him in this world or in the next.

This verse also strikes at the widespread belief among liberals that all of God's Old Testament promises to the Jew were made null and void because of Israel's rejection of Jesus. How much in error these teachers are, and this verse confirms it! Just because some Jews were unfaithful does not cause God to be unfaithful and to abandon His promises to them. After all, the covenant promises of God to Israel were all unilateral in nature; that is, they were not dependent upon the faithfulness of the Jew. They were solely dependent upon God's faithfulness. Therefore, if God chose to disregard His covenants with them, He would be as sinful as they!

Verse four is Paul's response to such a preposterous ideal He says, "God forbid!" In the original language, this phrase is the strongest phrase that can be used, short of blasphemy, to indicate a negative reaction. The ideas expressed in verse three are equal, in the eyes of Paul, to that of calling God a liar. Paul's quick response is to affirm that God is true. The word, "true," as used here, literally means, "totally trustworthy and beyond any hint of falsehood or deception at all." Here we have the graphic differences between the nature of God and the nature of man. God can always be trusted without reservation; man can never be afforded that kind of unqualified trust.

This inclination of man to place himself in a position of higher authority than God is an ages-old controversy that never ceases from generation to generation. Yet, in the final analysis, as Paul clearly states, God always prevails. Ultimately, if Jesus tarries in His coming, we will all die and our bodies will be deposited into a hole in the ground. How frail and feeble we are!

Verse five is a paraphrase by Paul of the faulty logic of the Jew. Surely Paul was often perplexed by these chosen ones of God who had been given so much light from the Lord but were still unable to see. Although he was fully aware that they were partially blinded, as we shall learn later in this study, Paul nevertheless is almost to the point of sarcasm in his response to their spiritual ignorance.

This verse indicates that the Jew felt that his sin glorified God. In other words, if a man fell into sin and God sent fiery judgment upon him, the society in which that man lived would be the better for having witnessed the chastising hand of God at work. Even the awful wrath of God in its worst manifestation would reveal God's pristine glory.

While there is an element of truth in that reasoning, we can all agree that the loving grace of God magnifies our wondrous Lord much more than His wrath. In no place in the Scriptures can _God's beauty be found more than at the ugly scene of Calvary. To answer Paul's rhetorical question, God is always found righteous in any of His acts, including those performed by Him in wrath, but His love and grace exceed His hatred for sin.

Verse six opens with that strangest of statements of negative emphasis — "God forbid!" The idea of God being unjust in any of His dealings with man evokes a sense of horror from the heart of Paul! It is blasphemous even to think such! The word, "judge," means "to separate by calling into account." It can also mean "to sentence by bringing to trial." God is the Righteous Judge! Whether we agree or not does not alter the fact that God will judge in absolute fairness every person who ever lives on the planet earth. And His judgment will be just!

Verse seven may be more clearly explained by using an illustration that regularly occurs in the lives of unconverted churchmembers. Here is a man who is a member of the social set. He enjoys his cocktails, his partying, and his occasional lapses into an extramarital affair. His justification for such waywardness is simple. He says, "Everybody can't live like a preacher. God needs folks like me so that people who are weak can use me as a model. Anybody can live like me if they'll just half way try. So, God is glorified by having a few fellows around like me to get those guys into the church who would otherwise be turned off!"

What absurdity! What folly! If that be the case, why is a man so severely punished for continuing in sin? If sin can actually bring others to God, it would not be sensible for the Lord to punish the sinner. And further, if the God of holiness ever accepted any measure of "glory" from an act of sin, he would cease to be a holy God. Lying for whatever reason, is never right.

Verse eight carries some overtones of predestination. The Jew who was being condemned by Paul in this section of this epistle to the Romans was radically committed to adhering strictly to the law. He knew right from wrong. The twisted thinking of his mind brought him to believe that his compliance to the law gave him the luxury to sin occasionally and that God would overlook his sin. How could anyone believe such heresy? Very simply, the Jew was so enveloped by his concept of the total sovereignty of God that he was convinced that his sins were just a natural part of the fabric of his life.

Somehow, the Jew, and later, the saved Jew, were perceived as preaching that since forgiveness of sin reveals the grace of God, the obvious lesson is that, once in God's family, it is a good thing to sin. As this verse indicates, that is slanderous! God is holy! He derives no glory from the praise of impure lips!

The next passage in chapter three is a declaration of the fundamental fact that the whole world lies under the sentence of condemnation.

9 What then? are we better than they? No, in no wise: for we have before proved both Jews and Gentiles, that they are all under sin;
10 As it is written, There is none righteous, no, not one:
11 There is none that understandeth, there is none that seeketh after God.
12 They are all gone out of the way, they are together become unprofitable; there is none that doeth good, no, not one.
13 Their throat is an open sepulcher; with their tongues they have used deceit; the poison of asps is under their lips:
14 Whose mouth is full of cursing and bitterness:
15 Their feet are swift to shed blood:
16 Destruction and misery are in their ways:
17 And the way of peace have they not known:
18 There is no fear of God before their eyes.
19 Now we know that what things so ever the law saith, it saith to them who are under the law: that every mouth may be stopped, and all the world may become guilty before God.
20 Therefore by the deeds of the law there shall no flesh be justified in his sight: for by the law is the knowledge of sin.

Verse nine is clear! Even though God gave the law to the Jew, the Jew is not in a place of superiority over the Gentile because of it. For example, I am a citizen of the State of Florida of the United States of America. I know our laws about automobile speed limits. I have known these laws from my earliest childhood years. On the other hand, there may be a person from another country who comes to America by plane and rents an automobile upon arrival. He knows virtually nothing about our speed laws. On a given day, if he is in one car and I am in another, and we are both stopped for speeding, will the arresting officer be more lenient towards me because of my knowledge of the law? Of course not! If anything, I would receive the harsher treatment.

Mark it well! The Jew had an initial advantage over the Gentile because God gave him a written law, but sin is sin!

The nine verses included in verses ten-eighteen constitute for us God's opinion of unsaved mankind. It is not necessary to comment on each individual verse; they are plain enough on their own merit. Please note that Paul condemns man's tongue, his feet, and his eyes. Man is pictured as totally depraved, entirely corrupt. Oh, dear reader, the very best that we are, we are far short of the standard of God's holiness. Do not be tempted to see yourself in a way that is different to that of God's estimation of you. Your only hope is to have, and live, in the daily activities and routines of your life by the perspective of you that is held by the Almighty. And a lifestyle outside the realm of God's grace and spirit is a lifestyle of degeneracy. Like Israel, you may have certain advantages. You may have been reared by godly parents. You may have been taken as a child to God-blessed churches. But those things do not make you right with God. The verses in this passage are a commentary on the inner condition of any unsaved person, whether that person is sitting on a church pew or riding on a donkey's back. No man is right before God!

Verse nineteen reminds us that the law was given by the Lord so that the "... world may be brought under judgment." The word, "world," is better translated from the original language as "world order." Do not become enamored with all that is happening in this world, it is under the critical eye of God. "Guilty" literally means that the world order is "under legal process." How can we understand that? Paul is saying that God Is aware of the world's ways and that He, as Eternal Judge, is presently in critical review of everything that is going on in the world. This verse indicates that He is in the process of determining this divine sentence that this world order deserves.

Verse twenty declares that the law brought man to the place of seeing his sins. The literal translation of "knowledge" means "full knowledge." We do not have a partial knowledge. God has been good to us! We do not have to wonder what must we question! We know what God expects of us!

I must emphasize repeatedly that the sole purpose of the law was to make all men aware of their lost state before God. The law does not now nor has it ever possessed any power at all to cleanse a man from his sin. Verse twenty is a statement of finality—-no man is right in the sight of God! The law is proof positive that we are all sinners.
Is it any wonder that Paul, as a saved Jew, glories in his salvation and credits the work of Christ so often? He had lived as meticulously as any man under the Mosaic code, but his experience on the road to Damascus was so dramatic that it caused him to bury his esteem for the law's requirements under the blossoms of grace. It is that to which he opens his comments concerning the doctrine of justification in Romans 3:21:
21 But now the righteousness of God without the law is manifested, being witnessed by the law and the prophets;

This verse is a confirmation of Christ as the subject of the entire Bible, not just the New Testament. Everywhere in the Scriptures, from Genesis to Revelation, we can find Jesus Christ as the instrument of God's choosing for man's justification.

This message of justification in Jesus Christ is available to everyone. God is no respecter of persons, and no man is in a superior position over other men so that he can excuse himself as not needing to be saved:
22 Even the righteousness of God which is by faith of Jesus Christ unto all and upon all them that believe: for there is no difference:
23 For all have sinned, and come short of the glory of God;

There it is! The dual truth of God with a negative side and a positive side. Negatively, we are all without merit! None has attained personal righteousness acceptable to God! All men everywhere are lost. Positively, every man can be saved. God has not determined to save certain men because of their moral standing by some other way than trusting in Jesus Christ. Belief is the sole act of man toward the cross of our Lord that justifies him before God.

Thank God for this universal remedy that is within the reach of all who desire salvation. No one can ever challenge God from hell by asserting that there were some who were too poor, too sick, or too sinful to be saved. Romans 3:23 makes it clear that " . . . all have sinned, and come short of the glory of God."

This brings us to the question of sin. Is man a sinner because he sins? Although that is the common view throughout most of the religious world, it is simply not true!
Man is not a sinner because he sins; he sins because he is a sinner. It is a little like the old illustration of the dog. Is he a dog because he barks? Of course not, he barks because he is a dog. Even so it is with man. Just as a dog's nature causes him to bark, man's unregenerated nature causes him to sin.

What is sin? How is it manifested in us? I believe that we can rightly understand sin by observing the various scriptural terms used to define it:
(1) TRANSGRESSION: the willful committing of an expressly forbidden act in either the written law or written Word of God;
(2) INIQUITY: an act that is obviously wrong, whether or not it is written as such;
(3) ERROR: a willful choice to depart from that which is right;
(4) MISSING THE MARK: an inability to live up to the standards of righteousness and personal conduct that God has established;
(5) TRESPASS: willful rebellion against the authority of God in a particular area;
(6) LAWLESSNESS: a general disregard for the authority of God in any or all areas;
UNBELIEF: a refusal to acknowledge God and whatever He says as ultimate truth to be acted upon and believed.

But what is the "glory of God" that man has fallen short of attaining? The word, "glory," can be accurately translated as the "outward expression of an inward reality." As far as God is concerned, the transfiguration of Jesus is an example of that which was in Christ (God) becoming truly outwardly visible over His humanity. The sheer manifestation of God in Him was easily recognized by Peter, James and John.

That same glory enveloped Adam and Eve but was lost by them through their transgression. No amount of religious exercise can reclaim that glory. Only by the new birth does an individual taste its sweetness again, and vividly display without even trying to do so the very character of God.

Because of that lost glory, we have only one person to whom we may turn for relief, and that is Jesus:
24 Being justified freely by his grace through the redemption that is in Christ Jesus:

Two words that emphasize the gift of nature of our justification which affords for us the marvelous glory of God are found in this verse. These words are "freely" and "grace." They are actually redundant, saying the same thing — God gives us justification through His generosity and Christ's work.

But what does "redemption" mean? It is the Greek word "agarazo" and means " to deliver by paying a price." Because of the federal head of our race, Adam, all mankind has been sold under sin: "For we know that the law is spiritual: but I am carnal, sold under sin" (Romans 7:14). The delivering of man from sin became the priority of the business of heaven. God's special creation, the human race, just had to be saved. No other means could be found that could redeem (deliver) man other than the death of God's only begotten Son:
25 Whom God hath set forth to be a propitiation through faith in his blood, to declare his righteousness for the remission of sins that are past, through the forbearance of God;
26 To declare, I say; at this time his righteousness: that he might be just, and the justifier of him which believeth in Jesus.

Jesus was "set forth" by the Father. Literally translated, "set forth" means "to state publicly." Christ has been presented by God as the answer to man's terrible dilemma. Much like a candidate who has been nominated to high office at one of our major political conventions, Jesus is offered by the Lord.

He is presented as "... a propitiation through faith in his blood." The word, "propitiation," means "that which satisfies God's demand for judgment of sin." When Christ died at Calvary, He received to Himself the death that had been intended for man. In so doing, He satisfied God's holy cry for sin to be punished.

Let me give you a little example. A neighbor's child is horribly attacked by some wicked person. When you hear of it, you are infuriated that such a thing could happen in your community. You telephone the police and demand that something be done to capture the one responsible for such a vile deed. To your cry for justice, the police respond, "Calm down. We have apprehended the guilty party, and we have sufficient evidence to convict him." That statement would satisfy your desire for punishment upon the wrongdoer. The police had "propitiated," they had satisfied, your outcry for justice.

Propitiation is a precious truth with even deeper meanings than that which I have just shared. In the Greek, it is "hilasterion," better translated "mercy-seat." Jesus Christ, according to Romans 3:25 became our mercy-seat; He was set forth to be our mercy-seat. In the innermost part of the Old Testament tabernacle could be found the mercy-seat of the Old Testament. Underneath it was the ark of the covenant, a box in which had been placed the broken tablets of the law, signifying man's inability to keep the requirements of the law. Above the mercy-seat was the area filled by the shekinah glory of Almighty God. But here was the problem faced by the Old Testament priest — God would not bring His celestial glory to a place inhabited by sin. What could be done? Only by sacrificial blood sprinkled upon the mercy-seat, thereby separating the broken law from God's presence, could the Almighty come to the level of men.

That sacrificial system required frequently repeated offerings of blood to propitiate, or satisfy, God. All of the sacrifices were actually a picture of the ultimate sacrifice for sins that would one day be found in Jesus

Christ at Calvary, and that offering of blood would never need to be repeated. It was once-for-all! The writer of Hebrews says it this way: "By the which will we are sanctified through the offering of the body of Jesus Christ once for all. And every priest standeth daily ministering and offering oftentimes the same sacrifices, which can never take away sins: But this man, after he had offered one sacrifice for sins for ever, sat down on the right hand of God" (Hebrews 10:10-12).

Returning to Romans 3:26, I see a wondrous truth indeed. Paul says that God is declaring the righteousness of Jesus so that all who believe upon Him may also be made righteous. Our Heavenly Father is limitless in H-is desire for all men to come to Him and be saved! He declares, He communicates, the gospel of salvation in a multitude of times and methods. By songs, sermons, and personal appeals, men and women are daily confronted with God's declaration of His willingness to save them.

His declaration is two-fold (v. 26). First, the Lord Jesus Christ is just (righteous); second, any who trust in the righteousness of Christ become righteous themselves. It is a staggering thought, yet scripturally true, that by simple trust in the conquering death of the Lord Jesus we can become as righteous as He is righteous.

It is little wonder that Paul asks a question of exclamation 1n verses twenty-seven and twenty-eight:
27 Where is boasting then? It is excluded. By what law? of works? Nay: but by the law of faith.
28. Therefore we conclude that a man is justified by faith without the deeds of the law.

In other words, since our righteousness is the result of the horrible death of Christ on the cross, what do we have as a basis for brag? As the hymnwriter has said:
"Jesus paid it all, All to Him I owe, Sin had left a crimson stain, He washed it white as snow."

Boasting of our moral uprightness is "excluded." The word, "excluded," means to "permanently close the door of entrance by one definitive effort." Is that what Jesus did when He died for us? It is indeed! A man is the worst of fools if he believes that there is any way that he can substitute another plan of salvation for the precious one that God has provided. Man cannot even add his most noble efforts to God's plan. The door has been forever shut to the arguments from puny man about his own mortal opinions of the best way to be saved. There is only one way, and that is faith in Jesus Christ!

Therefore, Paul reiterates in verse twenty-eight his position concerning man's ability to help himself in the matter of salvation. He emphasizes that a man is saved "without the deeds of the law." In the Greek, the word, "without," has a very strong meaning. It means, in relation to this verse, that a man's justification is as far removed from the deeds of the law as can possibly be imagined. There is absolutely no relationship between the good works of a man and his securing of salvation. Works are the fruit one bears for having already been saved; they are never the root for getting saved!

The final three verses in this chapter are a summary statement by Paul of the universal remedy of justification for the sins of all mankind:
29 Is he the God of the Jews only? is he not also of the Gentiles? Yes, of the Gentiles also:
30 Seeing it is one God, which shall justify the circumcision by faith, and uncircumcision through faith.
31 Do we then make void the law through faith? God forbid: yea, we establish the law.

Thank God, that our Father has chosen to provide salvation for all the people of the world, Jew and Gentile alike! Why does Paul make such an obvious statement of fact? He was attempting to show the Jew that if it was by the keeping of the law that a man could be saved, then non-Jews would have no hope because the law had been given to the Jews and the Jews alone! Even the Jew recognized that God was God to the Gentiles also! For example, Jeremiah had centuries earlier made this statement about the Gentiles: "O Lord, my strength, and my fortress, and my refuge in the day of affliction, the **GENTILES SHALL COME UNTO THEE FROM THE ENDS OF THE EARTH**" (Jeremiah 16:19). Paul's implication is clear! Since the Gentiles did not have the written law, if the keeping of the law was the only way to be right with God, how can it be explained that one day the Lord will draw the Gentile nations to Himself?

Verse thirty suddenly injects the ritual of circumcision into this discussion. Why? Remember that circumcision was to the Jew what baptism is to the Christian. It identified his acceptance of the teachings and traditions of the law. The one definite and outward difference between the Jew and the Gentile was circumcision. The Jew had submitted to circumcision; the Gentile had not.

So, Paul asserts that if a Jew will let the law be his schoolmaster as it was intended by the Lord, he can be brought "by faith" to Jesus Christ. But note clearly, he is not
saying that a man is saved "by faith" in the deeds of the law; that idea has already been forcefully rejected by him. He is here talking about the law being used as a guide in its deeper meanings of Jesus than in mere outer rituals of dead formalities.

In reference to the Gentile, Paul does not speak of salvation "by faith" as he has with the Jew. He speaks of salvation "through faith." The Gentile does not have access to the law as a schoolmaster. All that he knows of salvation must come through the proclamation of the gospel.

I am sure that many of Paul's readers of this Roman letter were of Jewish heritage. After having read all that he has written about the failure of the law to save anyone, I am certain that many of them had a very logical reaction by wondering why there should have ever been a law in the first place. Quite simply, if the law cannot save, why did not God allow Jesus Christ to come and save the world hundreds of years earlier?

That seems on the surface rather reasonable, except for one thing. The law brought man to a recognition of his utter inability to save himself, and thereby his need of a savior. Whenever a man, even someone today, is convicted of sin and looks to Jesus for salvation, it is because that he has been condemned either directly or indirectly by his violation of the commands of the law. In so doing, according to verse thirty-one, he has established it.

Chapter Four

Justification Continued

Paul is a master of apologetics —- the art of defending the faith. He has already given us an eloquent presentation of well-organized reasons why all mankind is condemned and why there is none, not even the most religious Jew, who can save himself. Now, in this fourth chapter, he brings this matter of justification from the level of the world and of national Israel to the level of individual humanity. He speaks of the beloved Abraham and Sarah; he quotes valiant David. As a skilled debater, Paul narrows the question of salvation from the arena of general application to the battlefield of the reader's own conscience and heart.

1 What shall we say then that Abraham our father, as pertaining to the flesh, hath found?
2 For if Abraham were justified by works, he hath whereof to glory; but not before God.
3 For what saith the scripture? Abraham believed God, and it was counted unto him for righteousness.

Faithful Abraham lived before the establishment of the law. Like the Gentile, he did not enjoy the privilege of God's guidance through written commands. He had no law. Yet, his blood was that of the Jew.

What was it that Abraham found of eternal value? Was it that he had done a great thing in fathering Isaac through whom it had been promised by God that the nations of the world would be blessed? No, because that birth was a miracle since Abraham was one hundred years old and Sarah was ninety at the time of Isaac's conception.

Really, Abraham did nothing out of the ordinary except believe God. Nothing of an extraordinary nature was ever done by him. Those things in his life that might be construed by the casual Bible student as being heroic or remarkable were in actuality the demonstration of God's power in working through the availability, not the ability, of this humble man. It was his simple faith in God that marked him as being different!

By daily walking with the Lord, Abraham entered new vistas of faith into which few humans ever tread. Jesus said of him: "Abraham rejoiced to see my day; and he saw it, and was glad" (john 8:56). By faith Abraham looked down the corridor of time, completely bypassing the era of the law, and he saw the Lord Jesus Christ! How wonderful! How magnificent! This Old Testament patriarch saw the Lord!

Paul says in verse three that Abraham's faith "was counted unto him for righteousness." The word, "counted," appears eleven times in chapter four (verses 3, 4, 5, 6, 8, 9, 10, ll, 22, 23, 24). It is the Greek word, "logizomai," and it can be accurately translated, "counted, imputed, reckoned." It literally means "to put on a person's account." Because of Abraham's trust in God, it was placed upon his account that heaven viewed him as a righteous man.

"Logizomai," (counted) has a beautiful meaning. It goes beyond the general definition that I have just given. As used in verse three, it conveys the picture of God taking the robe of Christ's righteousness and wrapping it completely around Abraham. Now read carefully! Abraham's faith did not save him! His faith was merely the vehicle through which he could see the One who could save.

We must understand that salvation always has been, is now, and always will be of grace, and not one bit of works:
4 Now to him that worketh is the reward not reckoned of grace, but of debt.
5 But to him that worketh not, but believeth on him that justifieth the ungodly, his faith is counted for righteousness.

These verses are so clear! Do you see the word, "reward"? It is better translated, "wages." Wages are earnings, what a person receives for services that he has rendered or for work that he has done. So, if a man says that salvation has been earned by him, either in whole or in part, he cannot say that he has been saved by the free gift of the grace of God. On the contrary, he must say that God was in debt to him, that salvation was owed to him. You cannot have it both ways. Either God has freely given you salvation, or you have earned it! And the one thing that millions do not seem to understand is that compared to all that the Lord has done for man, whatever a person might do to merit salvation would fall pitifully short. As we earlier saw in verse three, we are viewed by God as being righteous when we cease trying and start trusting!

Continuing Paul's personal references to familiar Old Testament characters, we are now introduced to David's concept of justification:
6 Even as David also describeth the blessedness of the man, unto whom God imputeth righteousness without works,
7 Saying, Blessed are they whose iniquities are forgiven, and whose sins are covered.
8 Blessed is the man to whom the Lord will not impute sin.

We have already examined Abraham's source of righteousness; now we turn to David. Both of these men lived before the death of Christ at Calvary. Why should they be considered at all in reference to salvation obtained by those who are now living after Calvary during "the Age of Grace"? Already in this study of Romans, I have tried to illustrate through the instructions of Paul that men have always been saved by the same plan of salvation and that the keeping of the works of the law never saved anyone. It is not correct to use the term, "Age of Grace," when referring to this period of history following Christ's death, the period in which we now live. Oh no, this is no more the Age of Grace than any other historical age. Man has always been saved by grace, either before or after Calvary. This is more accurately defined as "the Church Age," the period of years that God has determined to use in His special efforts to win the Gentile world, sandwiched between the Day of Pentecost and the future day of the rapture of the church. Therefore, it is perfectly in order to discuss the influence of righteous men of the Old Testament in relation to the doctrine of justification.

Verse six very clearly shows us that David was fully aware of the same fact of righteousness as Abraham had been centuries earlier. Works cannot save a man; they never have and never will. This recognition by David caused him to "pronounce blessing" upon any person who would discover this wonderful truth of the sheer simplicity of being right with God.

"Blessedness" is a very appropriate word. It means more than happiness. Happiness is dependent upon the pleasantness of whatever is happening around us in our environment. If our families are well and there is money in the bank, we are happy. But the good thing about being saved is that we can be in a state of blessedness even when we are not happy, because blessedness is the state of the heart. It does not mean that we have peace from trouble, but rather, peace in trouble. So it is with the individual who is saved. He is blessed.

Two exciting truths are declared by David in verse eight. First, sins are forgiven. Second, sins are covered. This principle of the forgiveness of sins must have been spoken into the heart of David by the Spirit of God. It was an unknown doctrine in the days of the Old Testament. This is important! The blood sacrifice merely shielded the sins of a man from the presence of God for a period of one year, after which the poor individual was held accountable for those same sins unless he offered another blood sacrifice. Never was he forgiven! He was only protected from the penalty of sin for twelve months at a time, but because of Calvary, sins are completely forgiven, thoroughly eradicated, for once and for all!

Second, the believer's sins are covered, never to trouble him again or ever to be remembered by the mind of God! Consider these verses: "As far as the east is from the west, so far hath he removed our transgressions from us (Psalm 103212). Also consider, " . . . and thou wilt cast all their sins into the depths of the sea" (Micah 7:19).

These verses reveal a wonderful attribute of God! Not only is He able to forgive sin, He is able to forget sin! Whenever a person is saved, all of the wickedness of his life is eradicated, completely covered, by the blood of the Lord Jesus Christ. God blots the very remembrance of that sin from His mind: "I, even I, am he who blotteth out thy transgressions for mine own sake, and will not remember thy sins" (Isaiah 43:25).

Of all the tremendous blessings that God has so bountifully poured upon the believer, I like this one best! My sins have been wiped away, even from the very mind of God! They are gone, forever!

I remember the story of the old saint who just could not contain himself in the worship services of his church. Whenever something good was said about Jesus, heaven, or the love of God, this dear old man would shout the praises of his heart. Finally, the pastor instructed the ushers to lock the old saint in a closet adjoining the vestibule if there should ever be another outburst. Well, sure enough, the day came when a hearty "Praise the Lord!" rolled from the lips of this dear man of God right in the middle of the pastor's sermon. So, up the aisle came the ushers, they retrieved the joyous offender and literally carried him out to the little closet. For a while, nothing happened! Then, a "Glory Hallelujah" fairly shook the building! Looking inside the closet, the ushers saw an unusual sight. The old man had found a stack of National Geographic Magazines». One, in particular, had caught his fancy. Pointing toward an article, he shouted to the ushers, "Bless Jesus, boys, here it says that the deepest point in the ocean is over 15,000 feet and that's where God has put all my sins!"

Verse eight expands upon the joy of sins forgiven. Literally translated, it says: "Blessed is the man whose sins the Lord will in no wise reckon." Never , not even at the judgment seat of Christ, will our sins confront us again. In other words, not only does God not remember our forgiven sins now, He will never at any time in the future recall them against us! That is indeed enough to make anybody happy and blessed!

Paul has stressed the futility of works in his assertion that salvation is by grace apart from the law, but he does not seem satisfied! It is as though he fears that somehow someone will misunderstand. So, in order to reinforce what he has just said in verses six through eight about David's discovery of the blessedness of righteousness, he follows up in verses nine through twelve with a well-reasoned argument that destroys anyone's belief that true inner peace can come about as a result of good works.

9 Cometh this blessedness then upon the circumcision only, or upon the uncircumcision also? for we say that faith was reckoned to Abraham for righteousness.
10 How was it then reckoned? when he was in circumcision, or in uncircumcision? Not in circumcision, but in uncircumcision.
11 And he received the sign of circumcision, a seal of the righteousness of the faith which he had yet being uncircumcised: that he might be the father of all them that believe, though they be not circumcised; that righteousness might be

imputed unto them also:
12 And the father of circumcision to them who are not of the circumcision only, but who also walk in the steps of that faith of our father Abraham, which he had being yet uncircumcised.

Why is this question of circumcision in relation to justification so important? To the Jew, the ritual of circumcision was the seal that bound him to God. It was the symbolic confirmation that the covenant promises between him and the Lord were valid and that God could be trusted. It also labeled God as "Jehovah, God of the Jews."

Such importance, therefore, was in direct opposition to uncircumcision. As far as the Jew believed and was concerned, there could be absolutely no hope for the uncircumcised because of the meanings of circumcision that I have just shared. Verse nine begins the argument of Paul on this point by emphatically declaring, " . . . to Abraham his faith was reckoned for righteousness."

Pursuing this discussion, we must arrive at the time of that reckoning — was it before Abraham's circumcision or after? Paul declared in verse ten that it was " . . . not in circumcision, but in uncircumcision."

To answer this question concerning Abraham's circumcision and Paul's statement concerning it, we must turn back to the Book of Genesis. There in Genesis 15:6 arethese words: "And he believed in the Lord; and he counted it to him for righteousness." When we move into the sixteenth chapter of Genesis, we find Abraham taking the Egyptian handmaiden as a sexual partner out of which sprang a son, Ishmael. Then, we move forward to the seventeenth chapter and find this account of Abraham's circumcision in verses 24 and 25: "And Abraham was ninety years old and nine, when he was circumcised in the flesh of his foreskin. And Ishmael, his son, was thirteen years old, when he was circumcised in the flesh of his foreskin." These verses give us a fact that cannot be refuted. Abraham's faith was counted for righteousness by the Lord at least thirteen years before his circumcision. That is very significant because it challenges the Jew's belief that no man could be right with God unless he had submitted himself to circumcision.

Verse eleven uses the word, "sign," which in the Greek means, "an emblem of, a token, a mark." Circumcision was not a ritual given to Abraham in order that he might gain righteousness; it was given to him as an outward display that he was already righteous. Even so it is with baptism. Just as Abraham's circumcision came after the Lord's acceptance of him as righteous, the believer is baptized after he is saved. Baptism is not essential to salvation; it is essential because of salvation.

The fact of Abraham's righteousness without circumcision was not merely coincidental! Nothing in the Scriptures ever is! Paul declares in verse eleven that Abraham could be " . . . the father of all them that believe . . . " because of his righteousness prior to his circumcision. The entire Gentile world would have been without his example if his righteousness was somehow related to his circumcision. In other words, according to Paul, since righteousness was bestowed upon Abraham by the Lord in the fashion that it was, all mankind, both circumcised and uncircumcised, can rejoice in that " . . . righteousness might be imputed unto them also"(v. 11).

This great truth of impartiality in saving all who come to God, 'whether they be circumcised or uncircumcised, is brought to an important conclusion in verse twelve. The emphasis of the verse is two-fold.

First, Abraham is said to be the "father of circumcision to them who are not of the circumcision only . . . " He understood the full meaning of circumcision and never connected it with his righteousness at all. Therefore, he was the father of all the millions of Jews who would follow him in that clear understanding of circumcision's meaning. They, like him, would be " . . . not of the circumcision only." By implication, then, Abraham was not the father of Jews who, like the Pharisees, were so careful to observe circumcision, somehow convincing themselves that they were making themselves right with God.

Second, Abraham can rightly be considered the father of every person who has been saved since his time, because verse twelve speaks of him being the father of all " . . . who walk in the steps of that faith." The word, "walk," is crucial to the meaning of this. In the Bible, salvation is never spoken of in the past tense. We are always to think in terms of salvation as a "right now" experience. If we are to share in the same victorious faith as Abraham,» we are to "walk," which implies a continual growth and use of the faith of our righteousness. When we do that, we are like Abraham.

For the remainder of our study of the fourth chapter, I think it would be wise for us to examine very carefully each verse, separating each one from adjoining verses so that we may fully appreciate its meaning. We left the subject of circumcision in verse twelve, and with verse thirteen we see that Paul has begun a new line of thought:

13 For the promise, that he should be the heir of the world, was not to Abraham, or to his seed, through the law, but through the righteousness of faith.

Most Jews, even today, have the mistaken notion that the promise of God to Abraham that the world would be blessed through his seed was a reference to Israel in its physical attachment to him because of the law. What we have already seen nullifies that argument. Nations and individuals become the recipients of God's promise to Abraham as they respond with the same kind of faith that brought righteousness to him. The channel of blessing has never been through what we do for Him, it has been and is now through what He has done for us! When we accept that by faith, God is pleased and abundant blessings that are almost unimaginable become ours to enjoy.

How righteousness becomes a reality and how it is afterwards maintained are fundamental to a correct understanding of man's union with God. This is the subject
of verse fourteen:
14 For if they which are of the law be heirs, faith is made void, and the promise made of none effect.

What is this verse saying? Very simply, if the Jew is able to keep the law and attain salvation, then there is another way to righteousness than faith. Remember, it was not Abraham's adherence to the law that was counted to him as righteousness; it was his faith. Therefore, to be able to trust the works of the law to bring righteousness does as verse fourteen says; it "voids" faith.

You cannot have it both ways. Either you will be saved by works, or you will be saved by grace. Later, we will look at this verse more thoroughly, but since it applies here, read Romans 11:6: "And if by grace, then is it no more of works: otherwise grace is no more grace. But if it be of works, then is it no more grace: otherwise work is no more work.

That is precisely the meaning of "void" in Romans 4:14. It means "empty, without strength, not existing." So very often, especially because of my media ministries, I will be criticized by sincere people who attack my narrow- mindedness when I say that Jesus Christ is the only way to heaven. I am urged to be more tolerant of other religions in the world. I am scolded for excluding other people of other faiths who have a different way to God. I am repeatedly told that there are many ways to God. It is not the purpose of this study before us to defend my position that Jesus Christ is man's only hope, except to remind you that Paul in this verse is warning us that if there is some other plan of salvation, it makes faith void (empty, without strength, not existing).

On one occasion I was invited to participate as a member of a panel that was to preview an upcoming television special concerning major evangelists. 'When the private viewing was completed, our reactions were asked by the religious editor of a major daily newspaper. Our panel included a Catholic nun, a Jewish rabbi, an Assembly of God preacher, and me. The rabbi was visibly upset. To the query of the reporter, he said, "I am upset that there are such people as these who believe that I am going to hell if I do not believe in Jesus Christ!" Looking at me, he said, "Do you believe that? Do you believe that I will go to hell?"

With as much compassion as I could muster, I said, "Yes, you will go to hell unless you trust Jesus Christ as your Savior and Lord. But please understand that that is not just my view. It is what Jesus said in John 14:6: "I am the way, the truth, and the life: no man cometh unto the Father, but by me." Continuing my answer to the rabbi, I said, "Please notice that Jesus did not say that He was a good way, or one of the ways, or even the best way. He said that He was "THE way."

This answer did not satisfy the rabbi. He retorted, "Maybe your Jesus looked upon Himself as the only way, but God never did."

Again, gently but firmly, I replied, "For God so loved the world that He gave His only begotten Son that whosoever believeth in Him should not perish but have everlasting life" (John 3:16).

My final statement to this sincere and morally fine rabbi was straight-to-the-point: "Sir, if your Jewish faith was sufficient to make you right with God because of your faithfulness in performing all of its laws and commands, then Jesus was the greatest of all fools for dying on the cross. You see, Jesus was a Jew and was sinless. Therefore, He had perfectly obeyed the law. That being so, if anyone could ever have testified to the law's ability to save a man-, it would have been Him. But no, He recognized that the law was never intended to save; but rather, it was an instructor, pointing those who seek salvation to the Only One who had the power to save."

Moreover, according to Romans 4:14, if the law-keepers can be made righteous, not only is "faith made void" but the "promise is made of none effect" also. What is the promise that is the subject of this concern? It is the promise God made to Abraham that through his seed all the nations of the world would be blessed. If we cannot depend on God's statement about Abraham's faith being counted unto him as righteousness, we cannot depend upon any of God's other promises, and the Word of God becomes a bundle of blunders.

After that solemn warning in verse fourteen, we come to the reason Paul gives in verse fifteen:
15 Because the law worketh wrath: for where no law is, there is no transgression.

This little verse sheds a tremendous truth! The law is God's red-light. It says to the sinner that he is a sinner. Please look at the word, "worketh." It is a present-tense verb form that actually means that the wrath of God is at work in the lost man's life every moment of every day, continually! Does the latter phrase mean that if a person is not exposed to the law, he is without sin? Of course not! We have already discussed that in chapter two of this study. This verse gives every man two alternatives from which he will choose one! He may either choose to reject Christ and live under the continual wrath of God, or he may choose to accept Christ and by His grace be justified so that he is looked upon as having never sinned at all.

There is a little play on words that is nevertheless true. Let me share it with you. Whenever you are studying the Bible and you come to the word, "therefore," find out what it is there for. Remember that little phrase. For example, you may use it in studying Romans 4:16. What Paul is saying in the verse is a result of everything that he has just said in the verses preceding. So, knowing that, read verse sixteen:

16 Therefore it is of faith, that it might be by grace; to the end the promise might be sure to all the seed; not to that only which is of the law, but to that also which is of the faith of Abraham; who is the father of us all.

"Seed," in this verse, gives a special insight to our discussion of how a person is made right with God. Seed has to do with reproduction. Why is that important? We have already seen that the promises of God for righteousness are not gained by a person faithfully keeping the works of the law. He cannot earn salvation. As verse fifteen has already declared, to attempt to become righteous by keeping the law "worketh wrath."

Therefore, righteousness does not result from what we have done but from who we are. It is a gift, not a wage! The "seed" indicates that! A man is an heir to the wealth of his father because of his birth into the family, a process which occurred without any effort by him at all. A man cannot earn an inheritance; he does nothing to deserve an inheritance. He receives it because of who he is, not what he has done.

Abraham is the "father of us all." That is, when we allow the grace of God to be exercised within us, we become the seed of Abraham's faith and heirs to the promises that God made to him. Just as we become heirs to our earthly parents by physical birth (a work that was totally their doing), we also become heirs to our Heavenly Father by spiritual birth (a work that was totally His doing).

Since what we enjoy in Christ is a result of His work and not ours, the "promise may be sure to all . . . " How comforting! "Sure" literally means "to be set, firmly fixed, definitely established." Oh, dear reader, we need not be concerned about the tomorrows of our lives in terms of how we will be viewed by our wonderful Lordl! As His own dear children, we are the recipients of firmly fixed promises.

That glorious truth is expanded by Paul in verse seventeen:
17 (As it is written, I have made thee a father of many nations,) before him whom he believed, even God, who quickeneth the dead, and calleth those things which be not as though they were.

The very name, "Abraham," conveys the same truth as is found in this verse. It means, "the father of vast numbers of peoples." In fact, his name does not exclude the Gentile nations. All the peoples of the world are included in his name and in this promise! God did not forget any of us!

And, think of it! This wonderful God before whom Abraham stood is the same wonderful God before whom we can stand these many centuries later. He is the "God who quickeneth the dead." In other words, He makes alive the dead! I earnestly believe that Abraham, by the end of his life and walk with the Lord, was able to visualize most of the ways that God would make alive the things and people who were dead. Let's consider a few possibilities:
(1) God would make alive the "dead" bodies of Abraham and Sarah so that Isaac could be born;
(2) God would make alive the settled fact in Abraham's mind that Isaac was to die a sacrificial death;
(3) God would make alive the Lord Jesus Christ as He would be resurrected from death;
(4) God would make alive future multitudes who would come from the deadness of spiritual darkness to the brightness of spiritual light;
God would make alive the physically dead believers who would come from
    death even as Christ had done before them.

Did you notice that God " . . . calleth things that are not as though they were?" That little statement of divine fact describes the omnipotence of Almighty God. Every created thing that exists, including man, came into being as a result of His call. But this is more than a reference to the material"! Those of us who have been saved know that we have been called to a new spiritual life in Christ, and that we are day-by-day being tugged by His wondrous call into new dimensions of growth in grace. It is impossible to comprehend in the mortal mind, but just as God brought me from nothing into existence as the physical son of my parents, I have also been called by God from a life that was not even a life to an existence as the spiritual son of the Most High God! Hallelujah!

With joy we can continue with Paul's commendation of the faith of Abraham in Romans 4:18:
18 Who against hope believed in hope, that he might become the father of many nations, according to that which was spoken, So shall thy seed be.

What had been God's special promise to Abraham? It was that this faithful man would become the father of many nations. I am sure that Abraham pondered that promise often, especially in light of the advanced age of his wife and of himself. He was one hundred years old; his wife was ninety. Human reason declared that it was a biological impossibility for the two of them to have children. As far as the experts of his day and the dictates of his own mind, either Abraham had misunderstood God or God had made a mistake.

Neither of the above was correct. Abraham had the right word from the Lord, and had not failed! "Hope against hope" can be accurately interpreted as "hoping in a situation so unbelievably difficult as to defy all odds in favor of an acceptable outcome!" Where God's Word is concerned, impossible circumstances become the incubators of victory!

When we study the Bible, we do not have to approach it with the formulas of the chemist, the records of the historian, the laws of the physicist, or the conclusion of the philosopher! God's Word was not given to us to make sense to us; it was given to us to make changes in us! The unfathomable depths of the Scriptures do not have to conform themselves to the puny probings of man. As the very Word of God, it is true in every point and detail, whether man sees fit to believe it or not. Abraham chose to believe what God had told him, so he lived in confidence with supernatural hope against the hopes of man.

That quiet confidence in the trustworthiness of God's promises strengthened his faith:

19 And being not weak in faith, he considered not his own body now dead, when he was about an hundred years old, neither yet the deadness of Sarah's womb:

The demonstration of the power of God in the believer's life is in direct proportion to that believer's personal will! You will be as energized by the Spirit as you choose. It was a reproductive fact that Abraham and Sarah were well beyond child bearing years. That was the way their neighbors saw them, and that was also the way they saw themselves.

If there was ever a man who lived that had a reason to be weak in faith, it would have certainly been Abraham. But real faith is not based on what appears to be obvious; it is, instead, founded upon a Word from God. Abraham's strength for the tests that he faced in his life was not a product of his own physical resources. His was a conviction of faith that relied upon the never-failing arm of the Lord.

So, it is not strange at all that Paul honors him in the twentieth verse by saying:

20 He staggered not at the promise of God through unbelief; but was strong in faith, giving glory to God.

I like the imagery employed by Paul on this description of Abraham's reaction to what God had promised. Most of us physically "stagger" or go into momentary shock when told of some extraordinary happening that is about to occur to us. Even Abraham laughed when first advised by the Lord of the future birth of Isaac. But that was an outward reaction.

The real Abraham, that man of faith inside his aged body, never wavered in conviction. His strength was youthful and vigorous because it had been placed within his heart by the Lord. The condition of his outer self had nothing at all to do with the condition of his inner self. While physically he was daily deteriorating, inwardly he was being daily renewed by the grace of our Lord. Realizing this important truth, Abraham gladly gave glory to God.

This means that he had passed from the passive level of intellectual

acceptance of the things that God had told him to the active arena of personal commitment:
21 And being fully persuaded that, what he had promised, he was able also to perform.
22 And therefore it was imputed to him for righteousness.

Note the phrase, "... being fully persuaded." This can be literally translated as "being totally established as a fact with no room for doubt or error." In other words, Abraham was "full" of the truth of God. What better picture could we have in the Old Testament of the profound truth in the New Testament of the filling of the Holy Spirit.

His confidence rested upon the sovereignty of God. Dear reader, you are destined for unnecessary trouble unless you can arrive at the same point of assurance. Since God is indeed the true God, we need not question His ability to do whatever He has said.

That is precisely the glad reason for the comforting statement of verse twenty-one. Faith in God is the foundation for the imputing of the righteousness of Christ into the life of the believer. By placing our faith solely upon what Christ did for us at Calvary, we have peace with God as Jesus comes to live within us in all of His righteousness! Glory!

Read again verses twenty-three and twenty-four in this chapter and see that it is really so! As verse twenty-four says, this imputing of righteousness is "for us also. . . . If we believe on him that raised up Jesus our Lord from the dead." Think of it! When I accepted Jesus Christ as my Savior and Lord, the same opinion that God had of Abraham, God now has of me! Even grander, the same opinion that God has of Jesus, He now has of me!

The last verse of this remarkable chapter stands like a beacon, towering above the confusion and sin of this world:
25 Who was delivered for our offences, and was raised again for our justification.

From the earliest intentions of God for the human race, there coursed through His mind the thought that Jesus would die for our sins. The pages of the Bible are a record of the unfolding of that plan. Beginning with God's provision of animal skins to cover the nakedness of Adam and through the entire sacrificial system of the Mosaic law we hear the Spirit whispering that Jesus will come. Finally, He does! And John the Baptist announces the glad tidings as he exults, "Behold, the Lamb of God that taketh away the sins of the world!"

When Jesus made His physical appearance among us, He affirmed the symbolism of every bloody sacrifice in the Old Testament era. He became the total fulfillment of every prophecy. He silenced the mouth of the skeptic who challenged God's Word in that day. All of these accomplishments are wonderful and more could be listed.

But more glorious than His sinless life and substitutionary death was our Lord's resurrection. No other religion can point to the physical resurrection of its founder. Therefore, every other religion must revolve around its founder's program. Our religion revolves around a person, Jesus Christ the Risen Lord.

His blood washed away sin, so that no man must ever stand guilty before God. His resurrection from the dead, moreover, proves that the blood really did destroy sin.
Unlike any other religion, we are not forced to hang our faith on what Jesus said, we have undeniable proof by what He did when He arose triumphantly from the dead!

Chapter Five

Justification Continued

Arriving at the fifth chapter, we can look backward over the path we have just traveled through the first four chapters and better describe the conflict in which we are all participants. A war is raging! This entire letter by Paul is an attempt to warn its readers of the deadly struggle that is presently in the world. The tragedy of our day is that only a minority within the church are aware that a battle is taking place. But there is no safety in such ignorance. Whether the believer recognizes that the powers of darkness and of light are at war, or whether he does not, changes none at all the biblical fact of its reality. His well-being in this world is directly affected by his involvement, or lack thereof, in this continual war. Many of the painful occurrences that an undiscerning believer calls "coincidental" or "accidental" are actually the unfortunate results of a spiritual war in which he is an unwitting participant, blindly being subjected to its awful results rather than being protected by a wise use of the whole armor of God.

As we shall see even more carefully defined in this chapter, we have:
TWO CHARACTERS: Adam (human) and Christ (divine);
TWO CHOICES: Condemnation or Justification;
TWO CONSEQUENCES: Death or Life.

These three options constitute the battlefield that is set before every man. His decision about each determines his role in the battle. He cannot be neutral, refusing to choose, because a refusal to choose is to choose.

1 Therefore being justified by faith, we have peace with God through our Lord Jesus Christ:
2 By whom also we have access by faith into this grace wherein we stand, and rejoice in hope of the glory of God.

The opening phrase is not as accurately translated from the Greek as it might have been. It really says, "having been justified by faith." Justification, unlike sanctification that we shall examine later, is not a progressive work. It happens once, when we are saved. It is an eternal pronouncement by God that the sinner is pardoned, never to be cast in peril of hell again. While he may lose fellowship with God, this act of justification provides that he will never lose his relationship with God.

As a result, we have "peace with God." No saint should ever again look at God through eyes of terror. He is a Father. Granted, we are wise indeed to fear His discipline, but even in those times of chastisement, God administers the rod with mercy and love.

Do you recall your battles with God before you were saved? Do you remember how thoughts of death brought anxiety? Do you ever think about those uncertain days when you were consumed with the dread awareness that your destiny was hell? Oh, dear friend, those days are over forever! You have peace with God! Now that you are saved, your struggle is no longer with Him! He is your friend, your ally, your defense, your guide, your companion, your hope, your consolation, and your comfort!

Verse two is one of those little verses that we often overlook even though it is full of nuggets of blessing. Do you see the little phrase, " . . . we have access . . . "? A better translation is, " . . . we have had access . . ." There was a fixed time that we entered the presence of God and His Spirit entered us. Like poor beggars who have entered a king's chambers never to leave, we will forever be in the presence of God throughout this life as well as the next.

This verse also tells us that this access to God was "through whom (Jesus)." He made it possible for us to enter the throne room! Such grand position cannot be bought or earned! It has been purchased by the blood.

Once we entered the presence of the Lord, this verse states that we continually do two things. We "stand" and "we rejoice." Both of these verbs in the Greek are in the indicative, which means that there was a time in the past when we actually began to stand and to rejoice in the presence of God, but beyond all that, the usage of these
words in the indicative means that we are still standing and rejoicing in His presence.

Three wondrous truths are implied in these opening verses of this

chapter:
(1) WE HAVE AN INCOMING SPIRIT (v. 1-2);
(2) WE HAVE AN IN DWELLING SPIRIT (v. 3);
(3) WE HAVE AN INFILLING SPIRIT (v. 5).

Is it any wonder that we have such cause as to stand and rejoice? The Spirit of God has come to live in us and to never leave us. He is ever abiding! On days of despondency, draw near to His presence and practice sweet communication with Him!

3 And not only so, but we glory in tribulations also: knowing that tribulation worketh patience;
4 And patience, experience; and experience, hope:
5 And hope maketh not ashamed; because the love of God is shed abroad in our hearts by the Holy Ghost which is given unto us.

Not many of us can follow Paul's example and glory in our tribulations. Tribulation is an interesting word. It means to be crushed. Paul says that he glories in those times of crushing in his life. How can that be?

Certainly he is not speaking of the experience itself. No one enjoys pain. Paul is sharing that he has learned to look beyond the trial of the moment to the blessed confidence that God will use temporary agonies to manifest His own eternal glory.

Tribulations are never easy. If they were, they would not be tribulations. Aside from the benefit they provide to the glory of God, they also produce patience in the suffering saint as he learns that "this too will pass." Be careful, therefore, when praying for patience because patience is the fruit that is plucked from the tree of tribulations.

Perhaps this explains why the church flourishes best when it is suffering its harshest persecution. The underground churches of the Iron Curtain countries put ours in this country to shame. There is a fragrance of faith that radiates from them that we do not possess. Just as biblical myrrh required crushing to produce a sweet smell, even so the believer.

There is a key word in verse four; it is the word "experience." Better translated, it is "the state of having been approved." Let's put the thoughts of Paul together.

Paul is saying that hardships produce patience as we expectantly watch for God to use our pain for His glory. That quiet, confident expectation (patience), brings pleasure to the heart of God and He writes over our heads, "approved." Somehow, in the deep recesses of our hearts, in spite of our pain, the Spirit lets us know that God is pleased. Now, with such approval, a new thrill bubbles from our innermost being as we "hope," or "with absolute confidence look," for our Lord's return!

Verse five continues this chain that began with tribulations. Shame or embarrassment are ours when we become too concerned about our own reputations. But when a man directs all of his energy toward magnifying Jesus, how men may criticize him no longer matters. He cares no more for the barbs of ridicule. What happens to him in the course of daily events may be good or bad, but they will not receive undue attention because he is busy for Jesus. If you are too mindful of yourself, dear friend, you will be often hurt.

Moreover, shame is not the inheritance of the saved because." . . . the love of God is shed abroad in our hearts . . . " (v. 5). "Shed abroad" literally means "to flow like a river" or "to gush out" or "to pour out." Again, as is often the case with verbs in the New Testament that are directly connected to blessings for the believer, this shedding abroad of God's love in our hearts is in the indicative tense. That means that there was a time that this began to happen and it continues to happen.

Since this love is gushing forth, there is no reason for the saint to be lacking in it. If he is, it is his own fault. There is sin somewhere in his life that is unconfessed. Actually, then, being filled with this river of love is to be filled with the Spirit, and the only times we are not filled are those sad periods in our daily walk when sin is allowed to reside within us unchallenged.

Please note that this love comes to us " . . . by the Holy Ghost which is given unto us" (v. 5). When we are saved, we are baptized with the Holy Ghost into the body of Christ (I Corinthians 12:13). By that baptism, the Spirit comes to RESIDE within us. Christ dying on the cross was God's ultimate gift to lost mankind; the Holy Ghost being given to indwell us was God's ultimate gift to saved mankind. And when we reject all known sin, the Spirit will no longer just reside within us, He will PRESIDE. When He presides, the flowing fountains of God's love begin to pour. Truly we become the recipients of showers of blessings.

6 For when we were yet without strength, in due time Christ died for the ungodly.
7 For scarcely for a righteous man will one die: yet peradventure for a good man some would even dare to die.
8 But God commendeth his love toward us, in that while we were yet sinners, Christ died for us.

Man was without hope in this world before Christ died. Thrashing about in despair, struggling to make himself acceptable to God but always failing to do so, man was indeed "without strength." It is no wonder that Job cried from his misery for a redeemer to represent him before Holy God.

For the people of God, those many years that they spanned in the Old Testament moved agonizingly slow. The law had done its job. It existed to show them the futility of their own efforts to gain righteousness. As a result, the faithful people of God in those days looked as anxiously for the first appearance of the Messiah as we do today for His second coming. Would He never come? Why did He tarry?

The answer for their questions is the same as for ours — "in due time Christ died for the ungodly" (v. 6). There was a definite time that had been established by the Father. Calvary was no unfortunate accident that took God by surprise as the liberal suggests. At the appropriate time, God gave the command, Jesus was born in Bethlehem, lived three years among us, and died for our sins. I take great comfort in knowing that God is right on schedule.

For a man to be born with the date of his violent death already set is in itself unique, but even more is it so if he lives a totally sinless life and then dies on behalf of people who are everything but sinless. Such was the death of Christ. Our hearts swell with patriotic pride because of soldiers who have died in the defense of our nation. We wipe tears of honor when we learn of someone exchanging his life for that of another in situations like burning houses that demand a commitment to valor. We applaud the man who steps quickly into the path of an assassin's bullet, attempting to spare the life of a leader. Some people, according to verse seven, will do that. These are all honorable, but will a man. as readily die for a child molester, or a rapist, or a murderer? Even more, will a father give his son for such vermin of society?

God did! Verse eight very simply states that fact — "God commendeth his own love toward us in that, while we were yet sinners, Christ died for us." Hyman Appelman, the late and very great Jewish evangelist, once told me, "Dr. Hunter, if an angel from heaven came to me and asked if I would lay down my life for some wretched sinner to be saved, I would tell him that I would be honored to mingle my unworthy blood with the worthy blood of the Lord Jesus. But if that angel asked me to allow my son to die in order that the most moral and upright sinner on earth might be saved, I would tell that angel to go back to heaven where he belonged! I would never agree!"

So often, but not nearly enough, we think of the price that Jesus paid, and it was horrendously great. But can you imagine the broken heart of the Father as He watched Jesus die? Surely, if you are a parent, you can understand why Calvary truly demonstrates God's love for us.

9 Much more then, being now justified by his blood, we shall be saved from wrath through him.
10 For if, when we were enemies, we were reconciled to God by the death of his Son, much more, being reconciled, we shall be saved by his life.
11 And not only so, but we also joy in God through our Lord Jesus Christ, by whom we have now received the atonement.

I think it is appropriate that I ask you to consider a very important point upon which all of faith hangs. Why was the blood sacrifice of Jesus necessary for our salvation? Could not God have chosen a less painful way?

There was no other way! Acts 20:28 informs us that the blood shed on the cross was God's blood. In spite of the often taught truth of the trinity, many believers somehow see Jesus as somewhat less than the Father. Oh, but that is not so! Jesus was not half God and half man. Neither was He all God and no man. Nor was He all man and no God. He was as much God as though He were not man at all, and He was as much man as though He were not God at all. Jesus was the perfect God-man. And since the Scriptures tell us that life is in the blood, and since it was God's blood that stained the cross, the crucifixion was God's way of giving all that He could possibly give that man might be saved! How wondrous was His love!

Ordinarily, we think of being saved from the wrath of God as speaking of hell. But the wrath of the Father is expressed in another way in the Scriptures. In the fourteenth chapter of Revelation, we see God's fury unleashed on a rebellious world during the seven years of Great Tribulation that are yet to come to our planet. Thankfully, Chris t's blood has not only saved us from hell, but it has also delivered us from the prospect of having to suffer the tortures of the Tribulation.

But there is more! The wrath of God is upon every man as we have previously seen in our study of the doctrine of condemnation. ' Some would argue that this wrath is undeserved since there are those who are not saved but still are not opposed to those who are saved. Humanly, there seems to be some sense to such assertions. But actually, any man who refuses to acknowledge Jesus as his own Lord and Master is in a state of rebellion against his Creator. Witness the displeasure of a parent as he spanks his child for ignoring some specific directions given by the parent. The child had not cursed his parent nor violently struck him. He simply ignored the instructions of the person to whom he owes his very existence.

To ignore God is to openly dishonor the Creator. It is to place oneself in opposition to the proclaimed laws of heaven. It is high treason of the worst sort.

Gloriously, and considering all that I have just said, it is incredible that God chose to reconcile us to himself while we were enemies to Him. Please note. God was never man's enemy. We were enemies of Him. It was our proud rebellion that drove a wedge between us. Therefore, God would have been just to cast us all into hell. Instead, he set in motion the death of His Son and the shedding of His own blood to reconcile us to Him.

But what does it mean " . . . to be saved by his life . . . "? Simply, since Jesus lives, our salvation is secure as He daily stands before the throne to intercede for us. His death paid the penalty for us and provided reconciliation. His life as our advocate maintains that reconciliation.

Verse eleven gives us the only place in which "atonement." can be found in the New Testament. A better translation is "covered." The emphasis of this verse is the fact that we can rejoice in this present hour because our sins are covered. And they are not covered for only a year as in the Old Testament. They are permanently covered! They are gone forever! Think of the most shameful thing that you have ever done, and right now rejoice! That sin is gone!

12 Wherefore, as by one man sin entered into the world, and death by sin; and so death passed upon all men, for that all have sinned:
13 For until the law sin was in the world: but sin is not imputed when there is no law.
14 Nevertheless death reigned from Adam to Moses, even over them that had not sinned after the similitude of Adam's transgression, who is the figure of him that was to come.

The man by whom sin entered the world was Adam. Verse twelve does not exclude Eve from her part in the original transgression, because Genesis 5:2 records that God " . . . called their name Adam." Both share awful blame for the sin that has poisoned mankind.

Would you please note that" . . . sin entered into the world . . . "? Sin did not begin with Adam and Eve. They did not create sin. Sin was already in existence. The satanic revolt against God declared that there was sin before there was man.

By man's fall in the garden, he became a slave to sin (Romans 6:16) and his ultimate payoff was death because of sin. Spiritual death, or separation from God, was immediate with Adam's sin. Physical death came over nine hundred years later. But both became our inheritance just as surely as they were his.

This verse, Romans 5:12, is an important verse for disclaiming a very popular theory concerning the creation. In an attempt to preserve the integrity of Bible instruction during the last century as evolution was first being taught, some preachers and theologians developed the "gap theory." Many staunch defenders of the faith have defended this theory. Quite simply, the gap theory says that there was a vast span of time between the first two verses of the first chapter of Genesis. It was during that period, they say, that dinosaurs and cavemen roamed the earth. Finally, God ended it all and in seven literal days created the world as we know it today. Romans 5:12 disproves the gap theory. We are explicitly shown that death did not enter the world until after Adam sinned. Therefore, no cavemen could have lived and died before Adam, and neither could there have been other creatures, like the dinosaurs, that lived and died. The first death was that of an animal that God slew to provide garments for Adam to cover his nakedness.

From Adam to Moses on Mt. Sinai sin was in the world. Man in those primitive days was having considerable difficulty defining sin. Sending Moses to the top of Sinai, God delivered the law by which He proposed to judge man. No more could man plead ignorance. The law was clear. If man had ever presumed to argue his moral innocency, he could no longer. Now when he sinned he knew it, and God judged him.

This brings another objection. If there was any credibility at all to the argument of moral innocency for those who lived between Adam and Moses, why did they suffer the penalty of death? We must understand that we are tied to our father Adam with a bond that can only be broken by the cross. Even in our day, small infants die and mentally retarded people die who have never reached the age of accountability. Why? Because they are bound to Adam. So, verse fourteen is accurate when it tells us that death reigned over people who never considered committing a sin such as that of Adam.

But now verse fourteen gives us a problem. How can a man like Adam be a figure (representation) of Jesus Christ? This representation we may call a contrasting similarity. Let me explain. Just as Adam's sin brought a dramatic reversal of life to death for all mankind, Jesus' sacrifice has brought a dramatic reversal of death to life.
15 But not as the offence, so also is the free gift. For if through the offence of one many be dead, much more the grace of God, and the gift by grace, which is by one man, Jesus Christ, hath abounded unto many.
16 And not as it was by one that sinned, so is the gift: for the judgment was by

one to condemnation, but the free gift is of many offences unto justification.
17 For if by one man's offence death reigned by one; much more they which receive abundance of grace and of the gift of righteousness shall reign in life by one, Jesus Christ.

Verse fifteen gives us two diametrically opposite conditions. On the one hand we have the trespass of Adam which was a willful act of disobedience and resulted in death. On the other hand we have the free gift of Christ which was purchased for us by His willful act of obedience and resulted in life.

One-half of one sin will separate a man from God. Verse sixteen seems to take that into consideration. Paul is suggesting, that if one seemingly innocent act brought such deadly consequences, should we not be deliriously happy as we look back upon our many vile deeds and recognize that God has forgiven us of them all and justified us completely in Christ Jesus?

Verse seventeen can bring "Hallelujah" to your lips when rightly understood. Paul displays his ability of logic as he allows the Holy Ghost to direct his writing. Paul is stating that if we can grasp how much devastation was wrought by the one sin of one mortal man, thereby causing sin to reign in the human family, how much more is the superiority of Christ's gift of righteousness than Adam's one sin so that Jesus can truly reign abundantly by grace in our hearts! In other words, think about the pain that sin has caused you. Now think about the joy that salvation has given you. Is not the latter infinitely superior to the former?

18 Therefore as by the offence of one judgment came upon all men to condemnation; even so by the righteousness of one the free gift came upon all men unto justification of life.
19 For as by one man's disobedience many were made sinners, so by the obedience of one shall many be made righteous.
20 Moreover the law entered, that the offence might abound. But where sin abounded, grace did much more abound:
21 That as sin hath reigned unto death, even so might grace reign through righteousness unto eternal life by Jesus Christ our Lord.

These concluding verses of chapter five summarize the differences between Adam and Jesus. We must understand that we are a fallen race because of Adam's disobedience. Contrary to the protests of those liberal theologians who teach that man is inherently good and can be brought to favor with God through education and reformation, these verses emphatically show that we are all separated from God and without any other hope in this world outside of Jesus Christ. Indeed, in their wild distortions of the Scriptures, these men suggest that verse eighteen teaches that all men will ultimately be saved.

Nothing could be farther from the truth. Their erroneous interpretation would tell us that Paul is here saying that since the entire human race came under condemnation after Adam's sin in which they had no part, even so the entire human race will be saved because of Jesus' sacrifice in which we had no part. How foolish!

What we really have in verse eighteen is "condemnation by appropriation" and "justification by appropriation." What do I mean? All mankind is under the sentence of condemnation, but that condemnation does not become an individual reality until a person reaches the age of accountability, that time in his life when he recognizes that the wrong he does is actually a sin against God. At that point, he is fully and forcefully condemned. And should he die, he would go to hell. That is why little babies and dear mentally retarded people go to heaven when they die. Although they were a part of the condemned human family, they were not individually condemned through a choice of their own will.

You must remember that names are not added to the Book of Life; they are blotted out. The name of every person who would ever be born into the world was placed in the Book of Life before the creation. If a man comes to the age of accountability, refuses God, and dies, his name is blotted out. If a man comes to the age of accountability, accepts Christ, and dies, his name is sealed by the Holy Spirit into the Book of life (Ephesians 4:30).

This clear doctrine of names being blotted out, but not added, is found in Exodus 32:32-33: "Yet now, if thou wilt forgive their sin — ; and if not, blot me, I pray thee, out of thy book which thou hast written. And the Lord said unto Moses, whosoever hath sinned against me, him will I blot out of my book." As you can see, this explains why the infants and the retarded are able to enter heaven. It also explains why the human race is also the beneficiary of what Jesus did. Salvation has been universally provided for all men by Him, but it only becomes an individual reality when a man asks Him for it.

It is a sad world of the church in our modern times where the Christian can so flagrantly disobey God, caring little for the results of that disobedience upon himself or upon others. Verse nineteen shows that such pitiful living is not in keeping with the example of the Lord Jesus. Adam was self-centered, choosing to do that which pleased himself. Jesus refused to accommodate Himself with the comforts of the "easy way," but through His selfless living and ignominious death made righteousness possible, within reach, of everyone.

Verse twenty is one of the most familiar verses in the Book of Romans. During these turbulent days when the filthiness of sin is apparently flourishing, we need to constantly recall this precious promise that where sin abounds, grace much more abounds. Why is this so? We are told here that the law entered so that sin might abound. Does this seem strange? As we have already seen, sin has been present before the world's creation. But it was not until the giving of the law that man was able to understand the vastness of sin. As he listened to the reading of the law, he was shocked at the seemingly endless list of sins. Surely he felt that sin did abound indeed.

With such a demoralizing awareness, man could only grope his way along, listening to the prophets, doing the best he could, but knowing it was never enough. But Jesus came! And His grace is to sin as light is to darkness. It abounds! There is grace to save the worst of sinners! Hallelujah!

A very important point is made in verse twenty-one. We are told that " . . . sin hath reigned . . . " Please note that this phrase is in the past tense. Now you may think that sin still controls you, but if you are saved, it does not. You may be confusing "sins" with "sin." "Sin" was your old nature that dominated you before you were saved. "Sins" are the manifestation of that nature. Before you accepted Christ, you were a slave to "sin." Now that you have been born again, the Spirit of God is in control, and you now deal with specific "sins."

The glory of salvation is not that we go to heaven when we die. It is that God's marvelous grace becomes the guiding light for us through a world darkened by sin. That is precisely the reason that people who are old when they are saved invariably say, "This is so much better than what I had, why didn't I get saved when I was young?" God's grace abounds, always, more than sin!

Chapter Six

Sanctification Introduced

We have now reached one of the high pinnacles in the Book of Romans. Nothing is more precious than our union with Christ. When we are able to understand that salvation is not just a change of mind and heart, but is an infusion of the Lord Jesus into us, we will respond with lives marked with supernatural power to live in victory. Think of it, at salvation, God just as surely entered our mortal bodies as He did when Christ was born at Bethlehem as the incarnate Son of God.

Chapter six is the "Victory Chapter." By following its simple suggestions, and accepting its fundamental teachings, we can be transformed from powerless, anemic
believers into flames of Spirit fire! If it were possible for me to teach one chapter to all the Christians of the world, I would immediately open my Bible to this one.

There are millions of beleaguered believers who struggle with the same recurring sins on a daily basis. Floundering about, they rush from one Bible conference to another, frantically searching for someone who may be able to provide an answer for the gnawing feelings of spiritual weakness and emptiness. Oh, dear friend, if this describes your plight, study carefully the words of Paul in this chapter. Do not allow Satan to continue his barrage of attacks -upon you without retaliation! Learn what you have because of your union with Christ!

1 What shall we say then? Shall we continue in sin that grace may abound?
2 God forbid. How shall we, that are dead to sin, live any longer therein?

With these verses, we have arrived at Paul's discussion of the third of the five major Christian doctrines, the doctrine of sanctification. His presentation of this truth is covered in Romans 6:1 - 8:39. Remember, condemnation is the result of Adam, justification is the result of Jesus, and sanctification is the result of the Holy Spirit.

Sanctification is to be "set apart." It is not an experience that is separate from the time of salvation. In fact, it is not an experience at all; it is a process, beginning with salvation and ending with the believer's entrance into heaven. As we grow in grace, we find ourselves being separated with an ever-increasing gap from the world and in an ever-closer walk with the things of God.

The very first verse has been the focal point for books and sermons galore. In the concluding verses of chapter five, we heard Paul say that where sin abounds, grace abounds the more. Here, in the first verse of chapter six, a very intriguing proposition is made. The logic is this -- if more sin brings more grace, we ought to sin more so that we can enjoy more grace. This is so utterly ridiculous that Paul answers it in strong words in the second verse with his exclamation of, "God forbid!"

These two words, so forcefully used, convey that the idea in verse one is totally without merit, never to be considered as even a remote possibility. Why? Because we are dead to sin. If we are dead to sin, how in the world can we continue to live in it! This condition is not only abnormal; it is a monstrosity!

Let me illustrate! Suppose you injured one of your legs. Infection developed and grew painfully worse day by day. In a effort to save your life, your physician finally is forced to amputate. You recover, and except for the loss of that leg, you enjoy good health. Would it make sense for you to dig that leg from its burial place and try to re-attach it to your body? Of course not! That which had at one time seemed perfectly natural would now be most unnatural. Just as unthinkable is it for a saved person to attempt to resume his old life of sin. That life is dead! It is gone!

Does this mean that a saved person should be in a state of sinless perfection? No, that is not the directive at all. The temptations of the devil are so many and so subtle that try as we might to live a totally consecrated life there will be occasion when we fall into sin. But though we may fall into sin, we are never to live there, making little effort to withdraw ourselves from its deadly tentacles. One of our sorest needs in the church is for holy living. Power with God is in direct proportion to purity of heart.

3 Know ye not, that so many of us as were baptized into Jesus Christ were baptized into his death?
4 Therefore we are buried with him by baptism into death: that like as Christ was raised up from the dead by the glory of the Father, even so we also should walk in newness of life.
5 For if we have been planted together in the likeness of his death, we shall be also in the likeness of his resurrection.

This passage is used as a proof-text by those who believe in baptismal regeneration. Such adherents teach that water baptism is a part of the salvation process, and regardless of whatever else a person may do in an attempt to be saved, he will be lost unless he is baptized.

Such is certainly not the case. Believer's baptism is a beautiful expression of our entrance into Christ, but it should never be understood as a part of salvation. Bible verses abound that prove the point I have just made, but two are sufficient. Romans 8:9 is clear when it says that " . . . if any man have not the Spirit of Christ, he is none of his." With that in mind, all we must do in order to determine the relationship of baptism to salvation is discover when the Spirit comes to indwell us. If this happens before water baptism, then baptism is not a part of being saved. If it happens following baptism, then baptism is a part of salvation.

Now, consider the witness of Peter to Cornelius in the tenth chapter of Acts. In this exchange between Peter and the inquiring Jews who had come up from Jerusalem, we get the answer for baptism's role. Peter asked the Jews this question, "Can any man forbid water, that these should not be baptized, which have received the Holy Ghost as well as we?" (Acts 10:47). There you have it! Cornelius had already received the Spirit, therefore in accordance with Romans 8:9, he was saved before baptism. In his case, as with ours, water baptism is an exquisitely beautiful symbol of a greater baptism, the baptism by the Holy Ghost with which we are brought into union with Christ.

Please note that in Romans 6:3 we are said to have been" . . . baptized into Jesus . . . " Since water baptism does not put us into Christ, as we have just shown, this passage must be talking about the other, and greater, baptism — that of the Holy Ghost. That baptism is the object of Paul's attention in I Corinthians 12:13 where he says, "For by one Spirit are we all baptized into one body. . . " This baptism is invisible and places us into the universal body of Christ at the time of our salvation. When that has happened, we then submit ourselves to the visible water baptism which places us into the visible body of Christ, the local New Testament church.

Does this minimize the importance of water baptism? Certainly not! Our Lord has given us the Great Commission in the twenty-eighth chapter of Matthew to go, and to teach, and to baptize! I do not believe that baptism is essential to salvation, but I do believe that it is essential because of salvation. I seriously question the validity of a man's salvation experience if he tries to excuse himself from baptism.

What happened when we were baptized by the Holy Spirit into Christ? First, our old nature was destroyed. The entrance of the Holy Spirit put to death in a practical sense the old man that was crucified with Christ in a positional sense. Friend, if you are saved, the Spirit's baptism buried and covered over your old man. But secondly, verse four tells us that immediately a brand new you burst forth.

Nothing to compare with the resurrection of Christ had ever previously happened! Stop for a moment and consider the uniqueness of it! A dead man came to life! Do not think of it in a biblical sense alone! Try to make it real! Suppose you were standing in a funeral parlor viewing the remains of a loved one when suddenly he begins to move, sits upright in the casket, gets out on the floor and walks away. Words would not be adequate to describe your emotional reaction to something so far removed from the normal sphere of human experiences. Such it was with the bodily resurrection of Jesus.

In verse four, Paul is saying that there is a definite parallel between Christ's resurrection and our salvation. In other words, it is just as far beyond human reason for us to become new creatures in Christ as it was for Him to come from the grave.

In similar fashion to His bodily resurrection, we have experienced a spiritual resurrection that is just as real. Please note Paul's comments in Ephesians 2:4-6: "But God, who is rich in mercy, for his great love wherewith he loved us, even when we were dead in sins, hath quickened us together with Christ, (by grace ye are saved;) And hath raised us up together, and made us sit together in heavenly places in Christ Jesus." When we were lost, the Bible says that we were spiritually dead (Ephesians 2:1). And what can a dead man do? Absolutely nothing!

That is precisely the reason that it is impossible to imitate the Christian life. The Christian life cannot be imitated because that really means that we would need to imitate the sinless Christ. Yet, multitudes answer the question of their personal salvation with, "Well, I'm doing the best I can." But remember, since a dead man can do nothing, your human efforts are doomed to failure.

The Christian life is not reformation; it is regeneration. It is not "turning over a new leaf" or living "like Jesus." The Christian life is a recognition that Christ lives within, and it is a day by day exercise of the will to let Him live out His life in the Christian's routine of life.

A very important word in Romans 6:4 is often overlooked. It is the little word "so." This word connects the fact of our spiritual resurrection to the reason for it. We were raised so we could "walk in newness of life." You see, it is utterly impossible to walk in the new life of a new creature in Christ unless you have been raised from spiritual death.

I am glad that Paul tells us that we can "walk." If he had said "run" we might have had difficulty in relating to this new life, because there are relatively few among us who seem to move so rapidly in Christian work, like the Billy Grahams or the Corrie Ten Booms. But everyone can "walk." Children and adults alike can walk. Walking implies steadiness and determination in moving forward.

But growth, real growth, is like that. We move upward — almost imperceptibly we move upward — so slowly that we are not even sure sometimes that any growth is taking place. Nevertheless, we can occasionally look back and be amazed at how far we have come. Thank God for our resurrection from deadness so that all of our days can be lived with the assurance of His working through us.

Move with me to verse five. Do you see the word, "planted"? A better translation is "grafted," or "grown together," or "intimate union." just like the similarity between our resurrection from spiritual death with His resurrection from physical death, even so is there a similarity between our choosing to die to our old life with Christ's choosing to die to His physical life. Our identification with Jesus in His death makes us one with Him. As a result the power that was generated in His bodily resurrection is the power in us that assures our walk with Him.

6 Knowing this, that our old man is crucified with him, that the body of sin might be destroyed, that henceforth we should not serve sin.
7 For he that is dead is freed from sin.
8 Now if we be dead with Christ, we believe that we shall also live with him:
9 Knowing that Christ being raised from the dead dieth no more; death hath no more dominion over him.
10 For in that he died, he died unto sin once: but in that he liveth, he liveth unto God.
11 Likewise reckon ye also yourselves to be dead indeed unto sin, but alive unto God through Jesus Christ our Lord.
12 Let not sin therefore reign in your mortal body, that ye should obey it in the lusts thereof.
13 Neither yield ye your members as instruments of unrighteousness unto sin: but yield yourselves unto God, as those that are alive from the dead, and your members as instruments of righteousness unto God.
14 For sin shall not have dominion over you: for ye are not under the law, but under grace.

This passage is one of the most important passages in the entire Bible in terms of practical value. We are constantly pounded by the ever-present bombardment of temptations. But the wise believer has the wherewithal to overcome these attacks. This passage shares the plan of action by urging the believer to:
(1) Know (v. 6);
(2) Reckon (v. 11);
(3) Yield (v. 13).

First, we must know that our old man has been crucified. We may not "feel" that our old man is dead, but we should not operate our lives on feelings anyway. "Feelings" is a term that is used only twice in the New Testament and in neither place does it have anything at all to do with our salvation. We must recognize as a fundamental biblical fact that our old man is dead. The Bible says it; that settles it.

What do we mean by "old man"? We see the term used here in the sixth chapter of Romans, but it can be translated as "evil imagination" or "old nature." That old man was actually the nature within you prior to your salvation by which you could comfortably sin without suffering pangs of remorse because you had violated the commands of God. Such is true no longer. Because the old nature has been replaced by the new nature, that ability to settle down with ease in this world is removed forever. That is the reason that the saved person is miserable trying to do the same sinful things that he had enjoyed before salvation without compunction.

This death of the old man must be viewed as already having taken place. The King James Version says that ". . . our old man is dead . . ." but the literal translation is that ". . . our old man was dead." The past tense is used which fixes this as a theological and historical fact. We can be fully confident our old nature is gone.

This presents tremendous difficulty for some believers. If the old man is gone, why is there sin in the believer's life? Read carefully. The old man speaks of the condition of sin. A lost man is totally immersed in sin. Since he has not taken the time to accept Christ and be saved, he is in a state of rebellion against God. Therefore, he is an enemy of God (Romans 5:10), and nothing he does can please God.

However, once that man is saved, he enjoys the imputed righteousness of Christ, and peace with God becomes a reality. From that point onward, he is not helplessly snared in a condition of sin. Now, he must face specific sins. Whereas the old man and condition of sin had dominion over the individual before his conversion, he now has dominion over sin after his conversion. That, dear friend, is the biblical fact we must know.

This truth is expanded in verse seven. If we are dead to sin, we can no longer be held accountable for that sin. In our modern judicial system, we have a similar policy called "double jeopardy." By this term, we mean that a man cannot be tried nor punished twice for the same crime. So it is in the spiritual realm. When we accept the "once-for-all" sacrificial death of Jesus Christ, we can never again be held in judgment for our sins. Why? Very simply, a man who is dead is not required to answer for anything. Once the old man has died, there is no one to charge.

Verse eight continues this theme. By using the word, "dead," we are again made to see that there was a definite action that has already taken place. Couple the past tense nature of the word with the present tense nature of the word, "believe," found in the same verse. Because our old man has died, we can now believe ". . . that we shall also live with him." Do you need freedom from doubts about the security of your salvation? Find assurance here. If your old man is dead, the penalty can never be exercised against you again, you are no longer a slave to sin, and you can look expectantly toward living now and in eternity with Christ.

Christ died only once, and will never die again! That being the case, the resurrection of our Lord resolved forever His power over death. The word "dominion" has a very strong meaning in the original language. It means to have the rights of a lord. It means to possess fullest authority. To a degree, death had power over the Lord Jesus until His wondrous resurrection. After His resurrection, our Lord assumed all of the power that He had originally limited within Himself when He was born into this world. It was after His resurrection that He heralded, "All power is given unto me in heaven and in earth!"

So, verse nine comes as another statement of blessing to the believer. Physically, we are yet subject to the influences of Satan and the certainty of death. But the glory of it all is that since Jesus now has power over death, He also has control over the manner and time of our deaths. Therefore, we can confidently rest without anxiety in the sweet and strong embrace of His care.

Verse ten may seem repetitious, but remember that repetition is the best form of learning. It is a pointed fact that Jesus died once, never to die again. In the Old Testament period, multiplied thousands of animals met bloody sacrificial deaths. Sins were never forgiven by their deaths but were only temporarily covered. Therefore, many animals were forced to shed their blood for the same sin. Only in the death of Christ do we have an absolute obliteration of sins, never to come against the transgressor again.

But the emphasis of verse ten is not on the death of Christ. On the contrary, it is on His life. Let this truth be yours; Jesus is alive right now as you read these very words! His life as our intercessor for us to God will span the full number of each believer's days in this world. A recurring message by Paul is that salvation is only the beginning of our wondrous love relationship with Jesus.

Oh, dear friend, if you would be victorious in this present life and overcome temptation, you must know (v. 6) that your old man is dead! You are not forced to sin anymore! Sin does not have dominion over you any longer! You are free from the shackles of sin although you must now deal with specific sins. The difference? Before salvation, you were without power to overcome; after salvation, you have the power of God within you.

\   The second word in the sixth chapter, after "knowing," that you must understand to overcome temptation, is the word "reckon," found in verse eleven. "Reckon" is an ancient bookkeeping term that means "to compare as in ledgers of assets and liabilities."

Now that you know that the old man is dead, and that you are now no longer a slave to sin, each time temptation comes your way, you must "reckon" the results of either yielding or refusing to yield. Why is this time of evaluation necessary? Very simply, sometimes it is extremely difficult to determine if "a particular activity is indeed a temptation or an opportunity. By reckoning about the results of participation in a certain activity, you can then determine whether this is an endeavor that is approved by God or whether it is a very subtle temptation by the devil.

We may illustrate it in this fashion. Here is a teenager in high school. His father is dead and his mother is barely able to support her family financially. A local service station offers him a job, but it would require his dropping out of school. Is this a temptation or an opportunity? By reckoning, he can get a better perspective of his decision. Very likely, he will come to the conclusion that to drop out will cost him dearly in the future. Therefore, this would be a temptation.

When we "reckon" in spiritual matters, we must engage in conversation with Jesus and determine His will for us. You are familiar with the word "supplication" which is often used in the Scriptures in connection with prayer. The primary» meaning of supplication conveys the idea of deliberation with God in a manner by which we offer our own conclusions as pertaining to the ways our needs may be met, but then waiting patiently for God's answer. To involve oneself in supplication is to prayerfully "think through" a problem as we present it before the Lord. That is also precisely the meaning that is attached to reckoning. It is important for spiritual growth because we learn to parallel our thought processes with those of the Lord.

The third of our significant words in this passage is found in verse thirteen where we are admonished to "yield" ourselves to God. In this same verse, we are warned to avoid yielding ourselves as instruments of unrighteousness. This moves our confrontation with temptation from the realm of the mind into the realm of action. When we have determined the mind of Christ by "reckoning," we can then obey Him outwardly by how we believe within.

Now, let me put all of this together for you and illustrate the entire process. Suppose you have been advised by your physician to eat no more sweets. One evening, however, while eating as a guest at the home of another, your hostess brings her delicious dessert to the table. Let us also suppose that the dessert is chocolate layer cake, and that happens to be your all-time favorite dessert. What are you to do?

First, you pause to remember that you "know" something. Since this dessert would not be good for your health, it would be a sin for you to eat it. You "know" that it is within your power to resist this temptation to sin. You are saved; and as a saved person, sin has no more dominion over you.

Second, you "reckon" the will of Christ. You might ask your "self" about the dessert. Of course, the answer will be an emphatic, "Yes, eat it!" Then, you ask the Lord Jesus if it is His will, and He will respond just as emphatically with, "No, don't eat it!" But, remember, whenever the Lord says, "Thou shalt not," it always means, "Don't hurt yourself." Therefore, if He asks you not to indulge in a particular activity, there is always a better and more satisfying way prepared for you.

Third, you "yield" yourself to whatever He directs you toward. Since He has vetoed the cake, He might then turn your attention to a bowl of fresh-cut fruit. Trust me, the sweetness of pleasing Jesus in obedience is far more flavorful than consuming the sugar of disobedience.

If you will read carefully verse twelve, you will see that we are commanded to "let not sin reign in our mortal bodies." After salvation occurs, the saint may occasionally sin, but he is never to allow sin to reign. That would be a monstrous contradiction. Once saved, the believer must recognize that Jesus Christ is now Lord and therefore must reign. That being so, a reigning Christ will not share His throne with any sin. He will not be a co-regent with the darkness of this world.

Paul affirms this truth in I Corinthians 6:20 when he says, "For ye are bought with a price: therefore glorify God in your body." If we do not even own ourselves, how can we presume to allow sin's reign in us? We cannot.

Nevertheless, it is a sad fact that many believers do fall into sin and continue therein in spite of the chastening of God. The subtle nature of sin is such that man can be horribly deceived. Generally, the believer is tempted to tolerate a given activity. If he falls prey to the devilish plea for tolerance, the downward direction of his own spiritual demise will begin.

We are created to worship something or someone. In other words, every person on this planet who reaches the age of accountability will choose to allow some entity to reign or to rule over him. Either it will be some form of sin, or it will be the Lord Jesus Christ. There is no neutral position.

Therefore, we are admonished to avoid obedience to the lusts of the flesh. In verse twelve, the word "obey" means more than actually yielding to some temptation to commit sin. It means to "willingly accept." Many believers would never participate in adultery, but they readily watch actors and actresses graphically portraying adultery in television dramas. By this definition of "obey," they have violated the command of this verse.

This same exhortation is continued in verse thirteen. Paul says that we are to present ourselves unto God. "Yield" is defined in the original language as "being in the position of readiness" or "at disposal of. The word in the tense it is used in this verse also conveys the idea of continual action, so that the one who is presenting himself to God will never do anything else but present himself to God.

What triumph we have in Jesus! Whereas sin had been our master, our new master is the Lord Jesus Christ! The glory of His presence within us provides us the unlimited sources of power that are His to bestow.

We have been redeemed! The Lord Jesus. Christ has become the object of our adoration and worship. No other person or organization should have a priority in our affections.

Because of the law, God had no choice but to be our Judge when we violated His commands. But now, because of grace, we are free and God has become our loving Father!

As we respond to the exhibition of God's love for us at Calvary, our appreciation and gratitude motivate us to do everything within our power to please Him. Unlike the solemn and forced obedience of the law, we can now gladly follow God's directives for us, knowing that whatever He asks of us is for our own good. Law brought bondage; grace brings freedom. Law brought restrictions; grace brings release. That being so, we should always do more for Jesus under grace than the Jew did for Jehovah under law.

15 *What then? shall we sin, because we are not under the law, but under grace? God forbid.*
16 *Know ye not, that to whom ye yield yourselves servants to obey, his servants ye are to whom ye obey; whether of sin unto death, or of obedience unto*

righteousness?
17 But God be thanked, that ye were the servants of sin, but ye have obeyed from the heart that form of doctrine which was delivered you.
18 Being then made free from sin, ye became the servants of righteousness.
19 I speak after the manner of men because of the infirmity of the flesh: for as ye have yielded your members servants to uncleanness and to iniquity unto iniquity; even so now yield your members servants to righteousness unto holiness.
20 For when ye were the servants of sin, ye were free from righteousness.
21 What fruit had ye then in those things whereof ye are now ashamed? for the end of those things is death.
22 But now being made free from sin, and become servants to God, ye have your fruit unto holiness, and the end everlasting life.
23 For the wages of sin is death; but the gift of God is eternal life through Jesus Christ our Lord.

    The leading question of this section has become a stumbling block for many dear people who believe in "falling from grace." That is, they believe that a person may lose his salvation because of sin. In theology, we call this faulty interpretation, Arminianism, which takes its name from Jacobus Arminius who lived from 1560-1609. This idea of falling from grace is actually a salvation built on works. But remember! However a person is saved is the way he stays saved. If a man is saved by grace, he is kept by grace. If he is saved by works, he is kept by works. therefore, if a man believes that he stays saved by what he does, then he must also concede, like it or not, that he was saved by works. Read Romans 11:6: ". . . And if by grace, then is it no more of works: otherwise grace is no more grace. But if it be of works, then is it no more grace: otherwise work is no more work." But, back to the original question in verse fifteen. Are we at liberty to sin because we are no longer under the law? Of course not! The strongest words of emphasis are employed to deny such an idea by the use of "God forbid!" The prohibition against sin has reached a new dimension for the saint. He does not sin because there is a dusty, musty law telling him not to sin. Oh no! He does not sin because there is a loving Lord Jesus who would be hurt by the sin.

    Perhaps this illustration might help. A happily married man does not commit adultery because of the command in the Ten Commandments. He does not commit adultery because it would break the heart of his dear wife. May we ever remind ourselves that we are the chaste bride of Christ, and that the commands of the law have a higher fulfillment in our love for Him, our Royal Bridegroom. Sin against Him is unthinkable because of our love relationship with Him!

Verse sixteen demonstrates the lordship of Christ. Please note that we are either servants of sin unto death or of obedience unto righteousness.

This word, "servant," is interesting. It is translated, "bond slave." A bond slave is a person who voluntarily sells himself to another person. This agreement could never be broken. He would be a bond slave to this particular master and to him alone. The agreement could be broken only by the bond slave's death. And that, therefore, was all that the slave had to look toward in his life.

However, when a man is saved, his "old man" dies (Romans 6:6). He is released as a bond slave from his old taskmaster, the devil. Now, he is a bond slave to Jesus. But no longer must he look drearily toward the dread prospects of death. Now, he can rejoice at the blessed prospect of eternal life in heaven.

It is important that we always remember that there is no neutrality as a bond slave. We cannot choose to obey Christ. He has the rightful expectation to have us, as His bond slaves, to perform for Him as He chooses! Simply, either Jesus is Lord of all or He is not Lord at all!

Verse seventeen declares Paul's joyous news for the Roman believers. They had previously been bond slaves to sin with an ultimate destiny of death. But now they belong to Jesus! A whole new life and Lord is theirs to enjoy.

Like these precious saints of centuries gone by, I believe it is a good thing for us to remember where we were when Jesus saved us. The first half of verse seventeen shows that we had been servants of sin. It was "a prison of iniquity from which there seemed to be no escape — indeed, there was not. It is no wonder that Paul gladly shouts the triumph of our own hearts, "God be thanked!"

Without the work of God in Christ at Calvary, we were as certainly headed for hell as though we were already there. There was no power of our own by which we could avoid that awful end. But God be thanked! By His intervention, we were set free!

Again, in verse seventeen, note what happened in us. We "... have obeyed from the heart..." This obedience was not of our own initiative. Oh no! There was a time that the Holy Spirit touched my heart because of God's grace directed toward me. He did not convict me by His Spirit because I deserved it, or because I was more upright than others, or because I was more favored by Him than others. By His sovereign choice, in a way that I shall never fully understand, God touched me in my heart by His Spirit. When that wondrous conviction upon me occurred in my heart, I obeyed from my heart, and was saved!

Now, all of this being true, what is the doctrine that we have obeyed, in our hearts? Basic to all other biblical teachings and principles is the gospel, the "good news." If we are wrong about that, it does not matter what other doctrines we are right about! We must have a correct definition of the gospel.

Disregarding the definitions of any other church or individual, let us see how the Bible defines this doctrine that verse seventeen says we have obeyed in the heart: "Moreover, brethren, I declare unto you the gospel which I preached unto you, which also ye have received, and wherein ye stand; By which also ye are saved, if ye keep in memory what I preached unto you, unless ye have believed in vain. For I delivered unto you first of all that which I also received, how that Christ died for our sins according to the scriptures; And that he was buried, and that he rose again the third day according to the scriptures (I Corinthians 15:1-4).

This passage, dear friend, is the gospel. In essence, the gospel is three-fold:
(1) Christ died for our sins according to the Scriptures;
(2) Christ was buried;
(3) Christ rose again the third day according to the Scriptures.

Obeying in the heart means that we fully believe that these three points of the gospel message are both historical fact and present-day reality. We obey, then, by living in response to this gospel.

Verse eighteen is very likely one of the least appreciated verses in the entire Bible, yet it is glorious indeed! "Being then made free from sin" is better translated, "and having been freed from sin." Just as definitely as there was a precise time that the umbilical cord that tied you to your mother was severed, even so there was a precise time when you were cut free from sin! Granted, we have continual war with sin, but no longer must we be slaves to it against our will. We are free to serve the Lord!

On the other hand, we just as emphatically became "servants of righteousness." I certainly do not understand the miracle of conversion that transforms me from a poor, hell-bound sinner to a son of the Most High God, allowed by His divine guidance to be honored as a choice servant of righteousness. If you could see the phrase, "'. . . became the servants of righteousness . . . " in its original language, you would find a wonderful nugget of truth. Because of the special Greek tense of "became," the idea is conveyed that God has made us the highest form of servant possible, and that even He cannot do better for us than He has already done!

Verse nineteen describes the human side of our servanthood. Verse eighteen has just given us God's side. God's side is positional truth; man's side is practical truth. These two verses should be studied as a couplet to understand Paul's declaration of Christian servitude.

Let me illustrate. On July 4, 1986, thousands of immigrants became citizens of the United States when they took an oath that renounced any desires on their parts to be affiliated with other nations in any manner whatever, however slight the attachment might be. In that same solemn oath, they pledged their allegiance to this country, promising to support and defend its laws. They changed "positions." That is positional truth. That is what Paul was saying in verse eighteen. Just as July 4, 1986 was a definite time in which citizens of other nations became citizens of this nation, even so the day you were saved, you became a servant to a new master, the Lord Jesus Christ. That is God's view.

Unfortunately, many of those who vowed allegiance to the United States will become murderers and rapists, criminals of the worst sort. Doing such vile deeds will not revoke their citizenship and return them to their previous countries, but it will be a cause for shame. Their new citizenship as an American also carries with it a responsibility to live honorably. That is Paul's teaching in verse nineteen.

Continuing our illustration, there was a time when these immigrants to the United States had actively submitted themselves to the laws of another country. Now, they should actively submit themselves to the laws of our land. Is it no less true for the believer? If he once served the devil in his flesh, ought he not now even more vigorously serve the Lord in holiness of character?

Verse twenty draws a very definite line of separation. No man can live in both worlds. Either he is saved, or he is lost. Either he is a servant of righteousness, or he is not. Ours is a religious society that cries out for tolerance and broadmindedness in matters of faith. Quite frankly, there can be none. The man that is lost is lost. Dr. Bailey Smith, former President of the Southern Baptist Convention has said, "To be 99% saved is to be 100% lost!" The man who is unsaved is " . . . free in regard of righteousness." There is nothing that he can do that meets with the approval of God. He is utterly and awfully separated from God. We may not in religious circles separate so sharply, but our Father does!

Verse twenty-one comes right to the point of the value of our lives before we were saved. It asks a very simple question, "What fruit had ye at that time in the things whereof ye are now ashamed?" Think about it! Are you not ashamed of your life as a lost man? Do you not remember with pain all your transgressions? Even if you were a morally decent person, do you not feel guilt because of the casual way that you treated Jesus?

As you look back on those days, you can now see how dark they really were. Had you died, you would have been eternally banished to the lake of fire. That is the meaning of the phrase in verse twenty-one, ". . . for the end of those things is death." The fruit of that previous life before salvation was artificial and tasteless. Though there were bright promises for the future, the life without God was empty and void. Now, praise the Lord, you are able to reflect upon those days and give Him thanks that they are all behind you, and even more, that God will never call them to remembrance against you.

Verse twenty-two concludes with more of a thrilling difference than does verse twenty-one. In verse twenty-one, we see that that the works of a lost man can be summarized as " . . . the end of those things is death." Verse twenty-two, on the other hand, speaks of the permanent nature of the believer's works by proclaiming, " . . ye have your fruit unto holiness, and the end everlasting life." There is such a difference between the final destinies of the man who chooses salvation in Jesus Christ and the man who rejects the same. No sane man would ever desire the lost state.

I would have you to note that because we have been freed from sin and have been made servants of God that the Bible teaches us that we are to " . . . have fruit unto sanctification._" This denotes a continual life of productivity for our Lord. It is not a matter of "on-again-off-again" spasmodic endeavor as so pervades the modern church. It is, instead, a statement of fact that we continually bear fruit.

Now we come to the most frequently quoted of the verses in this chapter. Verse twenty-three hammers home a never-changing truth. The paycheck for sin is death. Let it be clearly understood! Man is not sent to hell by the whims of a petty God. Man goes to hell, to his second death, because he has worked for sin and sin always pays in death.

For a man to miss heaven and end in hell, he must hurdle the obstacles laid 1n his path by godly friends and faithful preachers. He must persistently reject the wooing of the Spirit. But if he does so, hell becomes his rightly-deserved eternal home.

Such is not the case for those of us who have accepted God's free gift of salvation. We have laid ourselves prostrate before Him, repented of all sin, renounced all earthly considerations, and now we are, because of Him only, heaven bound!

Chapter Seven

Union With Christ

The first six verses of this chapter are used by Paul as an illustration of the advantages that belong to the believer because of the grace of God. That is also the theme of this chapter. I cannot emphasize strongly enough that this passage should never be studied in reference to marriage and divorce. Let me repeat. This passage is not a discourse on marriage and divorce. It is Paul's picture of the burden of the law as opposed to the freedom of grace in Christ.

1 Know ye not, brethren, (for I speak to them that know the law,) how that the law hath dominion over a man as long as he liveth?
2 For the woman which hath an husband is bound by the law to her husband so long as he liveth; but if the husband be dead, she is loosed from the law of her husband.
3 So then if, while her husband liveth, she be married to another man, she shall be called an adulteress: but if her husband be dead, she is free from that law; so that she is no adulteress, though she be married to another man.
4 Wherefore, my brethren, ye also are become dead to the law by the body of Christ; that ye should be married to another, even to him who is raised from the dead, that we should bring forth fruit unto God.
5 For when we were in the flesh, the motions of sins, which were by the law, did work in our members to bring forth fruit unto death.
6 But now we are delivered from the law, that being dead wherein we were held; that we should serve in newness of spirit, and not in the oldness of the letter.

These verses may be better understood if I explain them in short story form. For the story's sake, we enter the home of a very frustrated woman. She is married to a rigidly demanding man whom we shall call Mr. Law. It is not that she has not tried to be a devoted wife, because she has tried with all of her might to please him.

Each morning when Mr. Law leaves for work, he hands his weary wife a long list of chores that he expects her to have completed before he returns home in the evening. All day long she keeps one eye on the list as she relentlessly, but hopelessly, attacks her husband's commands. Finally, the day comes to an end. She has failed. Mr. Law harshly scolds her for her failure to fulfill the requirements for that day. She vows to work harder and do better, but each evening brings the same results — failure and despair.

One day, she finds herself wishing that she could have another man for her husband. But that is impossible: Her only hope is that her husband will die, and then she will be free, free to marry whomever she desires. To leave him while he is still alive and to marry someone else does nothing but make her an adulteress, out of the will of God.

Then, one memorable day, a miracle occurs. Death breaks her marriage to Mr. Law. No, he does not die; she does! That's right, she dies! And wondrously, another man with total and tender care for her, touches her and brings her to life. His name is Mr. Love. Can she marry him? Of course she can. Her marriage to Mr. Law is over because of her death, because death ends a marriage.

The wedding take place, and Mr. Love is everything that she had dreamed a husband would be. He is kind, considerate and loving. He delights in finding little ways to please her.

But one day, there is a strangely familiar scene. As Mr. Love leaves for work, he hands his wife a list of "responsibilities for her to complete before he returns home in the evening. In many ways, it seems to be the same list that her former husband, Mr. Law, had once given her. Old panic grips her heart as she sees the day coming to a close with jobs yet undone.

Hearing her husband's steps approaching the front door, this poor woman steels herself for a scathing rebuke. Upon his entry to their home, she begins to sob out her frustrations of trying so hard and working so hard but falling so short of his expectations. But a strange thing happens! Instead of cruelly scolding her, Mr. Love takes her in his arms and whispers in her ear that he is pleased with her.

How can this be? She knows that she has failed! Mr. Love sits her down, and taking her hands in his, he tells her that there are only two things he really expects of his wife. First, he wants her to love him more than anyone or anything else in the world. Second, he wants her to commit herself to make a total effort to please him whenever she does anything for him. He continues by reminding her that he will always do both of these same things for her. That being true, he tenderly shares his deepest love for the way she has worked all day, knowing that she approached each task because she truly loved him, not because of fear of him. Finally, Mr. Love does something that Mr. Law would never do. He pulls his wife to her feet and they joyfully finish all the work together. And so it goes day after day. When she has given her best effort, but still not quite succeeded, Mr. Love adds his strength and together each job is completed and nothing is lacking.

I hope that you are able to comprehend already the reason that this passage should never be studied in terms of marriage. No woman has ever been able to end a distasteful marriage and marry someone else as a result of her own death and subsequent resurrection. This is not a treatise on marriage, divorce and remarriage.

Paul uses this unique illustration to show us that man had no hope under the law. The law was demanding; it was oppressive. Pain and frustration, coupled with an absence of joyful vitality, made even the most ardent disciple of the law unbelievably miserable.

But since the law is God's Word to man, it has an eternal quality. Therefore, man seemed destined to trudge through his existence under its burden, trying in desperate futility to keep the letter of the law (v. 6).

Here was his dilemma. How could he escape the entanglements of law's load without at the same time doing despite to its author, Jehovah God? Unless God intervened, there was no way. But thank God, He did intervene!

What our Lord did was to use the law as a mirror to show man his inability to achieve righteousness under it. Then, through Jesus Christ and His marvelous grace (Mr. Love), God provided man a way to "die" to the law and be resurrected to a new life. In so doing, God fulfilled the law in Christ, but gave mankind a higher dimension of love upon which to build his life. That is the glorious reason that we no longer must vainly attempt to live by the letter but instead serve Him gladly with a "newness of spirit" (v. 6).

Unfortunately, this does not resolve our continual conflict with sin. This is quite clearly established in the balance of this seventh chapter of Romans. Let us consider Paul's assertion that sin had dealt him some cruel blows:

7 What shall we say then? Is the law sin? God forbid. Nay, I had not known sin, but by the law: for I had not known lust, except the law has said, Thou shalt not covet.
8 But sin, taking occasion by the commandment, wrought in me all manner of concupiscence. For without the law sin was dead.
9 For I was alive without the law once: but when the commandment came, sin revived, and I died.
10 And the commandment, which was ordained to live, I found to be unto death.
11 For sin, taking occasion by the commandment, deceived me, and by it slew me.
12 Wherefore the law is holy, and the commandment holy, and just, and good.

After all that Paul has said thus far in this letter to the Roman believers, one might assume that Paul would view the law as sin. Make no mistake! The law never has and never will save anyone! That is the ultimate weakness of the law. And it is the grossest of misunderstandings to believe that the Jews were saved by keeping the law and that we are saved by grace. Nevertheless, the law served a much-needed purpose in showing all mankind that we are indeed unholy.

Verse seven explicitly states this precept by Paul's contention that he would not have been able to clearly identify sin were it not for the teachings of the law. Since the revelation of the law at Mt. Sinai, no man can excuse himself from sin's penalties with the lame alibi that he did not know it was wrong.

I think it is interesting that Paul uses covetousness as his example of the law's clear teaching. Why? This tenth commandment of the Ten Commandments (the Decalogue) covers all the other nine and any other sin that may be named as well.

Covetousness is lust. And what is it that James tells us? He says, "But every man is tempted, when he is drawn away of his own lust, and enticed. Then when lust hath conceived, it bringeth forth sin: and sin, when it is finished, bringeth forth death" (James 1:14-15). So, rather logically it seems, Paul uses this mother of sins to support God's reason for having the law established.

Verse eight is a verse with which most spiritually-discerning believers can readily identify. There was a time, Paul says, that he had never studied the law and, therefore, " ". . . sin was dead," that is, he sensed no battle raging inside himself over any particular temptation or sin. Because of his ignorance of the law, sin lay dormant like a sleeping tiger. But when he became aware of the law's instructions, sin sprang with fierceness into action against him.

Two terms must be defined for you to fully interpret verse eight. "Taking occasion" means "starting point" in the original language. It is a military term usually employed to locate an enemy's place of attack. "Concupiscence" means "lust" or "desire."

Now we can accurately understand Paul here. Before he studied the law, there were no inner struggles with sin. After studying the law and finding its indictment of sins by naming them specifically, Paul found hidden sins in full warfare against the law. His mind would try to justify the committing of deeds that the law set forth as sin, and that became the starting point of the battle.

To clarify, imagine a visit to your physician's office. He informs you that milk and cheese should be eliminated from your diet. That does not seem to pose a problem for you because you scarcely ever eat dairy foods anyway. Until now! Now that you are not to eat them, dairy products are all that you crave — milkshakes, cheese sandwiches, butter.

Paul states that that experience occurred to him as he read the law. Sins that he had never thought of committing sprang to life. Here is a question to consider. Would it then be better to be ignorant of the law's requirements and thereby avoid conflict? No, it would not. Sin must be eliminated from the individual life if that person is to see God. The law exposes sin, and as painful as that may be, it is for the believer's good.

Verse nine sheds an interesting insight into Paul's view of his life before his salvation. He says that "... I was alive apart from the law once..." You must remember that he had been a strict adherent to the law. As a fanatic, he zealously kept the dictates of the law. No Pharisee ever dedicated himself to the law's compliance with any more fervor than did he. But that kind of submission had been to the dead letter of the law, instead of the joy that comes from doing God's will because of a love for God.

What kind of life could that have been, to which Paul is referring? It was a life with a purpose. While obviously it was a misdirected life, Paul awoke each day with a definite reason for living — the persecution and extermination of this new band of religious followers of Christ.

It is quite similar in our day with those who are saved out of very anti-Jesus cults. These converts often become flaming evangelists for the very Lord Jesus whom they once hated. Their frequent comment, after salvation, is that they were excited about life and enjoying it thoroughly while members of the cults, but it was an artificial happiness, devoid of real inner fulfillment.

But Paul continues in verse nine by asserting that "... when the commandment came, sin revived, and I died ..." Is it not an interesting phenomenon, true of Paul and all others of us who have been saved, that what we thought was "really living" outside of Christ cannot be compared with the real life we have in Jesus? It reminds me of the wedding at Cana of Galilee. There was a much more delicious flavor in the wine that Jesus provided than there was in the wine that had already been served.

Verse ten holds a terrible realization for Paul! Before his conversion, he had faithfully discharged the commands of the law. If ever there had been an outwardly upright man, it was Paul. What a sobering awareness must have been his when he was confronted with the fact that he was surely headed for hell and the law he had so vigorously defended could not keep him from that dread place!

Verse eleven begins by repeating part of verse eight: "For sin, taking occasion by the commandment . . . " Remember, "taking occasion" is better translated, "starting point." In verse eight, the starting point was the origin of sin's warfare in Paul's life. Here, in verse eleven, we have a different starting point.

It is the starting point of deception. Please note the word, "deceived." More accurately, in the original language, that word is "cheated" or "swindled." Sin cheated Paul. Sin swindled Paul. Beginning with Eve in the Garden of Eden, Satan has been in the business of destroying every person who has ever lived by the deceitfulness of sin.

That is why Paul says that " . . . it (sin) slew me." We are not only dead spiritually before salvation because of Adam's sin, but we are dead also because of our own sins. And the worst thing of all is that when we were dead, we thought we were alive. That is the terror of deception. A deceived man does not know that he is deceived.

Verse twelve brings us once again to the importance of the law. Had it not been for the clear denunciation of sin by the law, Paul would never have realized how separated he was from God and how desperately he needed a Savior. I must repeat again, for I fear that some reader may not fully understand, the law never saved anyone but that was not its purpose anyway. The law came to show us the true wretchedness of our condition. In doing that the law succeeded wonderfully well. Therefore, although the law cannot save, we must recognize its value.

The remaining verses in this chapter deal with the perpetual struggle between the two natures within the believer. Let us first read the verses:
13 Was then that which is good made death unto me? God forbid. But sin, that it might appear sin, working death in me by that which is good; that sin by the commandment might become exceeding sinful.
14 For we know that the law is spiritual: but I am carnal, sold under sin.
15 For that which I do I allow not: for what I would, that do I not; but what I hate, that do I.
16 If then I do that which I would not, I consent unto the law that it is good.
17 Now then it is no more I that do it, but sin that dwelleth in me.
18 For I know that in me (that is, in my flesh,) dwelleth no good thing: for to

will is present with me; but how to perform that which is good I find not.
19 For the good that I would I do not: but the evil which I would not, that I do.
20 Now if I do that I would not, it is no more I that do it, but sin that dwelleth in me.
21 I find then a law, that, when I would do good, evil is present with me.
22 For I delight in the law of God after the inward man:
23 But I see another law in my members, warring against the law of my mind, and bringing me into captivity to the law of sin which is in my members.
24 O wretched man that I am! who shall deliver me from the body of this death?
25 I thank God through Jesus Christ our Lord. So then with the mind I myself serve the law of God; but with the flesh the law of sin.

    Verse thirteen declares the subtle deceptiveness of sin. We have already seen that the law, when rightly understood, is good. Now Paul poses a hypothetical question. How could something that is good bring death? After all, the law came directly from God. It is God's Word. How could it be that God's Word for good could possibly cause death?

    It is clear! Satan realizes that there are many, like Paul, who will not blatantly oppose the commands of God. They will never yield themselves to drunkenness or sexual immorality. In every respect, they will conform to the very letter of the law. But in so doing, they are misusing and abusing God's law unless they trust Christ for salvation. As upright individuals, they are strutting their way to hell, thinking they are too good to go there. The worst form of sin is moral goodness when moral goodness is used as a substitute for being born again.

    So Satan very cunningly causes some poor souls to look so much to the law for salvation that they never look through the law for the giver of salvation. But once we understand this sinister ploy of the devil, we can echo Paul's words that the commandment makes sin exceeding sinful.

    Verse fourteen brings into sharp focus our basic problem as believers. The law is God-breathed; it is pure. It is a high and holy standard of outward righteousness. Paul, on the other hand, as consecrated a believer as ever lived, says that he is carnal.

Sometime you may hear sincere people speak of the "eradication of the flesh" or of "sinless perfection." You will recall in our study of chapter six that we saw that the 'old man ' was crucified with Christ. The two terms just mentioned result from a confusion by some dear folks of "the old man" in chapter six with "carnal" here in chapter seven.

Man is a trichotomous being; that is, he is body, soul, and spirit "The old man" has to do with man's innermost self his spirit. "Carnal" has to do with man's outer self — his body The word, "carnal," means "flesh." You have seen it used in connection with carnivorous (flesh-eating) animals or with chili con carne (chili with flesh or meat). That is why we have war within ourselves after salvation. Before we were saved the old man and our carnal nature got along rather well together. But no more! Now there is a declared war!

We must recognize that this body in which we live will one day die. It is not yet made ready for heaven, and will not be until either the rapture or the resurrection takes place. Have you considered that when a believer dies his spirit goes straight to heaven without having to pass through the judgement? This happens because the old man is dead and the believer cannot sin in his spirit (I John 3:9). There is nothing to be judged in his spirit. But when the rapture occurs and his spirit returns with Christ and is re-united with a glorified body being resurrected from the grave, then body and soul must appear before the judgment to answer for the things done in the body (II Corinthians 5:10).

To thoroughly understand verse fourteen, we must correctly translate the phrase, " . . . sold under sin." In the original, it has the meaning of a political prisoner sold as a slave to a foreign nation, never to return to his homeland. Can you imagine the misery of such an individual, forced to live in a place of strange customs, languages, and behavior? That is how we are as believers. We are sold under sin. Our spirits are forced to live in a body that has not yet been glorified. We, of the heavenly, are made to live in the earthly.

Verse fifteen expresses a familiar experience for every child of God. Our flesh has such powerful impulses that we find ourselves acting in wrong fashion before checking it in our spirits. How often have you found yourself saying, "I just hate myself for what I did!" Those are Paul's sentiments exactly! Oh, dear reader, how diligent, how careful we must be in this world! The flesh responds so readily to Satan's enticements. It is little wonder that we are so often advised in the Scriptures to "walk in the Spirit."

Verse sixteen is a compliment to the reason for the law. The law was, and is, a constant mirror by which we can see our own blemishes of sin that would otherwise go undetected. When we yield to temptation, but immediately recognize the wrongness of what we have done, it is because the law is activated by the Holy Spirit within and we are convicted of sin. Remember, the law is the Word of God. It is the written barb that the Spirit employs to forcefully remind us of our shortcomings. Therefore, it is good.

Verse seventeen has been construed by some as a license to sin. That is a perversion of the meaning here. Even though the believer is eternally secure in terms of his salvation, there is no situation in which he may excuse himself to habitually sin. Believers may fall into sin, but they do not "walk" in sin.

The Greek word used here for "do," 'means "to continually produce." That kind of evil activity is totally foreign to the man who knows Christ.

Please note Paul's use of "I." He says, by the use of "I," that the "real Paul" is not the one who is committing sin. Remember, according to I John 3:9, that part of us which is born of God at salvation "cannot" sin. It is impossible! So, that being true why do we fall into sin? Paul is quick to remind us in this verse that it is because sin dwells in us. "Dwelleth" is a present tense verb indicating continual action We have an on-going conflict that shall never reach a conclusion until we enter heaven.

Verse eighteen declares Paul's certainty about something that many believers arrogantly refuse to admit. He says that he knows that there is "no good thing" in his flesh. Oh, how often I hear someone say, "Well, maybe I'm not all I ought to be but I'm not all bad either." Or, I will be trying to lead some dear lady's lost husband to the Lord and she will say, "Now I know my husband is not a Christian, but he's really a good man." Such statements are utter foolishness and display a total ignorance of the Scriptures. My dear reader, you simply cannot trust your flesh, even in matters that seem perfectly acceptable. Why? Because Satan's instrument of defeat in your life is your flesh. Do not for one minute give occasion to yield to its most reasonable impulses.

And therein the battle lines are drawn. Our will is to do that which is noble and uplifting and God-honoring. But remember verse fourteen. Our flesh has been "sold under sin" as a prisoner forced to live in a foreign and strange land. Remember also Matthew 26:41 where our Lord warns us that the Spirit is willing, but the flesh is weak. Paul confesses, and you and I must sadly agree, that what we really knew we ought to do and what we ended up doing were worlds apart. For example, how often has God spoken to your heart about the urgency of speaking to some poor lost soul about his eternal destiny, but you just "never got around to it." Or, maybe the Spirit pressed upon you the need to give a substantial gift to the work of God, but you "just couldn't afford it right now." Such experiences as these are testimonies to the truthfulness of Paul's concern.

Verse nineteen continues Paul's dismay at the struggle within him. But this verse seems to have a contradiction within it. Paul says "that the evil I would not, that I do." We have already established that a believer may occasionally fall into sin but will not continue in it. Yet, Paul is in this verse apparently telling us otherwise. How can that be?

Please note that he does not use the word "sin" in reference to what he does. No, he uses "evil." Evil encompasses the entire dictionary of sins. Implied here is that as soon as Paul has conquered one sin into which he has fallen, before he can rejoice at his victory, he has fallen into another. He is not saying that he continues to commit some particular sin, but that he feels like he is being bombarded with a whole multitude of varied sins because of his flesh's bent toward evil.

Verse twenty provides some peace of mind for Paul. At least he recognizes that when he sins, it is not the "real Paul" who is sinning. This should not be viewed as a justifiable reason to sin. It is not. We cannot just simply throw up our hands and say, "Well, I'll just go ahead and sin because it's not really me who is sinning anyway! " We must make every valiant effort to overcome the temptations in our lives. But in order to avoid hopeless despair, we must identify the enemy. And as Pogo of comic strip fame once said, We have found the enemy, and he is us!

Verse twenty-one has been variously interpreted by good men of the Word. Where you see "a law," it should be more accurately "the law." The two dominant, and different interpretations are based upon these two words, the law. Some say that this is a reference to the law of the Old Testament. Some say that this is a reference to the law of evil, which if so, is a new term and concept used here.

It is my opinion that the latter is the case. I do not believe that Paul would have said, "I find the law," if he had been speaking of the Mosaic law. "Find" indicates that he has made a discovery. A law, unlike a theory, is unchanging and universally applicable. The law that he has discovered is the result of years in a bitter, spiritual war. Simply stated, this law that is true in every believer is two-fold: there is a new nature that cannot sin produced at salvation within man and there is an old nature that can do nothing but sin residing in his flesh. Hence, there is a perpetual war.

Verse twenty-two is an expression that only a saved man can understand. The Word of God, even in its thunderings of judgment, has a sweetness that the unregenerated man can never know. The word "delight" can be pictured as a small child jumping up and down, clapping his hands with joy. That is the reason that the believer so enjoys the preaching of the Word of God and attendance at the house of God.

Verse twenty-three, with its reference to the "law of my mind " is better understood by remembering Paul's words in Philippians 2:5 where he says that the believer is to have within himself the mind of Christ. Three laws are mentioned in this verse. There is the law of our members which is the continual inclination of our flesh to commit sin. There is the law of our mind (the mind of Christ in us) that is the continual inclination of our Spirit to do good and overcome sin. There is the law of sin which is merely a reiteration of Paul's earlier observation that there is nothing good that dwells within our flesh. That law of sin is anti-God, anti-righteousness, anti-holiness.

This is the state of war between these three laws, and Paul's ultimate discouragement also. The law of our members sometimes pulls so hard in its fleshly impulses that we yield to those impulses in spite of the spiritual resistance of the law of our minds, and this yielding results in our being taken as captives into the law of sin which, in turn, brings inner conviction and sorrow of the Spirit.

Verse twenty-four is Paul's cry for relief from this agony of heart. "Wretched" is used only one other time in the New Testament and that is in Revelation 3: 17. The word is better understood in the original to convey the image of a man hopelessly caught in a trap from which there is no escape. "Body of this death" is more accurately "this body of death." Perhaps Paul had in mind an ancient Roman practice of tying a murderer face-to-face with the dead body of his victim and allowing him to starve to death. Whatever the case, Paul feels the same awful dilemma.

There is only one hope, and that hope is in a person. Paul says, "who shall deliver me . . . " The moment he uses the word, "who," he is implying that he cannot deliver himself, no plan can deliver him, no creed can deliver him, and since every other person on this planet is in precisely the same condition, no other human being of Adam's race can deliver him. The "who" refers to a person, and that person is the Lord Jesus Christ!

But since Paul is already saved, has not Christ already delivered him? No, our deliverance will not be complete until we enter heaven. Our salvation, our deliverance, is in
three tenses: we have been delivered from the penalty of sin, we are being delivered from the power of sin, we will be delivered from the presence of sin. It is that third deliverance of which Paul speaks — deliverance from this body of sin.

Verse twenty-five closes this chapter seven with an exuberant shout of Joy! Paul clearly draws the line of difference between the inner man and the outer man. This outer man is not going to heaven in the shape it is in anyway. Thank God the "real us" will never have sin laid to its charge because of the substitutionary death of Jesus. We cannot be conquered by the law of sin in our flesh! We are the conquerors through Him who loved us!

Chapter Eight

Deliverance And Assurance

Of all the noteworthy passages in this remarkable book, none seems to capture the readers' hearts quite like this one. Great sermon series have been preached from this chapter alone. In it is shared in graphic design the wondrous sovereign love of God. Other than John 3:16, a reigning favorite verse is tucked into this chapter. It is Romans 8:28 and we shall study it in some detail later. The challenge for me is the selection of pertinent information that you should incorporate into your basic Bible skills and which information is less essential. I have attempted to illuminate this chapter sufficiently enough in detail that you will know the sovereign care of the Lord for you.

Paul begins in the first eight verses with a general statement concerning the freedom that belongs to the believer who is no longer under the sentence of condemnation:

1 There is therefore now no condemnation to them which are in Christ Jesus, who walk not after the flesh, but after the Spirit.
2 For the law of the Spirit of life in Christ Jesus hath made me free from the law of sin and death.
3 For what the law could not do, in that it was weak through the flesh, God sending his own Son in the likeness of sinful flesh, and for sin, condemned sin in the flesh:
4 That the righteousness of the law might be fulfilled in us, who walk not after the flesh, but after the Spirit.
5 For they that are after the flesh do mind the things of the flesh; but they that are after the Spirit the things of the Spirit.
6 For to be carnally minded is death; but to be spiritually minded is life and peace.
7 Because the carnal mind is enmity against God: for it is not subject to the law of God, neither indeed can be.
8 So then they that are in the flesh cannot please God.

Verse one is the badge of distinction for the saved. There is "no condemnation to them which are in Christ Jesus." This wonderful truth is even better enjoyed when we understand that "condemnation" is more accurately translated "judgment" in the original. While it is true that we must all appear before the judgment seat of Christ to answer for the works done in this body, it is not of that judgment that this verse speaks. The condemnation, the judgment, of verse one is reserved for the unsaved who have never appropriated to themselves the pardon for their sins so graciously offered through the atoning death of the Lord Jesus. This promise is for those of us who are "in Christ Jesus."

That phrase "in Christ Jesus" is important if you are to understand the rest of verse one. We are in Christ as a result of His grace. Under no circumstances whatever do we gain access into Him because of any works that we do. We have already seen in chapter seven that the flesh is totally depraved ("in it dwells no good thing") and is alienated from Christ. Therefore, that part of us that is "in Christ" is the innermost man which cannot sin (I John 3:9). It, "the real us," need not fear the judgment.

Those who espouse the doctrine of Arminianism, falling from grace, use this verse to promote this faulty interpretation by asserting that if a believer fails to walk in the Spirit, but persists in walking after the flesh, he will be lost again; he will lose his salvation. This verse knows nothing of losing salvation. Instead of a warning to the saved man that he could yet be relegated to hell, this verse is a statement of fact.

We have already discussed that a believer may "fall" into sin, but he will not continue to "walk" in it. Note that this verse emphatically designates that the ones who are not under condemnation are those who "walk not after the flesh, but walk after the Spirit." This is not a verse that threatens the loss of salvation. It is a verse that gives us a perfect gauge by which to determine our own relationship with God. Regardless of the fact of occasional sin, are your patterns of living marked by Christ-honoring motives, habits, and deeds? That is, do you, in overwhelming fashion, "walk" in the Spirit? If so, praise your dear Lord that Jesus has borne your sins away and you need not fear the judgment!

Verse two presents Paul using the term, "law," again. He seems to enjoy the use of this particular word to describe certain of God's unchanging principles. For example, he has spoken of the law of Moses, the law of sin, the law of the mind, etc. This verse now shows us that there are two more laws — the "law of the Spirit of life" and the "law of sin and of death." The reason that we are not destined for condemnation (v. 1) is because the law of the Spirit of life has made us free.

How do these two laws influence us? Let me illustrate it in this way. The law of sin and of death we shall compare to the physical law of gravity which is always a downward pull. The law of the Spirit of life we shall compare to the law of aerodynamics which provides an upward thrust for aircraft. As long as an airplane provides enough inner energy and operates according to the law of aerodynamics, it overcomes the downward pull of the law of gravity. Even so it is also with the believer. He must depend totally upon the power of the Spirit of life within himself to overcome the downward pull of the law of sin and of death. Just as with the airplane, he cannot cease in that upward drive of the Spirit or else he will fall rapidly. That failure, in essence, is what we call "backsliding."

The term, "made free," in the original, means "something that has actually already happened in the past that so provides total liberty that nothing can ever be done to improve upon it." That is how free we are in Christ by the law of the Spirit of life!

Verse three shows us again an important fact that we have seen repeatedly already in this study. The law could not save! In reality, it is not the fault of the law that it could not save because the law was perfect since it was the Word of God No, the reason that the law could not save was because of the inability of our own sinful flesh to live up to its holy standards.

There is a second reason that the law could not save. Simply, it was never in the mind of God for it to do so. He had a different purpose for it: "Wherefore the law was our schoolmaster to bring us unto Christ, that we might be justified by faith" (Galatians 3:24).

Once man came to understand his failure to meet the requirements of the law, the law had fulfilled its reason for its existence. Man could clearly see that he was a sinner incapable of pulling himself from his low state of unholiness to the high state of God's holiness. What a dilemma! What is he to do?

Enter Jesus! In verse three, you see the phrase, " . . . God, sending 'His own Son . . . " This speaks of the doctrine of incarnation, which literally means that God enveloped Himself in human flesh. That is the glory of the virgin birth.

Moreover, the very importance of Christ's virgin birth is directly implied here. The Bible says that He was sent in "the likeness of sinful flesh." Jesus was not sinful flesh by virtue of the nature of His birth; He was born with the "likeness" of our own frail limitations. If you have never read M. R. DeHaan's book, The Chemistry of the Blood, you should do it as soon as possible, and you will be thrilled at the way Dr. DeHaan, a medical doctor, shows that the blood of a child is contributed by the father. That is why Acts 20;28 is such glorious truth when it tells us that the blood of Calvary's cross was God's blood. If you remove the virgin birth, you remove that wonderful truth from the Bible, and in so doing, you remove your own salvation from the Bible. Make no mistake! It was God's "own Son" who gave us our greatest gift —- salvation!

As the sinless Son of God, yet in the likeness of sinful flesh, Jesus was thoroughly qualified to die on the cross for us. When He did, He overcame the law of sin that is universal in every human being that we discussed earlier in chapter seven. When He cried, "It is finished," the one narrow escape from a hitherto unbreakable law was provided. Jesus Christ lived a sinless life in His flesh —— that repudiated the law of sin. Jesus Christ died a substitutionary sacrificial death — that released us from the law of sin.

Do you remember David and Goliath? David was the representative of the Israelites. Goliath was the representative of the Philistines. If David won, the Israelites won. If Goliath won, the Philistines won. Jesus was our representative against the forces of hell. When He won at Calvary in the condemnation of sin in the flesh, we all won!

Verse four continues to describe what Christ did for us. The law concerned itself with the righteousness of the outer man, and indeed, that is all that it could do. But verse four declares that the righteousness of the law is fulfilled "in us." That is possible because Jesus not only died for us, but He also indwells us with the Spirit. This is what we call "the imputed righteousness of Christ."

Again, this same verse gives an identifying mark for those who have Christ "in" them. It is the fact that they will "walk" in the Spirit and not in the flesh. Oh, how badly this principle should be preached again and again! While we may occasionally "fall" into sin, we cannot as believers habitually practice, or "walk," in it!

Verse five sets forth this clear teaching. There is flesh and there is Spirit. This just happens not to be the false line that is drawn by the average church member. He thinks in terms of secular and religious. Most of the days of his life are spent in the secular world; a few of the days of his life are spent in the religious world.

But Paul says that a man is either of the flesh or he is of the Spirit. The mind of flesh takes its delight in the unspiritual things of this world. The mind of Spirit takes its delight in the things of God. A good question for you to ask yourself is, Is there anything at all I would rather do than contemplate the Lord Jesus Christ through the Word of God or prayer?"

How readily do churches re-arrange worship services to accommodate athletic events, like Super Bowl football games! How easily do church members find excuses to miss church bible studies or evangelistic services! How unhesitatingly do professed followers of Christ take vacations with no thought of attendance in worship while away!

These characteristics of minding either the things of the flesh or the things of the Spirit do not make a believer, but they do mark a believer. By this means of identification, we must honestly admit that many who profess Christ have never known Him at all. A sad commentary of the modern church is that our buildings are filled with those who are really members of the "cult of the comfortable." They have the mind of flesh, and given the right circumstances exhibit it.

Verse six affirms what I have just said in verse five The man with the mind of flesh is lost; the second death of separation from God in hell will be his final destiny because he is spiritually dead right now. He has never become a "new creature in Christ. (II Corinthians 5:17). Sadly, what he thinks is really living it up is really "dying it down." He is doomed in his dancing through this life.

But what peace and life there is for the man who is saved! He may not have peace from trouble, but he has peace in trouble! Like the artist's rendering of a violent, wild storm, but with a sparrow fast asleep in a small crevice of a rock, the believer is secure in the bosom of the sure Rock of Ages. To the world, it may seem that he is living a joyless life, devoid of the much-publicized gusto of living, but in his heart is the tranquility that only God provides.

Verse seven is a reiteration of the truths we have seen previously in the latter verses of chapter seven. The flesh is an enemy of God. It refuses to respect and submit to the law of God. You can try to educate it, to refine it, to subdue it, to reform it, to discipline it, or to adorn it, but the flesh will always be anti-God. It is an alien of our Lord. If you do not come to grips with the certainty of that truth, you will be destined for a life of total frustration.

Verse eight tells us why! If the flesh is an enemy of God, alienated from the things of the Spirit, it only stands to reason that anyone who lives in the flesh and enjoys the things that the flesh enjoys cannot please God.

Now Paul turns his attention to the power of the Spirit:
9 But ye are not in the flesh, but in the Spirit, if so be that the Spirit of God dwell in you. Now if any man have not the Spirit of Christ, he is none of his.
10 And if Christ be in you, the body is dead because of sin; but the Spirit is life because of righteousness.
11 But if the Spirit of him that raised up Jesus from the dead dwell in you, he that raised up Christ from the dead shall also quicken your mortal bodies by his Spirit that dwelleth in you.
12 Therefore, brethren, we are debtors, not to the flesh, to live after the flesh.
13 For if ye live after the flesh, ye shall die: but if ye through the Spirit do

mortify the deeds of the body, ye shall live.
14 For as many as are led by the Spirit of God, they are the sons of God.

Verse nine is very pointedly directed at the life of the believer. It is comforting to know that there need be no question concerning our relationship with God, Even though we are engaged in a struggle with the flesh that will continue all the days of our lives, we can still march confidently toward the day that we meet Jesus because of the blessed presence of the Spirit within us. He would not be there if we were not saved! The absence of the Spirit on the other hand, is proof positive of being lost.

Since that is true, how can a person know whether the Spirit is indwelling him? The Spirit will not share living quarters with sin. If you, dear reader, are born again, you cannot commit sin without terrible conviction by the Spirit coming upon you. If you are able to continue in sin without is conviction, it means that the Holy Spirit does not live in your heart. So, consider your daily life. Are you able to sin with no pangs of the Spirit in your heart that make you know immediately that you have violated a law of God? Are you not thrust into remorseful repentance when you sin? If this is indeed the condition of your spiritual life, you are lost! The Spirit does not indwell you!

This verse also refutes a very popular modem error. Often we hear sincere individuals speak of "the baptism with the Holy Ghost as a second work of grace." My dear friend, it is by the Holy Ghost baptism that we are brought "into" the body of Christ (I Corinthians 12:13). That is the work of God that occurs at the time of salvation and brings us into a "son" relationship with the Father because of the work of Christ at Calvary.

Look carefully at the last sentence in verse nine: "But if any man have not the Spirit of Christ, he is none of his." That being so, which of course it is because this is the Word of God, the baptism with the Holy Ghost cannot possibly come "after" salvation. To be without Him at all is to be lost. Moreover, and read this very carefully, there is not one single place in the Bible where a saved person is commanded to be baptized with the Holy Ghost! Why? Because the believer has already been baptized with the Holy Ghost at the time of his salvation. Of course, as believers we are commanded to be "filled," or controlled by the Holy Ghost (Ephesians 5:18); there are many times in our Christian journey that we need to be "filled." But there is only one baptism and that is at our salvation or else Romans 8:9 is not true!

Verse ten, and also verse eleven as we shall see in a moment, confidently and gloriously state that when the Spirit indwells us, our salvation is assured. These verses are a continuation of Paul's declaration in verse nine.

When he uses "Christ" in verse ten, it is as though he had used "Spirit." Sometimes Paul will use one term, and sometimes he will use another, when he means the same thing. This is to reinforce the fact of God's trinity. The Holy Ghost (Spirit) indwells us. Christ indwells us. God indwells us. The blessed truth of it all is that because of God's triune nature, when we use one term, we could just as easily refer to all three. And think of it! Because of that nature of the Godhead, there is as much of God in the heart of each believer as -there is of God in heaven!

We have, in verse ten, a positional truth — "the body is dead." Practically speaking, that does not happen until the heart stops and a man is declared "dead." But remember Adam, the Lord told him that in the day - that he ate of the forbidden fruit he would die. Adam lived over nine hundred years after that awful day! Was God wrong? Of course not! On that day, Adam did die spiritually by his separation from God. He also lost the eternal quality of his body. For the next nine hundred years and more, Adam suffered the knowledge of impending physical death. Disease, pain, and aging became grim reminders that he would not physically live forever. So, it is true in Romans 8:10 — the body is dead.

The latter part of verse ten gives us the other side of the coin. Spirit, as used here, should not be capitalized; this verse is talking about man's eternal spirit, not the Holy Spirit. Our spirit, because of the imputed righteousness of Christ, will live forever. And it is all because of the righteousness of Christ within us.

Verse eleven is such an encouragement to all of us are saved. Oh, but to enjoy the comfort of this verse you must first know that you have been born again. Surely you have settled that question by the time you have reached this point in our study of the Book of Romans. Do not ever again let anyone try to tell you that you cannot know for certain that you are saved. To listen to such a misinformed and biblically ignorant person is to contradict the words of John: "These things have I written unto you, that ye may know that ye have eternal life . . . " (I John 5:13). We do not have to guess that we are saved or hope that we will be in heaven. Dear reader, the Bible says we can know it! Already in our study of this eighth chapter alone, we have shown definite questions that you may ask yourself in order that you can be sure.

To understand verse eleven, please remember that Paul tells us in I Corinthians 6:19 that our bodies are the temples of the Holy Ghost. Although this body will ultimately die, Satan will not even be able to brag about its destruction because of sin. Our bodies will die, unless the rapture occurs first. Make no mistake of that! But we are blessed beyond measure! We will in our bodies, yet to be glorified at the resurrection, see our Savior face to face!

How will this happen? Please read carefully one of the most exciting lines that I shall write in this entire study. This verse plainly teaches that the same Holy Spirit that brought Jesus from that musty tomb almost two thousand years ago is the exact same Holy Spirit that lives within me this very moment and will bring this body to a glorious resurrection life even if I should die before Jesus comes! Think of it! The same Holy Spirit in Christ is in me!

The assurance that we will be raised from the dead lies in the fact that Christ himself was resurrected. Therein is the vital importance of the bodily resurrection of our Lord. Although some suggest that it makes no difference whether He was raised in His body just as long as His Spirit was raised, I protest that it does make a big difference. Paul points this out in I Thessalonians 4:13-14 when he says, "I would not have you to be ignorant, brethren, concerning them which are asleep, that ye sorrow not, even as others which have no hope. For if we believe that Jesus died and rose again, even so them also which sleep in Jesus will God bring with him." The fact of our resurrection is certain because Jesus was raised!

Verse twelve is a short, but direct, statement of our responsibilities. Since the flesh is the enemy of God, we owe it nothing. We have no commitment to meet its selfish demands. Our allegiance is on a higher plane, and that is to the Holy Ghost within us. By His power we are able to live holy lives and force our flesh into subjection to Him.

Verse thirteen is another of the verses in this letter to the Romans that is so often misconstrued to mean that we can lose our salvation. Paul is reasserting again the clear distinction between being saved and being lost. How badly we need that same line drawn today! I am thoroughly convinced that our pews are packed with unregenerated people. This verse, I believe, is especially for them.

Note that we are told that if a man makes a continual habit of living after the flesh, he "must die." There is no question about it! He "must" die. For him to live after the flesh and still go to heaven would reduce the Bible into a book of blunders. The flesh is the enemy of God. Our study has already firmly established that. If a man follows God's enemy, he will not follow him to heaven but he will follow him to hell.

On the other hand, if we live after the Spirit and continually destroy the desires and deeds of our flesh, we "shall" live. That word, "shall," eliminates any guesswork about our salvation. We "shall" live. In following the Spirit, we become the enemy of the enemy of God. Since the Holy Spirit is God, to follow Him is to go to God.

Verse fourteen settles the question of our power as believers. The Holy Spirit is our strength! He is our guide! He is our motivation. Please note that we "are led by the Spirit." This means that our will has been yielded to His will. Similar to a child being led by an adult across a busy intersection, we are led by the Spirit through this treacherous world. We do not have to chart our own course! For successful living, all we must do is follow Him! How gloriously simple!

This willingness to be led by the Spirit is his identifying mark, for himself and for those around him. Only a son of God will follow the Spirit! Often I hear people exclaim that it is so hard to live the Christian life. No, it is not hard; it is impossible! The Christian life is only possible by Christ living through us. Therefore, no man can follow the Spirit unless the Spirit is within him. And, according to Romans 8:9, the Spirit is not there unless that man is saved!

The next three verses reveal our blessed position with Christ:
15 For ye have not received the spirit of bondage again to fear; but ye have received the Spirit of adoption, whereby we cry, Abba, Father.
16 The Spirit itself beareth witness with our spirit, that we are the children of God:
17 And if children, then heirs; heirs of God, and joint-heirs with Christ; if so be that we suffer with him, that we may be also glorified together.

Verse fifteen describes the plight of the unsaved by informing us that they do not have the same glad situation as believers in Christ. Paul says that the unsaved are in " . . . bondage . . . to fear." Thank God, we are not! The lost man has no security financially, physically, emotionally, or spiritually. He must live under a cloud of dread. Fear is his live-in companion. But as the hymn writer has said, "My hope is built on nothing less than Jesus' blood and righteousness; I dare not trust the sweetest frame, but wholly lean on Jesus' name." That means that I have placed all the cares and fears of this world upon Him, and now I am free from their bondage.

God is not a demanding slave driver. He very tenderly cares for us. Never feel that the "Thou shalt nots" of our Lord in the Scriptures are there to bind us! When God says, "Thou shalt not," the real expression of His heart is, "Child, don't hurt yourself!" When you were saved, you did not exchange the treachery of the devil for the tyranny of God. You are not under bondage. You are free to be all that you were designed to be.

In fact, this same verse shows clearly how much the Lord cares for us. In the human family, a parent-child relationship comes into existence by one of two ways — birth or adoption. Only in God's family does this relationship occur both ways. We are born into His family by the experience of the new birth; that gives us His nature. We are adopted into His family by His sovereign choice; that gives us our position as joint-heirs with Christ.

Further, our Lord grants us the privilege of calling Him, "Abba; Father." "Abba" is an Aramaic word. It is a term of endearment. As a child, how did you address your father? Was it Daddy? Was it Papa? Because of God's wonderful love for you, He permits you to refer to Him with those same, sweet, affectionate words. Stop right now, and pray to Him, using your "Abba," whatever you called your earthly father, as you talk to your Heavenly Father. Does a God who smiles upon us with such fatherly warmth as this sound like a God of hard demands? Of course not!

Verse sixteen is more accurately translated in its opening phrase as, "The Spirit Himself." He is a person, not an emotional feeling. We have previously shown in this study how the Spirit, as the third person of the Godhead, proves our relationship with God. He bears witness that we are children of God. This phrase, "beareth witness," in the original Greek, means to "testify that something is so." One of the many jobs of the Spirit is to testify that my salvation is sure. Another verse that confirms this is I John 5:10: "He that believeth on the Son of God hath the witness in him."

As I have pointed out to you, there are good, definitive ways to know by the Spirit that you have truly been born again (see my comments on Romans 8:9). However, down deep inside of me in a manner that I have no words to describe, there is a settled conviction and peace by the Spirit of God that I belong to Jesus. I cannot explain it, but I know it!

Verse seventeen continues Paul's declaration of what we have in Christ. Ours is an exalted position, high in honor! Can you imagine being an heir of God? As unbelievable as that is to comprehend, what about being a joint-heir with Christ? Do you know what that means? It means that everything God will do for Jesus, He will also do for you! If a man has four sons, his will may decree that their inheritances are to be unevenly distributed. One son could receive everything and the other sons nothing. But if his will stipulated that all four sons were to be joint-heirs that would mean that they would all share and share alike. That is the position we have with Christ! He receives no more from the Father; we receive no less! What a staggering revelation!

That position as joint-heir has two extremes. On the one hand, we suffer with Christ. The words, "if so be," are more correctly translated, "because we do." Friend, every follower of Jesus is destined to suffer: "They that live Godly in Christ Jesus shall suffer persecution" (II Timothy 3: 1 1). But do not be dismayed! If you would be like Jesus, just remember that He suffered here on earth. As a joint-heir with Christ, our earthly inheritance is suffering.

On the other hand, we will be glorified with Him. "Glorified" means that our bodies will be raised in perfection so that we can dwell in heaven. As a joint-heir with Christ, our heavenly inheritance is a perfect body, free from the limitations of time and space, pain and death, sin and sorrow!

Now we move to our next section of verses in this chapter. These deal with the coming deliverance of God's total creation — including us - from the curse of this world:

18 For I reckon that the sufferings of this present time are not worthy to be compared with the glory which shall be revealed in us.
19 For the earnest expectation of the creature waiteth for the manifestation of the sons of God.
20 For the creature was made subject to vanity, not willingly, but by reason of him who hath subjected the same in hope,
21 Because the creature itself also shall be delivered from the bondage of corruption into the glorious liberty of the children of God.
22 For we know that the whole creation groaneth and travaileth in pain together until now.
23 And not only they, but ourselves also, which have the first fruits of the Spirit, even we ourselves groan within ourselves, waiting for the adoption, to wit, the redemption of our body.
24 For we are saved by hope: but hope that is seen is yet hope: for what a man seeth, why doth he yet hope or?
25 But if we hope for. that we see not, then do we with patience wait for it.

Verse eighteen continues the comparison of our earthly inheritance with our heavenly inheritance. Sufferings on earth are temporary; glorification in heaven is forever. The word, "reckon," is a term that had its origin in the Greek as a bookkeeping term. It conveys the idea, as used here, that Paul has sat down and systematically, as in a ledger of assets and liabilities, compared the pain he has suffered for Christ with all the rewards he will one day receive. The result of his study?. He is ecstatic that the profits are going to be so great that his personal losses in suffering are almost nonexistent; they are "unworthy to be compared."

Verse nineteen speaks of the "earnest expectation of the creature." "Creature" should be read as "creation." When Adam fell, he brought upon the entire creation the curse of God. However, one day the curse will be lifted. That is the expectation of creation. This curse upon the creation was four-fold in nature. We have already discussed one of them — the curse of condemnation that was brought upon man. Saved in his spirit, man's curse is partially lifted when he accepts the price paid for his sins at Calvary; the curse upon man's body will be removed at the resurrection, thereby freeing man entirely from the curse of Adam's sin.

The second curse of creation was placed upon the animal kingdom. In Genesis 3:14 we find: "And the Lord God said unto the serpent, because thou hast done this, thou art cursed above all cattle, and above every beast of the field . . . " This tells us something very important! Not only was there a curse placed upon the serpent, but also to a lesser degree but still very definitely " . . . every beast of the field." That is the reason we have some animals that are predators and other animals that are prey. That is the reason that dogs chase cats and cats chase mice. There is a curse upon them.

But one day, during the thousand-year millennial reign of Christ, the curse upon the animal kingdom will be removed. That is found prophesied by Isaiah in Isaiah 11:6-9: "The wolf also shall dwell with the Lamb, and the leopard shall lie down with the kid; and the calf and the young lion and the fatling together; -and a little child shall lead them. And the cow and the bear shall feed; and their young ones shall lie down together: and the lion shall eat straw like the ox. And the sulking child shall play on the hole of the asp, and the weaned child shall put his hand on the cockatrice den. They shall not hurt nor destroy in all my holy mountain: for the earth shall be full of the knowledge of the Lord as the waters cover the sea."

The third curse of creation was placed upon the mineral kingdom. The very ground upon which we walk is cursed. That is the reason we have earthquakes, volcanoes, tidal waves, droughts, erosions, and floods. A cataclysmic and terrible effect occurred to the ground as a result of Adam's transgression. Genesis 3:17 tells us: "And unto Adam he said, because thou hast hearkened unto the voice of thy wife, and hast eaten of the tree, of which I commanded thee, saying, thou shalt not eat of it: cursed is the ground for thy sake; in sorrow thou shalt eat of it all the days of thy life."

But during our Lord's blessed millennial reign upon the earth, that curse will be lifted. Isaiah declares it by saying, "The wilderness and the solitary place shall be glad for them; and the desert shall rejoice, and blossom as the rose" (Isaiah 35:1).

The fourth curse was placed upon the vegetable kingdom. That is the reason such hard work is required for good crops to flourish, but weeds grow with no encouragement whatever. Plants have blights, and roses have thorns. After speaking of the curse upon the ground, the writer of Genesis records God saying to Adam in Genesis 3:18-19: "Thorns also and thistles shall it bring forth to thee; and thou shalt eat the herb of the field: in the sweat of thy face shalt thou eat bread, till thou return to the ground . . . "

Again, during the millennium, this curse will be lifted. Read the words of Isaiah as he says: "F or ye shall go out with joy, and be led forth with peace; the mountains and the hills shall break forth before you into singing, and all the trees of the field shall clap their hands. Instead of the thorn shall come up the fir tree, and instead of the brier shall come up the myrtle tree: and it shall be to the Lord for a name, for an everlasting sign that shall not be cut off" (Isaiah 55:12-13).

Now, returning to Romans 8:19, please note again the term, "earnest expectation." It literally means "straining to see" or "totally concentrating." Our mortal bodies, the animal, plant, and mineral kingdoms are all "totally concentrating" with delicious anticipation upon one future event — the return of the Lord in glory with all of His saints. When will this happen? Jesus will come at the rapture to remove all the saints from the world. That is the next event in prophecy that is scheduled. Then, there will be seven years of great tribulation upon the earth while we, the saved, are being judged before Christ at His throne. Then, we will return with Him in glory for the victory at Armageddon and the introduction of the Millennial Kingdom. Since the curse will be lifted from all creation during that kingdom age, it is no wonder that the creation can hardly wait for our return with the Lord from heaven.

Verse twenty reminds us that the creation is under a curse, but not of its own choice. All of earth's created beings had been placed under the dominion of Adam. They were "subjected" to him. But he sadly failed in this God-given responsibility. And when he tumbled underneath the wheels of God's curse, the creation over which he had authority tumbled with him.

Two words in verse twenty stand out as twin lifeguards for a drowning creation. Those words are " . . . in hope." God has a way, an exit, from all the deadness and judgment and curse of this life. That exit is in Jesus Christ and the "blessed hope" of His return. It is no wonder that the creation, could it speak, is, in a way that only God knows, excited about Jesus coming again!

Verse twenty-one comforts the weary believer as he looks about himself at a scarred and ravaged world. As the redeemed we have liberty in our spirits, but at the present time we are forced to live in a body and a creation that are cursed and in slavery to sin and sin's devastating effects. Will it not be wonderful indeed to dwell for a thousand years with our Lord and be in perfect harmony with a creation that has been, like us, delivered from a corrupting, death-delivering servitude into the very glory of our Risen Christ?

Verse twenty-two repeats and emphasizes what I have already said about creation's curse. There is perpetual unrest and bitter conflict in the body of man, in the animal kingdom, in the mineral kingdom, and in the plant kingdom. Everywhere we dare to look can be seen nothing but a creation that has something terribly wrong with it. Like a pregnant woman with intense labor pains, nothing else matters but to be delivered. Creation longs to be delivered into the joy of peace when Jesus comes!

Verse twenty-three is Paul's exclamation that the saints of God also groan in anxious anticipation of the day that all the curse will be lifted . Some believe that the phrase " . . '. first-fruits of the Spirit . . . " is a reference to the fruit of the Spirit as found in Galatians 5:22. I do not believe that to be the case. If you will read carefully Galatians 5:22, you will find that "fruit" of the Spirit is singular, not plural as is this phrase in this verse. Second, although I would never under value the importance of Galatians 5:22, it still does not harmonize with this passage in terms of contextual meaning. The fruit of the Spirit (Galatians 5:22) is an inner evidence that we have been filled with the Spirit in order to live victoriously in this present world. But here, in verse twenty-three, "first fruits of the Spirit," has to do with the end-time.

"First fruits" is a term that has its origin in the Old Testament period when a farmer would bring the first, tender fruit of his crop to the temple as a symbol of his confidence and gratitude for the greater harvest yet to come. As used here in reference to the Spirit, it is my belief that it refers to the same fact expressed in the second chapter of Ephesians where we are seen to have already been resurrected with Christ in the Spirit. We were resurrected spiritually from deadness when we were saved. No wonder we groan for the "redemption of the body." "Redemption" means "liberation" — a condition that will exist when the body is resurrected. We are alive spiritually; we are carrying with us a body of death.

Verse twenty-four should begin with this better translation: "For we were saved by hope . . . " Our salvation has already taken place. I was saved on August 2, 1953. On that blessed day, I was saved "by hope." Since I was only eight years old at the time, there was much that I could not understand about the Scriptures. There is much about God and the things eternal that I cannot grasp today. But I have always, even since my early childhood days been able to look through eyes of hope.

"Hope," as used in the Bible, means "a certainty based upon the faithfulness of God." It is not merely wishful thinking as used in daily language. The excitement of looking ahead to all that the Lord has for us is intensified because we cannot see it all yet. Like a huge, beautifully-wrapped Christmas present, heaven and all of its riches remain a delicious mystery for us to anticipate.

Verse twenty-five strikes a nerve for me with its reference to patience. Oh, how badly I need patience. Most people need more than they have. One of the ways that God increases it in us is by keeping us in a world of discomfort while promising us a life free from pain in the hereafter. As I get older, I find my attitudes about heaven changing. I am moving from the state of "willing to go but wanting to stay" to the state of "wanting to go but willing stay."

In the next three verses of this chapter we have some of the most comforting truths that can be found anywhere in the Word of God:
26 Likewise the Spirit also helpeth our infirmities: for we know not what we should pray for as we ought: but the Spirit itself maketh intercession for us with groanings which cannot be uttered.
27 And he that searcheth the hearts knoweth what is the mind of the Spirit, because he maketh intercession for the saints according to the will of God.
28 And we know that all things work together for good to them that love God, to them who are the called according to his purpose.

Verse twenty-six is a wonderful promise. I am so glad that the Spirit helps me in my weakness and time of distress. I am so glad that He intercedes for me, that He prays for me. Have you ever stood outside an emergency room waiting for a report from the doctors about someone you dearly love whose life is in the balance? At those times, it is so hard to pray, if not impossible. The words just will not come. But the Spirit is quietly carrying the cry of your heart to the very throne of God!

We get so confused about our "needs" and our "wants." It is a consolation to know that the Spirit does know the difference. My father sometimes thought I needed a whipping; I do not ever recall wanting one. As an adult now, I can look back and appreciate his wisdom. One day from the vantage point of eternity, we will be able to look back and "understand it better by and by."

We often hear people speaking of "praying in the Spirit," and relate it to speaking in tongues as it is taught in the modern charismatic movement. Genuine praying in the Spirit, however, requires no verbal communication at all - known or unknown. It is of the inner man with " . . . groanings that cannot be uttered." The most eloquent sermons, the most beautiful singing, or the most sincere praying are puny and feeble compared to the majestic power of the prayer of the Spirit within us.

Verse twenty-seven states a very important, and at the same time, a very practical principle. It speaks of " . . . he that searcheth the hearts." Sometimes I hear godly preachers implore their hearers to examine their hearts. The only difficulty with that is that sin camouflages itself so well that we are unable to detect its presence. Better is the prayer of a man who says, "Lord, I don't trust myself to look into my heart. I want your Spirit to direct His mighty flood lights of illumination straight into my mind and heart. Whatever He shows me in there that is inconsistent with your teachings, I vow to reject." In so doing, the intercession by the Spirit as seen in verse twenty-six will be "according to the will of God." As a result, the answer to the Spirit's prayer on our behalf will be to our good and to God's glory.

Verse twenty-eight is probably the most-frequently quoted verse in the Bible by the average believer. It is a precious verse, but it cannot be appropriated in power by just anybody and everybody. The first requirement for the man that would use this verse is that he be saved. That is the meaning of " . . . the called according to his purpose." This phrase says two things of importance. A man must be one of "the called," not- just "called." God calls everyone to salvation, but "the called" are those who by our Lord's sovereign grace accept salvation as their own. Notice also that we are the called " . . . according to his purpose." The initiative for each man's salvation was God's doing, not that man's. God chose us! God had a purpose for choosing us! Verse twenty-eight is an introduction of sorts to a discussion of the sovereignty of God that is to follow in upcoming verses. For right now, just remember, to be able to employ Romans 8:28, you must be saved as one of "the called."

The second requirement is that you not only be one of the called but that you are also daily demonstrating your love for God by your obedience to Him. No backslidden saint, though he is saved, can look to the heavens and piously declare from besetting difficulties, "Well, you know all things work together for good just like the Bible says!" The Bible does not say that! It says if we love God, as His children, all things will work together for good.

Dear reader, if you are living a Spirit-filled life, let me encourage you! This verse says that "all" things are working for your good. The sweet and the sour, the good and the bad, the pleasant and the unpleasant, the friendships and the betrayals, are all working together for good. I love good homemade biscuits. I do not like baking powder alone, or salt alone, or flour alone. But if you take these ingredients and mix them with some others, you will produce a biscuit that I do like. So it is with our lives! Even the sins God will use to our advantage. An old proverb is that God uses the ax that the devil sharpens to strike the devil.

The next five verses are the most controversial verses in this chapter:
29 For whom he did foreknow, he also did predestinate to be conformed to the image of his Son, that he might be the firstborn among many brethren.
30 Moreover whom he did predestinate, them he also called: and whom he called, them he also justified: and whom he justified, them he also glorified.
31 What shall we then say to these things? If God be for us, who can be against us?
32 He that spared not his own Son, but delivered him up for us all, how shall he not with him also freely give us all things?
33 Who shall lay anything to the charge of God's elect? It is God that justifleth.

Verse twenty-nine opens with a declaration that God "foreknew" us. This word, in the original, means "a voluntary action of prior knowledge that is motivated by affection." Is it not wonderful that He foreknew us and chose us with great love for us before the foundations of the world (Ephesians 1:4)? Here the question is always raised about predestination. As someone has well-said, "If you try to understand predestination, you will lose your mind; if you reject it, you will lose your soul." Dr. Harry Ironsides put it this way: "Over the door of salvation is written, 'Whosoever will may come.' After passing through, one sees over the inside of the door, 'Chosen in Him before the foundation of the world.' " Like the old-timer, I harmonize predestination and the free will of man by suggesting that we pray like it all depends on God and work like it all depends on us. More will be said about predestination in chapter nine.

Verse thirty takes us step-by-step through the procedure by which we are saved as viewed from the perspective of God. Those God foreknew were predestined, were called, were justified, and one day will be glorified. Dr. W. A. Criswell says that each of these conditions can be further broken down into other conditions, or aspects, that reveal God's work in each of us from eternity past to eternity future. These aspects sometimes occur in us one after another; some of them occur simultaneously with each other. They are:

(1) foreknowledge;
(2) predestination;
(3) calling;
(4) contrition;
(5) repentance;
(6) faith;
(7) regeneration;
(8) justification;
(9) reconciliation;
(10)~sanctification;
(11) adoption;
(12) glorification.

    Whenever I think of verse thirty, the word that most quickly comes to my mind is "glorified." As I have shared earlier in this study, "glorified" means "to be made fit for heaven." By glorification, these very bodies that now give us such difficulty will be made perfect. That has not happened yet. But if you will look again, the word is used here in its past tense rather than future tense. How can that be?.

    Here is a truth so wondrous that I thrill every time I consider it! Some things are so certain in the mind of God that He speaks of them as though they have already occurred! For example, our best picture of the crucifixion is not found in the New Testament but in the fifty-third chapter of Isaiah which was written seven hundred years before the birth of Jesus. In that chapter we are told that Christ "was wounded" and "was bruised." These are past tense terms used for a future event, but Calvary was so fixed in God's mind that He spoke about it as a historical event that had already happened!

    Dear reader, if you are saved, the fact of your going to heaven is likewise so fixed in the mind of God that He speaks of you as already having been glorified. Does that not make you glad? We are so blissfully secure in Jesus!

Verse thirty-one is Paul's answer of a question with a question. Since God has been working for each of us who are saved from before the creation of the world, since all things work together for us who love God and are the called according to his purpose, and since God speaks of us as though we are already with Him in heaven, why in this world should we ever feel for even one minute that Satan will gain victory over us? He may win a few battles, but he will never win the war!

Verse thirty-two is a statement of God's wondrous love for the saved. He could not love us more than to give His own dear Son as a sacrifice for our sins. Nothing more can be expected of Him to show His deep affection for us. That being so, God would not possibly consider leaving us helpless before our enemy.

He operates jointly "with him," with Christ, to provide us with whatever means are necessary to overcome the Evil One. This provision is not based upon our faithfulness. It is always there for us to claim and use whenever we turn with whole hearts to God. Note "freely give." There is no pressure upon God for Him to extend His helping hand. There is nothing that we could ever do that is good enough to deserve it. He "freely" gives it! Therefore, never let Satan tell you that you are not good enough or that you do not have enough faith to live victoriously. God's supply is never measured to us by what we are or by what we do. It is "freely" given "with Christ" l To explain this marvelous grace, we might do an acrostic of the word. G-R-A-C-E —— God's Riches At Christ's Expense!

Verse thirty-three may be employed as a defense against the devil. "Charge" means, in the original, "to accuse someone as in a court of law. " In context, verse thirty-three is written in terms of relationship to God. So the question is one that is better addressed to Satan or whomever Satan may use to attack the salvation of a believer. The question may be asked in this manner, "Satan, who do you think you are to try to challenge my salvation? You say that I am unworthy and that I fall into sin; therefore, I am not qualified to be saved. But, Satan, you don't seem to understand that my relationship with God is His doing, not mine. Since that is true, you don't need to waste your time accusing my failures. If you've got to attack anybody, attack God for His lack of wisdom in choosing me and saving me in spite of my failures."

Why can you tell the devil something of this sort? Verse thirty-three tells us we are "God's elect"; that is, we are not the responsible agent for our salvation; He is! This verse also uses the phrase, "It is God that justifieth." This means that since our salvation, God continues to justify us as His children. How can He do that? He can do it only upon our faith in Jesus' shed blood for our sins, which makes Jesus our advocate (defense attorney) when accusations from the devil are hurled against us (I john 2:1).

34 Who is he that condemneth? It is Christ that died, yea rather, that is risen again, who is ever at the right hand of God, who also maketh intercession for us.
35 Who shall separate us from the love of Christ? shall tribulation, or distress, or persecution, of famine, or nakedness, or peril, or sword?
36 As it is written For thy sake we are killed all the day long; we are accounted as sheep for the slaughter.
37 Nay, in all these things we are more than conquerors through him that loved us.
38 For l am persuaded, that neither death, nor life, nor angels nor principalities, nor powers, nor things present, nor things to come,
39 Nor height, nor depth, nor any other creature, shall be able to separate us from the love of God, which is in Christ Jesus our Lord.

Verse thirty-four presents another interesting rebuttal to the attacks of Satan. It opens by asking the question, "Who is he that condemneth?" better translated, "Who is he that is condemning?" To paraphrase, who has the right to place any person under condemnation? Only one has the authority of condemnation, and that is Jesus Christ who died for us, was resurrected, and now " . . . Maketh intercession for us." Note the interesting logic shared here by Paul. I think it is fascinating! Since Jesus is the only one who can condemn us, and since He is busy interceding for us, there can be no condemnation against us! To use a simple picture, if there is only one lawyer in town and he has already been chosen to defend you, who is going to prosecute? Nobody.

Verse thirty-five begins the grand finale to this eighth chapter. In it, Paul lists several conditions that some might think would break our relationship with God. Please note that he makes no comment concerning our faithfulness or unfaithfulness in these areas. That is not the issue, as we have just seen. Look at each of these conditions. Some may apply to you:

(1) Tribulation: any crushing experiences in life that are generally from outer circumstances;
(2) Distress (anguish): inner fears and anxieties;
(3) Persecution: being followed by harsh critics and fault-finders;
(4) Famine: starvation;
(5) Nakedness: poverty;
(6) Peril: continual presence of dangers;
(7) Sword: threats from governing authorities.

Can any of these separate us from the love of God? The answer in verse thirty-nine is a resounding, "No!"

Verse thirty-six may seem out of place in this passage; but, of course, it is not. It is a quote from Psalm 44:22 where the psalmist is lamenting Israel's failure to remember its covenant vows before God. It suggests that although Israel had forgotten its vows, the God of Israel had not forgotten His vows. True, chastisement had come upon the nation; chastisement so hard that it seemed like certain destruction. But this chastisement was being used to bring Israel back to God.

We may fail. Indeed, we will fail! But like Israel of old, that will not sever the glorious tie that we have with God. Even if He must exercise discipline (Hebrews 12), it will be for our good to bring us back to Him. Whatever occurs, even our sin will not destroy our relationship with God although it may destroy our fellowship with Him!

Verse thirty-seven tells us that we are "... more than conquerors through him ... " That means that we are gloriously victorious. When wars are won and parades welcome the weary soldiers home, it is the generals who receive the most lavish praise, and his tired troops join in glad applause. One day, when the wars of this life are over, we can throw our crowns down at His blessed feet!

Verses thirty-eight and thirty-nine should actually be one verse;

there should be no division. It is not necessary to take each item listed. Multitudes of other items that have occurred in your walk with God could be listed by you. The glad result would still be the same. It is the summary conclusion of this eighth chapter — absolutely nothing can separate us from the love of God!

Chapter Nine

The Sovereignty of God

Chapters nine, ten, and eleven should be studied as a unit. These three chapters depart from God's dealings with the individual and his personal salvation and move to the program that God has outlined for the nation of Israel. In these chapters can be found some rather direct statements concerning the elective purpose of God. While these certainly may have overtones that apply to the individual, we must never forget the primary context of these chapters, and that is the plan of God for Israel. Some try too hard to make these verses "fit" individuals, but it is faulty biblical scholarship to do so.

The first five verses display Paul's burden for the Jews. He says:
1 I say the truth in Christ, I lie not, my conscience also bearing me witness in the Holy Ghost,
2 That I have great heaviness and continual sorrow in my heart.
3 For I could wish that myself were accursed from Christ for my brethren, my kinsmen according to the flesh:
4 Who are Israelites; to whom pertaineth the adoption, and the glory, and the covenants, and the giving of the law, and the service of God, and the promises;
5 Whose are the fathers, and of whom as concerning the flesh Christ came, who is over all, God blessed for ever. Amen.

Verse one is a preface to a startling burden in Paul's heart that is found in verse three. It is such an unbelievable burden that Paul feels he must underscore the validity of it before sharing the fact of it. Paul, therefore, calls upon three unimpeachable witnesses to stand in support of the truthfulness of his burden. These three are Christ, his conscience, and the Comforter (the Holy Ghost). When Paul speaks of his concern for the lost nation of Israel, he wants his readers to know that he does not speak trivially. There isa deep inner pain within him for the nation to be saved.

Verse two shares an important truth that we all should learn. His burden for them is a "continuing sorrow." Oh, how often are we caught up with "great heaviness" over the lost state of some acquaintance, especially if we are involved in a season of revival at our church. But when the scheduled days of revival come to an end, so also does the "heaviness" end. Not so with Paul! His was a relentless, never-ending compassion that churned within his very soul for the salvation of Israel.

Verse three brings us to that aforementioned burden. Paul makes an astounding statement: " . . . I could wish that myself were accursed from Christ for my brethren . . . " The word, "accursed," means "devoted to destruction." In other words, Paul has become so caught up in the sacrificial love of Christ for the world that he now is willing to place himself in the same role of substitution as did Jesus. _Just as Jesus devoted Himself to destruction for lost mankind, Paul is now crying the same desire to be "accursed" (anathema, in the original); that is, "devoted to destruction," if by doing so, the nation of Israel would be saved.

Please note that the verse says that Paul "could" wish it, not that he did wish it. There is a difference. He knew that to actually wish to be accursed would run counter with, and contradict, everything that he has said about the sovereignty of God, particularly in the eighth chapter. It would also insult his previous teaching that nothing can separate us from the love of God, and that would even include a self-imposed separation as a result of our love for sinners. He does not wish to be accursed, but he says that he is at thepoint of burden for Israel that he could wish it.

Verse four emphasizes the identity of the people toward whom this burden is directed. Ordinarily in Paul's letters, he uses "brethren" to mean fellow believers. This is not the case in this passage. He says that they are:
(1) "My brethren";
(2) "My kinsmen according to the flesh";
(3) "Israelites."

Make no mistake! This burden is for national Israel!

Before we continue, I think it is important to point out that God still has a plan for the nation of Israel although they rejected Jesus. There are many false teachers who try to make the church the recipient of all the covenant promises made to Israel in the Old Testament. I have always found it amusing that such teachers are willing to take Israel's blessings and are just as willing to leave Israel all the curse.

The simple fact of the matter is that there are two kinds of covenant promises. One is bilateral which means that the agreement is based upon the faithfulness of both parties entering the covenant. Another is unilateral which means that the agreement is based upon the faithfulness of which ever party is initiating the covenant, regardless of the faithfulness of the other party. The latter was the case with the covenants that God made with Israel. Regardless of the faithfulness of Israel, and they were indeed unfaithful, the Lord will honor his unilateral covenants and never break or transfer His promises from them to another. Not even to the church! We have more already than could ever be imagined!

In verses four and five are listed seven special gifts that the Lord has given Israel:
(1) Adoption;
(2) Glory;
(3) Covenants;
(4) Giving of the law;
(5) Service of God;
(6) Promises;
(7) Fathers.

Israel has not yet claimed their adoption as sons, but God has already established that as the nation's ultimate relationship with Him (Jeremiah 31:9). God has previously given Israel the second gift, His glory, and He will return it to them during the end-time (Haggai 2:7). The third of God's gifts to Israel are covenants, those special unilateral promises of God (II Samuel 7:16). The giving of the law was the nation's fourth gift, and it was this code of ethics that is the basis for the judicial codes and laws of virtually every modern civilized nation. The fifth gift was their privilege to serve God as demonstrated in the tabernacle and temple (Isaiah 61:6). His promises to Israel, especially highlighted by His promise to restore them to the land, is the sixth gift (Ezekiel 20:33-38). The seventh gift was our Lord's giving to Israel such fathers to help shape them — men like Abraham, Isaac, and Jacob.

Verse five has another little special nugget in it, other than the seventh gift of the fathers by God to the Jews. Christ was of the nation of Israel in the flesh. The name, "Christ," literally means, "Messiah." To be the Messiah, it was necessary that Jesus be born into the Jewish race. That He was! Had He had not been a Jew, Jesus could not have won salvation for us at Calvary because John 4:22 says that "... salvation 'is from the Jews." Eventually, the Jews will discover that Jesus is not only the promised Messiah but that He is also God of Very God, "... over all." He is the omnipotent God Almighty!

Now we move to a section in this ninth chapter that has given rise to much controversy about the sovereign choice of God as it affected Jacob and Esau:

6 Not as though the word of God hath taken none effect. For they are not all Israel, which are of Israel:
*7 Neither, because they are the seed of Abraham are they all children: but, In Isaac shall thy seed be called_*
8 That is, They which are the children of the flesh, these are not the children of God: but the children of the promise are counted for the seed.
9 For this is the word of promise, At this time will I come, and Sarah shall have a son.
10 And not only this; but when Rebecca also had conceived by one, even by our father Isaac;
11 (For the children being not yet born, neither having done any good or evil, that the purpose of God according to election might stand, not of works but of him that calleth;) ,
12 It was said unto her, The elder shall serve the younger.
13 As it is written, Jacob have I loved, but Esau have hated.

Verse six is a reminder for us that we not become anti-Semitic (anti Jew)' in our attitude toward these people because of their rejection of Jesus. By the time that Paul writes this Roman letter, thousands upon thousands of Jews had been Saved In fact, Acts 21:20 confirms that fact by telling of "Thousands" of Jews who had believed. The day Of Pentecost had even previous to that statement witnessed three thousand Jews come to the Lord And while the Pharisees, scribes, and high priests hated Jesus we are told that the common people loved Him.

This verse directs us to remember always that God's Word was not voided because of Israel's rejection. Verse six explicitly declares that there were those in Israel who loved God, honored His commandments, and had no direct part in the crucifixion of our Lord. They were the "true" Israel a remnant within the nation that was faithful to God. '

Verse seven implies that some Jew might respond that He belongs to God because of his physical, blood tie to Abraham. That is just not true! If it were, then it would mean that an Arab Moslem would have just as much right to call himself a child of God because of his relationship to Abraham through Ishmael, as a Jew would because of his relationship to Abraham through Isaac. But there is a special meaning attached to "children" as used here in this verse. It does not mean "biological offspring." It means "offspring of inheritance" or "children of promise." Therefore, like it or not, since Isaac was designated by God as the child of Abraham through whom the Lord would bless the nations, only the Jew as a descendant of Isaac can be the "children of promise."

If you understand that, then you can understand why the Arabs have no legitimate claim to one inch of the land of Israel. They sprang from Ishmael; they are not the nation who were promised the land of Palestine. They can be saved by accepting Jesus as Savior just as we can who are Gentiles. But only the Jew is entitled by God to possess that special land.

Verse eight gives us two "children." We have the "children of the flesh" who were the result of Abraham and Sarah's disbelief. As they considered the circumstances of their aged bodies, it could not be, so they reasoned that an old woman like Sarah could ever bear a child. So, in order to assist God, they developed their own plan. Abraham would have sexual intercourse with Hagar, Sarah's handmaiden, and the resulting child would become the child of promise. But that was not God's plan, and since it was not, Ishmael could never qualify to be the channel through which God would bless the world.

Verse nine looks back upon the promise of God found in Genesis

18:10: "And he said, I will certainly return unto thee according to the time of life: and lo, Sarah thy wife shall have a son. And Sarah heard it in the tent door, which was behind him." God promised Abraham two things in this verse.

First, Abraham could expect a visitation from the Lord at a set time, "... according to the time of life." Second, Sarah, not her handmaiden, would be the woman who would be the mother of the child of promise.

In light of the low regard for women in his culture, Abraham reasoned that it really should not make any difference which woman bore him a son. As far as the timing was concerned, surely God would understand that since he and Sarah were so old, they were about to run out of time. Reasonable? Sure! But these were not God's ways, and unless we follow the directions of God, we cannot please Him! When Abraham did that which seemed perfectly logical, it was really an act of blatant unbelief in God's promise to return and to-give Sarah a child.

Verse ten brings us another perspective in God's sovereignty to choose. We have just seen the Lord choose between the sons of two mothers. In this verse, we watch Him begin the process of choosing between sons of one mother. Isaac's birth to Sarah was a miracle because Sarah was far past the child-bearing years. On the other hand, Rebecca was young, able to conceive, and delivered twin sons. From our standpoint, it is easier to see the reason behind God's choice of Isaac (because of his miraculous birth) over Ishmael, than it is to see the reason God chose Jacob over Esau, particularly in view of the fact that Jacob was younger than Esau. But we must not allow ourselves to respond as Abraham who felt he must understand the ways of God. If they are indeed God's ways, our minds will never fully comprehend them. Our position is simply to believe,

Verse eleven defies the Bible teacher who suggests that salvation is of works. Here, it is clearly stated that God's choice of Jacob to be the continuation of the children of promise begun in Isaac was made while these two boys were still in their mother's womb! Therefore, they could not possibly have done anything to deserve the respective positions that God would later give them.

Now do not be like Abraham! Whether you understand the method or even the rightness of God's choosing, believe it anyway! Note II Timothy 1:9 "Who hath saved us, and called us with an holy calling, not according to our works, but according to his own purpose and grace, which was given us in Christ Jesus before the world began." Remember, if you try to understand it, you will lose your mind; reject it and you will lose your soul.

Verse twelve runs counter with the legal custom of the day. The older son was always the favored son, in every way. Such was not the case with Jacob and Esau. I do not have sufficient time, nor is it necessary for this study, to detail completely the conflict that erupted between these two brothers. At the bottom line of it all, Jacob emerged as the one with the birthright and as the one that God had chosen to bless even though he was the younger.

One very important point should be made. A common thread in the Scriptures is that wherever you find two sons, the younger will represent the Spirit and the older will represent the flesh. Abel pictured Spirit; Cain pictured flesh. Jacob pictured Spirit; Esau pictured flesh. The prodigal son pictured Spirit; the older brother pictured flesh. The birth of the Spirit in man always follows the birth of the flesh.

Verse thirteen causes great difficulty for some who do not carefully study the scriptural methods of expression. How can God speak of hating anyone? Does this not seem contradictory to His very personality? After all, the Lord also went a bit farther in the first chapter of Malachi where He said that He not only hated Esau but that He also hated Esau's descendants forever!

First, we must consider the literal interpretation. The words, "love" and "hate," as used here, are hyperboles. In strict grammar, in fact, we call such words of extreme to show a thought. a "hyperbolic antithesis." This was a frequently used literary device among the writers of Paul's day, and to a great degree still is.

Jesus employed the same device in Luke 14:26 where He warned that unless a man loved Him enough to hate father and mother, then that man could not follow Him. Was our Lord teaching that we should actually hate our parents? No, of course not! He was Showing, by hyperbolic antithesis, that our love for Him should be so great that it would make our love for them appear as hate.

The same device is employed here in Roman 9:13. God blessed Isaac so much as His selected child of promise that it made His love for Esau seem as hate. But God did love Esau. If you will examine scriptural accounts, you will find that Esau became a very prosperous man at the hand of God.

Second, other than the literal interpretation, we also have the spiritual application. I have already shown you that Jacob pictured the Spirit and Esau pictured flesh. Puny Jacob came to recognize during his struggle with the angel at Peniel that unless God came to his defense, Esau would slay him. Esau, as a self-made man, needed no one's aid. Do you see? Arrogant flesh always tries to destroy the Spirit. And man, like Jacob, is at his spiritual high point when he realizes how desperately he needs God. That is why the Lord has said that He is at perpetual warfare with the descendants of Esau (Malachi 1). They represent flesh, and God hates the flesh!

Our next section of verses in this chapter continues the scheme of God's elective choice:
14 What shall we say then? Is there unrighteousness with God? God forbid.
15 For he saith to Moses, I will have mercy on whom I will have mercy, and I will have compassion on whom I will have compassion.
16 So then it is not of him that willeth, nor of him that runneth, but of God that sheweth mercy.
17 For the scripture saith unto Pharaoh, Even for this same purpose have I raised thee up, that I might shew my power in thee, and that my name might be declared throughout all the earth.
18 Therefore hath he mercy on whom he will have mercy, and whom he will he hardeneth.

Verse fourteen poses the question of the carnal mind. To paraphrase it, "Can God be fair by choosing one and rejecting another?" Do not try to bring God's reasoning down to the level of your own. It is impossible to do! God is God! He may do as He chooses since He alone can see the end from the beginning.

When a governor of a state chooses to pardon a man from death row, does that mean that he is unfair to the men who are left there? Of course not! We were all under the sentence of condemnation. All have sinned. The fact that God chooses, for reasons unknown to us, to save anyone from hell is a remarkable display of divine grace. He, as unblemished holiness, is not required to give a reason to any condemned man of unholiness.

Verse fifteen quotes the words of God spoken to Moses in Exodus 33:19. His emphatic declaration to Israel's great lawgiver was very direct. To say it another way, God said, "I will choose to bless whomever I choose to bless. Whether a man thinks I have done right or not does not matter to me. I am God, and I will do exactly what I want to do." Dear reader, this verse is clear! I would suggest that you not try to make it say something other than is found here. Having studied the opinions of some of the world's best theologians on the subject of God's elective choice, I must confess to you that there is as much of the doctrine that I do not understand as there is of the doctrine that I do. But I will not be an Abraham in this matter and try to develop a "reasonable plan" for God because I do not fully understand His!

Verse sixteen continues Paul's view of divine election, really God's view since this is all the Word of God. The grace of God is never extended to a man because that man has willed it to be so. Neither has the grace of God been bestowed upon a man because he has run hard in his zeal to serve the Lord. This verse strikes down the false notion that a man can be saved at the time of his own choosing. It also voids a salvation that is based on works. God grants salvation, He grants mercy, in accord with His elective choice to do so.

Verse seventeen quotes Exodus 9:16. If you will read Exodus 5:2, you will find Pharaoh opposing the will of God for the children of Israel to be released. Later, in response, God begins to harden the heart of Pharaoh (Exodus 7:3).

But even before Pharaoh began to argue against God in the fifth chapter of Exodus, the Lord had already determined to harden his heart. In fact, God made that determination before Moses ever returned to Egypt (Exodus 4:21).

God had a plan in His mind as Moses was sent back into Egypt to retrieve Israel. That plan was the plan of redemption that has wondrously touched the life of every believer. Had it not been for the hardening of Pharaoh's heart, there would have been no Passover. Without the Passover, there would have been no need for the shedding of the blood of a lamb as a protection for the first-born against the death angel. Had it not been for that lamb, we could never have embraced with full appreciation the Lamb of God. Had we not accepted the Lamb of God, we would have been forever lost. Every time we break bread and partake of the cup at the Lord's Supper, we are, in a manner of speaking, continuing the story that began with the conflict between Moses and Pharaoh ——— the old, old story of redemption that has been " . . . published abroad in all the earth."

Verse eighteen is a summary of these verses. Two times is the phrase, "I will," found here. It refers to God's determined and deliberate choice. The opinion of the liberal is that since man is the creation of God, then God "owes" man. Friend, the conclusion of these verses is that God "owes" man nothing! It is clear that God will harden some. In the original, "hardeneth," means "to make arrogantly stubborn."

Now we turn our attention to Paul's illustration of God's elective choice:

19 Thou wilt say then unto me, Why doth he yet find fault? For who hath resisted his will?
20 Nay but, O man, who art thou that repliest against God? Shall the thing formed say to him that formed it, Why hast thou made me thus?
21 Hath not the potter power over the clay, of the same lump to make one vessel unto honour, and another unto dishonour?
22 What if God, willing to shew his wrath, and to make his power known, endured with much long-suffering the vessels of wrath fitted to destruction:
23 And that he might make known the riches of his glory on the vessels of mercy, which he had afore prepared unto glory,
24 Even us, whom he hath called, not of the Jews only, but also of the Gentiles?

Before I proceed with a verse-by-verse analysis of this passage particularly, I must emphasize again that although there are overtones of God's election in individual lives that may be drawn from this analogy of the potter and his lump, the primary interpretation has to do with God's dealings with Israel.

Verse nineteen echoes the questions of the liberal who will not simply believe God. Asked in another way, these questions are, "Why is God so concerned with finding fault?"; and, "How can anyone find favor with God if God has already decided by His own will not to favor them?"

Both of these questions are absurd and have already been answered previously. As for the first, sin breaks man's fellowship with God. If I were sick with cancer, I would much rather my physician take dramatic and painful measures with me in this disease's early stages rather than trying to compliment me on the places in my body that are well. As for the second, do as the Apostle Peter suggested and make your own calling and election sure, then thank God for it! Do not continue to force answers where there are none!

Verse twenty begins with, "Nay but. . . " This phrase is difficult to translate from the original but is suggestive of total shock or utter disbelief. Paul is answering the question of an imaginary skeptic by saying that it is incomprehensible that any person would take issue with God on anything that God chooses to do. It is as useless as a dog barking at the moon to flee the sky! Just because we are God's creation gives us no right to challenge the way He deals with us! Paul is shocked that any rational person would.

Verse twenty-one has caused sermons innumerable to be preached and multitudes of lectures to be taught. A potter takes a lump and uses part of it to make vessels " . . . unto honor." This word, "honor," in the original, can be translated, "preciousness." Those of us who are saved are the preciousness of God. We are the vessels unto honor during this church age. Some, like Pharaoh, are made from the same lump but are made to dishonor. I could write reams of paper on this subject, but Paul has already covered the truth of election in detail.

Verse twenty-two may seem somewhat unclear at first glance, but closer examination shows it to be quite clear. The implication is that there may be those who are critical of God because He waits to punish someone like Pharaoh. In other words, if a person is chosen by God to be destroyed, why does God let that person live, particularly if that person is a very wicked person who is barbaric in his treatment to others? The answer is here in verse twenty-two. Sometimes God waits in exercising His wrath, so that when He finally does, multitudes will be gratefully amazed because of His intervention. As an example, I cite the rise of Adolph Hitler. By God willing to wait with His judgment until Hitler posed a real threat to the world, the glory of God was extended.

Verse twenty-three provides us the reason for the elective choice of God in destroying some. It is so that He can . . . make known the riches of his glory upon vessels of mercy . . . " Those vessels of mercy are, during this church age, the saints of God who have trusted Jesus Christ. God is not a capricious old man, sitting up in a cloud impishly figuring out new ways to torture people. Whenever He judges. God judges in holiness. And He always judges the wicked, so that we, the elect, can be blessed by His grace.

Verse twenty-four brings God's diverse household of faith together as one body in Christ. Note that he called us. When the term, "called," is used, it is the same as if He had used the term, "elected." God elects, God chooses, Jew and Gentile, male and female, rich and poor, religious and non-religious. This is very important for you to note. God's election of individuals is totally without influence from those individuals. Not one single person of any race or position has an "edge" over any other person in terms of God's election.

The final section in this chapter is full of biblical quotations. All of them are designed to support this doctrine of election:
25 *As he saith also in Hosea, I will call them my people, which were not my people; and her beloved, which was not beloved.*
26 *And it shall come to pass, that in the place where it was said unto them, Ye are not my people; there shall they be called the children of the living God.*
27 *Esaias also crieth concerning Israel, Though the number of the children of*

Israel be as the sand of the sea, a remnant shall be saved:
28 For he will finish the work, and cut it short in righteousness: because a short work will the Lord make upon the earth.
29 And as Esaias said before, Except the Lord of Sabbath had left us a seed, we had been as Sodom and been made like unto Gomorrah.
30 What shall we say then? That the Gentiles, which followed not after righteousness, have attained to righteousness, even the righteousness which is of faith.
31 But Israel, which followed after the law of righteousness, hath not attained to the law of righteousness.
32 'Wherefore? Because they sought it not by faith, but as lf were by the works of the law. For they stumbled at that stumbling stone;
33 As it is written, Behold, I lay in Sion a stumbling stone and rock of offence: and whosoever believeth on him shall not be ashamed.

Verse twenty-five quotes Hosea 2:23, which prophesies Israel regaining its blessed position before the Lord. This verse from Hosea is a direct statement regarding the certainty of Israel's restoration. But watch this! Paul uses this verse in application to all of us who have been saved and belong to the church of our Lord. Please note the calling of the Jews and Gentiles together as one — that has only taken place in the church.

So, two truths are found here. First, Israel, who had been put aside as God' people and His beloved during the church age, WILL be restored to a place of honor and trust as the Lord's beloved at the close of the great tribulation period. Second, we who were spiritually alienated from the Lord are now His very loved bride.

Verse twenty-six quotes Hosea 1:10. It is my conviction that this verse applies solely to the nation of Israel by virtue of the use of the term, "the place." This term can have no other fulfillment than in Israel returning to the land that was promised them. This return is predicted in various places in the Word of God; one of the best is Ezekiel 37:21.

This does not mean that everything Israel does is right in the sight of God, but it does mean that ultimately they will totally inherit, possess, and be recognized as the legitimate government of the land. More than that, they will be loved by the Father as His own dear children.

      Verse twenty-seven quotes Isaiah 10:22. I think that it is very important that you understand a point of prophecy that many casual Bible students do not understand. All of Israel will not be saved. Do not confuse the restoration of the nation to the land with the condition of their spiritual salvation. Each Jew must be saved in precisely the same 'way as any other person, by trusting the shed blood of Jesus Christ for the remission of sins. Even after the nation has returned to the land of promise, only a remnant shall be saved.

      Verse twenty-eight is a quote that comes from Isaiah 10:20-23. The world is an evil place, and the conditions are growing worse every day. Man has tried philosophies, religions, and strategems of every sort to bring some sanity into this world order. But everything has failed. Each day seems to find our condition a little bleaker than the day before. Only God can stop the madness that besets us! Please note His method. He uses His word to finish the work of iniquity upon the earth and to establish righteousness. This should not appear strange, because God's precious Word is indeed the ultimate weapon; and it shall prevail. There is a brighter day coming for the saint.

      Verse twenty-nine is a quote from Isaiah 1:9. God had left "a seed" to Israel. Had it not been so, Israel would have long ago perished along with the likes of such pagan people as those of Sodom and Gomorrah. What was that seed? "The seed" is a reference to the promise that our Lord made to Abraham that in his seed, that is through the birth of Isaac, all the nations of the world would be blessed. Therefore, since the Jewish nation sprang from Abraham through Isaac, Israel was not destroyed from the face of the earth, as have been other nations, because of their sins. Only God's promise, a promise made by His grace, preserved them. Those of us who are saved ought to thank God daily that He likewise keeps us by His grace.

      Verse thirty has the words in it that can be translated more accurately. The first word is "followed," and it is more correctly, "following." The second word is "attained," and it should be "attaining." The message is clear. All of us who are Gentiles were never blessed with the moral code of the

Mosaic law as were the Jews. We are not following that rigid standard for outward righteousness during this church age. Nevertheless, we are attaining to the righteousness which God requires, inner righteousness, through our faith in the Lord Jesus Christ.

This is, of course, the better form of righteousness. It is the "imputed righteousness" of Christ that I have discussed earlier in this study in the discussion of justification. The righteousness of the law will ultimately fail. The righteousness of Christ by faith in His blood shed for us can never fail. Praise His dear name!

Verses thirty-one through thirty-three actually should be one verse, so let us study them as such. The Jew has never been able to understand the position of faith in his relationship with God. Strict Judaism produces high levels of morality. Family ties are strong and social evils are avoided. But this will not produce salvation. With such a meticulous conformity to the standards of the law, he still misses the reason for the existence of the law, which is to point him toward the Savior.

They made a fatal mistake and concentrated solely upon the rituals of the law instead of looking through the law to find the same kind of saving faith that was exemplified in Abraham. Abraham by faith looked through the corridors of time and saw Jesus. Faith saves, not faithfulness. Therein lies a big difference.

Verse thirty-three is a reminder of the old story connected with the building of the temple. The workers at the temple site sent word to the quarry that the cornerstone should be sent. Such an unusual stone with an odd shape was brought to the workers that they felt that surely a mistake had been made and threw it down the hill into the Kidron Valley below. Later, discovering their error, they dragged it back to the work site. What a picture of Jesus! He just did not fit intothe scheme of the law, or so these ancient Jews felt. But one day they will discover their mistake and will accept Him!

Chapter Ten

God's Plan For Righteousness

    This is one of the best known chapters in the Bible because of its frequent use in soul-winning. While there is no question of its effectiveness in that area, it still must be remembered that chapters nine, ten and eleven have their primary application with the nation of Israel. Their blatant disregard of God's clear commands brought devastating results. Such disobedience, as depicted in chapter nine, has its results in chapter ten. The plaintive plea of the Apostle is found in the opening seven verses:

1 Brethren, my heart's desire and prayer to God for Israel is, that they might be saved
2 For I bear them record that they have a zeal for God, but not according to knowledge.
3 For they being ignorant of God's righteousness, and going about to establish their own righteousness, have not submitted themselves to the righteousness of God.
4 For Christ is the end of the law for righteousness to everyone that believeth.
5 For Moses describeth the righteousness which is of the law, that the man which doeth those things shall live by them.
6 But the righteousness which is of faith speaketh on this wise, Say not in thine heart, Who shall ascend into heaven? (that is, to bring Christ down from above:)
7 Or, Who shall descend into the deep? (that is, to bring up Christ again from the dead.)

    Verse one should be read by looking back to the opening verses of chapter nine where Paul is found wishing himself to be accursed that Israel might be saved. The word "desire" has a double meaning in the original language. It conveys a thought with deep emotion of the heart, and, at the same time, a clear intellectual choice of the mind. This was no statement of concern that was only lip service. Paul is sharing a deep burden for Israel's salvation; and he is sharing his mental awareness of the plight of their lost state.

    Verse two confirms the religious zeal of the Jews. Should anybody ever question their sincerity and thorough compliance to the details of the law? Paul says that he stands ready "to bear them record that they have zeal for God..." If anybody could ever qualify for salvation based upon what he did, it would have been the Apostle Paul. Therefore, he could easily recognize that same trait in others. How horrifying it must have been for him, who had had such a fervor for the keeping of the law before his salvation, to watch his own people in Israel walk the same path as he had walked of self-destruction. He watched their refusal to hear about Jesus.

Make no mistake! They were sincere, but they were sincerely wrong! It matters none how much a man may think he is right if he is wrong. I come from the mountains of Tennessee. In those mountains can be found churches that believe snake-handling is important as a test of a man's relationship with God. Of course, the Bible does not teach any such doctrine. But these dear people are absolutely sincere; they are not phonies in the practice of what they believe, but they are ignorant of the truth.

In somewhat the same way, the Jew looks into the Old Testament and sees without seeing. He fails to understand that the Old Testament is the New Testament concealed; the New Testament is the Old Testament revealed. It is sad. The Jew has partial knowledge of the law, but not the complete knowledge that includes the person toward whom the law points, Jesus Christ the Lord.

Verse three uses the word "ignorant" about the Jew. This word, in the original, carries the idea of being willingly ignorant of a particular truth or of purposefully trying to miss. How did Israel manage to be so "ignorant"? It was by their stubborn resolve to work enough on their own that they would deserve the approval of God, and thereby be righteous.

This type of twisted thinking has not changed. People, in multitudes, refuse the Savior's gracious offer of salvation, believing that, somehow their own moral goodness is sufficient. If a man tries in any manner whatever to make himself acceptable to God, he will not "subject himself to the righteousness of God." His pride will not let him! Basic to Christianity is that grace and works are opposites. They can never be mixed together. They are like oil and water. Grace has no element of works at all. Works have no element of grace at all. And salvation is solely by grace.

Verses six and seven are a quote from Deuteronomy 30:12- 13. Moses was coming to the end of his life. In the thirtieth chapter of Deuteronomy, he left some observations and summary directions for Israel to follow after he was gone. Among other important issues, he dealt in these two verses with the law's sufficiency, namely, that Israel was to look for no more revelations of the law. They were not to look to heaven, and they were not to look beyond the sea. Israel had all of the law that they would ever have.

Paul parallels the law with Christ, the law's end. He says that the comments of Moses, that I have just discussed, were in relation to the outward righteousness of works. But Paul's parallel comments are in relation to the inward righteousness of faith. Just as Moses taught that the law was complete, Paul says that Christ is complete. Just as Moses taught that there would be no more revelations from beyond the sea, Paul goes a little farther; he says that we are not to look for more revelations of Christ from the world of the dead by another resurrection.

We now move into our next section of verses in the chapter. These form the very core of the passage and are some of the most vital verses in the entire Bible in reference to the plan of salvation:
8 But what saith it? The word is nigh thee, even in thy mouth, and in thy heart:that is, the word of faith, which we preach;
9 That if thou shalt confess with thy mouth the Lord Jesus, and shalt believe in thine heart that God hath raised him from the dead, thou shalt be saved.
10 For with the heart man believeth unto righteousness; and with the mouth confession is madeunto salvation.
11 For the scripture saith, Whosoever believeth on him shall not be ashamed.
12 For there is no difference between the Jew and the Greek: for the same Lord over all is rich unto all that call upon him.
13 For whosoever shall call upon the name of the Lord shall be saved.

Verse eight opens with a rhetorical question by Paul in attempting to find a conclusive and reliable authority about God's plan for righteousness. My opinion is no better than yours and yours is no better than mine. We need to know God's thinking on this most important of all subjects. So, Paul asks,"

What saith it?" That is, "What saith the Word of God?"

These are not just words; they are words "...of faith." When a man reads the Bible, he will have a different inner response than when he reads any other kind of literature. Therefore, since the Bible was written by the Spirit, the authority of God becomes clear when we read the Word with our mouths and let the Spirit say, "Amen," from our hearts.

Verse nine is a very precious promise for those of us who have done as it instructs, and have found that it is true! Two fundamentals of the faith are declared here as this verse is a continuation of verses six and seven. One truth expressed is the incarnation of Jesus. When the Bible uses His earthly name "Jesus" and His heavenly title "Lord" you have the combination of the human and the divine in one man; you have the incarnation. Another truth expressed is the obvious reference to His resurrection from the dead. Paul declares that any man who confesses these two truths to be living realities shall be saved.

But what does it mean to confess? It means more than simply to walk down an aisle. Confession is a total commitment in every way to a daily walk with Christ. Confession should never be viewed as a one-time experience. "Confess" used here means a continual action of displaying. That includes a public profession of faith, consecrated living, personal devotional habits and a ready witness to the unsaved.

The implication of this verse is abundantly clear. If a man does not have the fruits of faith in his life, it is proof positive that he does not have faith. Such is the teaching of Paul here as it is also the teaching of James in his letter (James 2: 14-17). Confession, which is the outward proclamation that Jesus is Lord in word and deed, is the fruit of salvation while faith is the root of salvation.

Verse ten continues the same thought begun in verse nine. Conviction of the heart and confession in the mouth lead to conversion of the soul. Matthew 12:34 tells us the same thing by asserting "...for out of the abundance of the heart the mouth speaketh."The old-timers were prone to say, "Whatever is down in the well will come up in the bucket." If faith is really within us, we will gladly proclaim it. There is. no such thing in the Scriptures as a silent believer.

That is why we may have two men of similar backgrounds, who have similar dispositions, sit in the same service, hear the same sermon come down the same aisle, pray the same prayer, and talk with the same counselor; one is saved, the other is not. How can that be? Upon rising from their knees at the altar, one man confessed joyfully that he had indeed been born again while the other confessed that he had not. When a man is really saved, his lips cannot help but speak it is so.

Verse eleven is a quotation of Isaiah 28:16. There is one difference. Isaiah says "He that believeth..." Paul says, "Whosoever believeth..." Oh, what a wonderful difference! "He" is singular. It refers to an individual. But "whosoever" includes everybody! How often I have rejoiced with great congregations in singing, "Whosoever Meaneth Me."

And what does "whosoever" mean in this verse? It means that if we trust Christ we will not be put to shame. I have met many shameful Christians who were so because of the disgraceful ways that they have lived their lives, but I have never known a person who lived a separated life of disbelief in Christ who ever had to be ashamed. Our Lord stands for the right, for the noble, for the just, for the good. Whenever we follow that kind of pattern for living, we never have to suffer the pangs of guilty shame.

Verse twelve affirms the universal aspect of this "whosoever" gospel. There had been an invisible, impenetrable wall between the Jews and the Greeks. It seemed as though God had only one group of people on earth that He cherished, and that group was the nation of Israel. God loves the Jew no more than He does the Greek, and vice-versa. He is no respecter of persons.

Does that mean that God has been forced to reduce the blessings for one group because He is now merciful to all groups? Of course not! God has all the riches of heaven and earth at His disposal! He owns the cattle on a thousand hills, the wealth in every land! This verse says that He is"...rich unto all that call upon him." Dear reader, there is no shortage of any kind in heaven. Whatever your need may be, the Lord has riches enough more than amply to provide. Why will a man continue to live so sparingly when God has so much He desires to give!

Verse thirteen repeats the "whosoever" theme. This is a quotation from Numbers 12:7 and Joel 2:32. How could God possibly be any clearer than in this short statement, "Whosoever shall call upon the name of the Lord shall be saved."

God cannot lie! When doubts of your security in Christ are thrown your way by the devil, use this verse to repel him. Have you ever, with an earnest heart, called out to God for salvation? If you have, then rest assured in God's faithfulness in keeping His Word.

We have arrived at the final section of verses in this chapter:
14 How then shall they call on him in whom they have not believed? and how shall they believe in him of whom they have not heard? and how shall they hear without a preacher?
15 And how shall they preach, except they be sent? as it is written, How beautiful are the feet of them that preach the gospel of peace and bring glad tidings of good things.
16 But they have not all obeyed the gospel. For Esaias saith, Lord, who hath believeth our report?
17 So then faith cometh by hearing, and hearing by the word of God.
18 But I say, have they not heard? Yes verily, their sound went into all the earth, and their words unto the ends of the world.
19 But I say, Did not Israel know? First Moses saith, I will provoke you to jealousy by them that are no people, and by a foolish nation I will anger you.
20 But Esaias is very bold, and saith, I was found of them that sought me not; I was made manifest unto
21 But to Israel he saith, all day long I have stretched forth my hands unto a disobedient and gain saying people".

Verse fourteen presents three questions. We must remember that chapters nine, ten and eleven are primarily directed toward Israel. No single verse in any of these chapters more graphically describes the terrible plight of the Jew in our day. Unfortunately, he sees very little of the true gospel emanating from the Christian community around the world. This verse is clear that unless someone, a preacher, has enough love for these dear people to declare in simple terms the story of Jesus, they will never believe and be saved.

The great need of this present age is for more preachers who will faithfully proclaim the good news that Jesus saves. God's program for salvation has not changed. With the Holy Spirit in full control, a man is called to preach the gospel at a designated time and place, and to a designated audience. This audience, whether it be one person or thousands, will hear the message. By the impartation of truth by the Spirit of God, they will respond in belief and be saved. It has always been the divine plan to use people to reach people for Jesus.

Verse fifteen states one thing about any effective preacher that is absolutely imperative. He must be sent. This, of course, means that be must be called by the Lord to preach. A sad evolution has been taking place for some time now in Bible colleges and seminaries. The necessity of a call upon a young man to surrender to preach is no longer taught with the same vigor as once it was. Men are choosing to enter full-time ministry in just about the same way that they would choose to sell aluminum siding. Yet we must remember that a seminary can train a preacher, but it cannot train a man to be a preacher——only God can do that!

In this verse, Paul quotes Isaiah 52:7 and Nahum 1:15. These Old Testament verses are taken from much longer passages where the future fulfillment of God's promise to David about the Messiah's everlasting kingdom is discussed. For the poor, beleaguered Jew of that ancient day, such Joyful proclamations of better days to come were thrilling indeed. Therefore, when he heard a real prophet of God instead of the phony ones who seemed so numerous and who were preaching for popularity or financial gain, the Jew was made glad. He was able to differentiate between the genuine man of God and the imposter. And such good news from a man of God caused him to love that man and ecstatically shout, "How beautiful are even his feet!"

During this church age, we are just as grateful for the person who shared Christ with us and led us to Jesus. I must tell you that I would not want to be unsaved during these critical days. There seems to be such a shortage of people who care about a man's lost state. But how good it is to hear the old, old story of Jesus and His love.

Verse sixteen makes a sad observation about Israel. By the time that Paul began writing this letter to Rome, it is very safe to assume that the entire nation of Israel had been exposed to the gospel of Jesus Christ. After the reality of the resurrection had really "come home" to the disciples, they fearlessly threw themselves into the task of taking the good news worldwide. The Book of Acts is a record of the explosive growth that took place after Pentecost. Following that inaugural day for the church when three thousand were saved, it has been variously estimated by excellent Bible scholars that between sixty-five thousand and five hundred thousand came to know the Lord in the following six months.

Yet, Israel "...did not all hearken." It is one thing never to be given the opportunity of hearing salvation's story, but it is another thing to hear it and still refuse. Such was the sad case with many in Israel. However, Paul quotes Isaiah 53:1 and asks, "...who hath believed our report?" The answer was given in my preceding paragraph. Multiplied thousands have believed it through the centuries, but multiplied thousands had already believed it by the time of Paul's statement here. But like the Good Shepherd, Paul's concern is for the sheep still out of the fold.

Verse seventeen is a statement of fact. Some people spend countless hours in prayer, calling upon God to increase their faith. This is certainly not an indictment of prayer; if anything, we should be doing far more praying than we are. Nevertheless, this verse is quite clear. We receive faith, and we grow in our faith, in only one way----by the Word of God!

We are often told by the liberal denominationalist that doctrinal purity is relatively unimportant, that our major concern should be sending missionaries around the world to reach the masses. Let me ask you a question, when the missionary finally reaches that far land, what is he going to tell that poor pagan if doctrine is unimportant? It is not the missionary that brings faith to a lost heart. It is the message he bears. If that message is not the Word of God, whatever else that lost man is told will never produce the faith necessary for salvation.

Verse eighteen should actually be the opening verse for the eleventh chapter. It describes an interesting phenomenon. As a result of God's work through the nation of Israel, the entire world has been privileged to hear the wonderful story of redemption. But the irony of it all is that Israel herself refused the very gospel that vast multitudes in the rest of the world so readily embraced. We have already seen in our study of this book that Israel's partial blindness to the Messiah was all a part of God's plan to release the gospel worldwide.

Verse nineteen recalls Deuteronomy 32:20-21 from the Old Testament. The Gentile nations are almost in total obscurity in the Old Testament. The blessings of God are seen being poured out almost exclusively on the Jew. When the Jew rejected Christ, however, God began sharing the good news throughout the length and breadth of the earth. Because the Gentile world had not been blessed with the enlightenment of the law, they were "...void of understanding." This resulted in a jealousy that can be seen in our modern day, a jealousy that in part fueled the truth of this verse.

Verse twenty is another of the many, many verses in the Word of God in which the grace of our wonderful Lord is taught. Here in this verse, God declares that He revealed Himself to the Gentiles although they were not even seeking Him. We only need to remember the account of Peter's witness to Cornelius as an excellent example. When first approached by the Lord in that memorable scene on the rooftop in Joppa, Peter could not believe that God was actually sending him to share the gospel with a Gentile. Such a missionary enterprise was totally unthinkable to him, a Jew. But God had already visited the heart of Cornelius, and such conviction by the Holy Spirit is indeed a manifestation of God's marvelous grace. One of the miracles of heaven's communication with man is that God convicts a lost man's heart and shows him his need of a Savior. This miracle is as much by grace today as it was two thousand years ago.

Verse twenty-one is the concluding verse in chapter ten. It is taken from Isaiah 65:2. It is a summary of sorts in which God makes one simple explanation for his turning to the Gentiles. He had repeatedly through the centuries tried to bring a rebellious House of Israel to Himself. But unfortunately, they refused His every gracious invitation.

Does this mean that God's plan has failed? Oh, no! This rejection of God, and of the Messiah (Jesus Christ), was all a part of the divine plan. The hardness of the Jew's stubborn heart was used by God to reveal His love for all mankind.

Chapter Eleven

The Blindness Of Israel

This is a fascinating chapter. I hope that you will savor the study of it. As we move through it, we will see again the sovereignty of God and His plan for all of us---Jew and Gentile alike. Our opening section of verses shows that God has not cast away Israel:

1 I say then, hath God cast away his people? God forbid. For I also am an Israelite, of the seed of Abraham, of the tribe of Benjamin.
2 God hath not cast away his people which he foreknew. Wot ye not what the scripture saith of
Elijah? How he maketh intercession to God against Israel, saying,
3 Lord, they have killed thy prophets, and digged down thine altars; and I am left alone, and they seek my life.
4 But what saith the answer of God to him? I have reserved to myself seven thousand men, who have not bowed the knee to the image of Baal.
5 Even so then at this present time also there is a remnant according to the election of grace.
6 And if by grace, then is it no more of works: otherwise grace is no more grace. But if it be of works, then is it no more grace: otherwise work is no more work.
7 What then? Israel hath not obtained that which he seeketh for; but the election hath obtained it, and the rest were blinded
8 According as it is written, God hath given them the spirit of slumber, eyes that they should not see, and ears that they should not hear; unto this day.
9 And David saith, let their table be made a snare, and a trap, and a stumbling block, and a recompense unto them,
10 Let their eyes be darkened, that they may not see, and bow down their back always"

Verse one provides a clear, definitive answer to the multitudes of anti-Semitics who have through the centuries blamed the Jews for rejecting Christ and crucifying Him; the just result, in their distorted estimation, being the revoking of all God's promises in the Old Testament from Israel. Again, I must emphasize that Israel is still in God's plan for the ages. Again, I must emphasize that all of the unilateral covenant promises to Israel by the Lord will be fulfilled. That is the affirmation of Paul in this verse also.

We must never, even indirectly, place more blame upon the Jew for the death of Christ than we are willing to take upon ourselves. That would be contradictory with Acts 4:27- 28 which tells us, "For of a truth against the holy child Jesus, whom thou hast anointed, both Herod, and Pontius Pilate, with the Gentiles, and the people of Israel, were gathered together, for to do whatsoever thy hand and thy counsel determined before to be done." Dear reader, your sins just as surely nailed Jesus to the cross as did the hands of the ones who hammered home the bits of metal through His flesh.

The best answer that Paul could give is given in this verse. Since he is a Jew himself of the tribe of Benjamin, the king-making tribe, Paul declared that if God has cast away the Jew, then he has been cast away. If Paul has been cast away, then the great thrust of evangelism to the Gentiles led by him has been cast away. If that thrust has been cast away, then all of us who are Gentiles are without hope. Obviously, therefore, God has not cast away Israel.

Verse two brings us again to the doctrine of the sovereign foreknowledge of God. He knew that Israel would stubbornly rebel. It did not take our Lord by surprise that His son, Jesus, would be slain at Jerusalem. The details of the death of Christ were a foregone conclusion (See Psalm 22 and Isaiah 53). God knows the end from the beginning and everything 1S operating precisely on His predetermined schedule.

However, because of our feeble perceptual abilities, we can draw wrong conclusions about situations we may see unfolding before us. Paul looks back into I Kings 19:14-18 and reminds us of Elijah who sincerely thought he was the only righteous person left in Israel. How wrong he was! His fear of Jezebel was so great that rather than trusting God to reveal others of faith to him, he cowardly blurted out his exasperation of loneliness. Yet, there were seven thousand who were faithful in the land.

Paul uses this story of Elijah as an illustration to the believers in Rome. Regardless of the news that comes to them from Israel, they are to believe always the ultimate victory that the Jew will enjoy. Too, regardless of the horror and torturous martyrdom that may threaten the Roman believer, he is never to lack faith in God's plan for the ages.

Verse three continues the analogy that Paul is using of Elijah. Indeed, this analogy shows _us the humanity of the prophet. He is seen protesting to the Lord that Ahab and Jezebel have killed all the prophets. That was not true! There were other prophets yet alive. We know, for example, that Obadiah had hidden a hundred prophets in a cave (I Kings 18:4).

In this verse, we have a good, old fashioned "pity party." Even great men and women of God can fall victim to this malady by jumping to a wrong conclusion. It reminds me of a little limerick that says, "There was once a dog named August, who was always jumping to conclusions. One day he jumped at the conclusion of a mule, and that was the last day of August!"

Verse four explains why this matter of making quick assumptions can be so wrong. Elijah really, earnestly believed that he was the only righteous man left in the entire nation. In so doing, he was forgetting the Word of God. The Lord had many, many years previous to Elijah's conflict with Jezebel promised Abraham that his seed would be like the sands of the sea in number. It would be rather ridiculous to presume that such a grand promise had now dwindled down to only one man.

It has been my experience that faith does indeed come by the Word of God; but just as surely, fear comes by an absence of the Word of God. And in our continual warfare with the devil we must never forget where our real strength lies. It is in the trustworthiness of God's infallible Word.

Verse five is applicable only to the Jew. This parallel that has been drawn by Paul in recalling Elijah's frustration is just as relevant today as it was back then. Within the great, world-wide body of people that we call Jews, there is a remnant that will be saved. It has always been so. It is today. While I recognize the tremendous difficulty that exists in trying to share the gospel with these dear people, their frequent refusal does not speak for all of them by any stretch of the imagination.

A dear friend of mine, Dr. Hyman Appelman, is now with the Lord. This Jewish evangelist circled our globe bearing the good news that Jesus saves. Christian history will remember him as one of the greatest preachers of all time. But it was not without personal loss to him. His conversion put a barrier between him and many within his own family. Dr. Appelman is just one wonderful example of the remnant of Jews who truly know the Lord.

Verse six, to be understood correctly, must be viewed in the light of the things I have just said concerning the remnant in Israel that are saved. The Jew has tremendous difficulty in accepting a salvation that is totally of grace. Because of his upbringing, he insists that there must be something he must do in order to inherit eternal life. The Book of Hebrews is almost entirely devoted to this problem. Study that book and you will find it addressed to Jewish converts who believe that Christianity can be embraced by grace, but if a man sins after salvation, he is required to offer the blood sacrifice of an animal to be forgiven.

In this verse, we see Paul briefly deal with that same Jewish mind-set. Very simply, grace and works do not mix. If you have one, you cannot have the other. If I hand you a check for a certain specified amount of money, it is either a gift or it is pay for work that you have done. So it is also with grace and works. And praise God for His grace! Grace, unlike works, originated with God, is preserved by God, and will culminate when we stand before God. It is all because of what He has done--not what we have done!

Verse seven establishes the continued plight of Israel. Three groups within the nation are listed in relation to their respective responses to salvation. The first group sought for righteousness, but " . . . obtained it not . . . " This is the group that worked so diligently to meet the requirements of the law. They really wanted to know God but got themselves caught up in the program of God rather than the person of God.

The second group received righteousness as a gift of grace from God. This is the remnant that we mentioned earlier. They are the redeemed, fully aware that their exalted standing is a work of God, not of anything that they have done.

The third group in this verse became the unfortunate recipients of hardness. In our next verse, we shall see that the hardening was a condition brought upon them by God. "Hardened" is sometimes translated, "blinded." How desperately we need to turn back to the words of Psalm 95:7-8 which says, "Today, oh that you would hear his voice! Harden not your heart." As awful as hardness of the heart was for ancient Israel, it is equally so for the lost sinner today. Dear reader, in which of these three groups do you find yourself? Are you trying to work enough in church-related activities to win salvation, are you neglecting to respond to the conviction of salvation unto salvation, or are you saved by the grace of God? To be in any of these except the last one is to consign yourself to hell.

Verse eight is a quote from Deuteronomy 29:4 and Isaiah 29:10. This verse is a short, to-the-point, explanation of the source of Israel's hardening. It is God. He gave them a spirit of "slumber." Better translated, the Lord gave them a-spirit of "stupor." Like a person who has been drugged, the Jew thinks that Christianity is the religion of the Gentile. He cannot see its importance for himself. He just does not see that Christianity is in the same category as that of his ancient faith of somber rituals, Judaism. It is too simple, too humble, and too easy for the works-ridden Jew to accept.

At this point it is good to remind you that the hardening of the Jew's heart did not occur because he was more wicked than others. This hardening was in accord with the plan of God. That is the point of this chapter. God's plan included the hardening of the Jewish heart. It was his sovereign, elective purpose to do so.

Verses nine and ten should be coupled together and considered as one verse. They quote Psalm 69:22-23. There are three phrases found here that are better understood from the perspective of the original language. "Let their table be made a snare. . ," and "let their eyes be darkened," and "bow down their back" are all written in the imperative mood. This indicates that they are commands issued by one person upon another person.

These seem hard words for the nation of Israel. But always remember that God's great love for this nation has always been the reason for His dealing with them. Just as a surgeon must cut, and hack, and saw on a person's limbs, it is for that person's ultimate good health. By turning His attention toward the Gentile, the Lord in a spiritual sense is doing to Israel what He did in a physical sense when He sent them into slavery in Egypt. He is preparing them through His apparent affection for other people to assume again their exalted position at a later time.

Israel had become proud. Their self-exaltation reached its zenith in the crucifixion of the Savior. Verses nine and ten reveal the indignation of God at the very thought that His people would have such a stubborn turn toward sin. And sin must be punished, even among those of God's favorite nation. That is why the Jew has suffered such cruel treatment and terrible pain since their rejection of Christ. We must underscore the ageless truth that" . . . the way of the transgressor is hard" (Proverbs 13:15). So, because of sin, which was within the sovereign plan of God, their eyes have been darkened and their backs bowed.

This blinding of Jewish eyes, partial as it may be, opened the door of salvation to the Gentiles as indicated in the following verses in this chapter:
11 I say then, Have they stumbled that they should fall? God forbid: but rather through their fall salvation is come unto the Gentiles, for to provoke them to jealousy.
12 Now if the fall of them be the riches of the world, and the diminishing of them the riches of the Gentiles; how much more their fullness?

Verse eleven provides the answer to the question we considered in the opening verses of this chapter; that is, "Has God cast away Israel?" Is Israel forever banished from the fulfillment of God's promises to Abraham and David?

Two words answer that question — "God forbid." I can write dozens of pages explaining why Israel has not been forsaken by the Lord, but this little two-word phrase should sufficiently settle the question with finality — "God forbid." It never occurred to God and should not occur to us that He will not, even yet, do a mighty work in this little nation.

This verse also gives us a very interesting situation. The word, "fall," is found twice in it, but it comes from two different Greek words and therefore has two different meanings. The first time it is used, "fall" has a better translation of "falling completely down to the point of being prostrate."

In its second usage, "fall" means merely "to stumble." Understanding these differences provides a brand new meaning to the verse.

We may now accurately paraphrase the verse to say, "Did they stumble that they may fall completely to their destruction? God forbid: but by their stumbling salvation is come to the Gentiles." As you can see, we have a considerable difference in meanings. Quite literally, Paul is saying two things. First, the fall of Israel is not permanent; and second, their fall made it possible for the Gentiles to hear.

Another phrase in verse eleven also needs a clearer translation. This phrase, "to provoke them to jealousy," is more accurately, "to admire to the point of desperately trying to have." As used here, "jealousy" has a somewhat different meaning than is common in the English language. When a partially-blinded Jew comes in contact with a genuinely-converted Gentile, the impact is so great that he cannot ignore the dramatic presence of Jesus Christ in that person's life. The result? He is touched by the Spirit to want the same for himself.

I hope that you will consider the importance of what Paul has said here. God has partially blinded the Jew. There is no question about that. However, lest you think that He was unfair in doing so, please note that He also provided a way for those blinded eyes to be opened, and that is through the evidence of Gentile lives that have been changed through the power of the Lord Jesus Christ. Listen carefully! If a Jew to whom we might personally witness, dies and goes to hell, we cannot simply write him off because God had blinded his eyes. We must bear the burden of his lost soul because the provision for his enlightenment was made in us.

Verse twelve poses an interesting question. If Israel has proven to be such an unfathomable blessing to the world through a remnant's faith and in spite of the majority's hardness, what can we expect when all of Israel responds to God at the end of the age? Israel has had a profound effect for good in our world as a "nobody." Imagine the glory that will be showered all over the world when she becomes a "somebody."

Beginning in verse thirteen, and moving through verse twenty-four, we have some serious warnings presented to the Gentile world by Paul:

13 For I speak to you Gentiles, inasmuch as I am the apostle of the Gentiles, I magnify mine office:

14 If by any means I may provoke to emulation them which are my flesh, and might save some of them.

15 For if the casting away of them be the reconciling of the world, what shall the receiving of them be, but life from the dead?

16 For if the firstfruit be holy, the lump is also holy: and if the root be holy, so are the branches.

17 And if some of the branches be broken off, and thou, being a wild olive tree, wert grafted in among them, and with them partakest of the root and fatness of the olive tree;

18 Boast not against the branches. But if thou boast, thou bearest not the root, but the root thee.

19 Thou wilt say then, The branches were broken off, that I might be grafted in.

20 Well; because of unbelief they were broken off, and thou standest by faith. Be not high-minded, but fear:

21 For if God spared not the natural branches, take heed lest he also spare not thee.

22 Behold therefore the goodness and severity of God: on them which fell, severity; but toward thee, goodness, if thou continue in his goodness: otherwise thou also shalt be cut off.

23 And they also, if they abide not still in unbelief, shall be grafted in: for God is able to graft them in again.

24 For if thou wert cut out of the olive tree which is wild by nature, and wert grafted contrary to nature into a good olive tree: how much more shall these, which be the natural branches, be grafted into their own olive tree?

Verse thirteen is Paul's statement of his respect for the position that God has given him. He says, "I magnify mine office." He is not seeking praise for himself. He recognizes that the authority that he is exercising in this letter to the Gentiles at Rome is not a result of anything that he has done. Paul is quick to direct their attention to the office of apostle to the Gen tiles, which he holds, as the source of his authority over them. Paul had been made an apostle by the Lord. To receive his instruction, therefore, was to receive God. To reject him was to reject God.

This is paralleled in the church. The Bible knows nothing of a ruling board of deacons, stewards, or elders. No church can attain all that God has for it unless -that church does it God's way. And God's way is to work through the pastor that He has given to the church. We ought not follow a man because of his personality or ability, but we ought to follow a man because it is the scriptural thing to do. The pastor's office is that of God's undershepherd. If the pastor abuses his high and holy calling, God will deal with him. But if the pastor is to be effective, he must be allowed to do so in the free exercise of the gifts of his office.

Verse fourteen repeats a continual burden that Paul has already expressed in the opening verses of chapters nine and ten. If we combine this verse with verse thirteen, Paul is found saying that one of the reasons that he is preaching to the Gentiles with such zeal is because he is hoping that the Jews will see the conversion of those Gentile and, as a result, want that same experience for themselves. He fully realizes that not every Jew will be saved, but he " . . . might save some of them."

Verse fifteen presents a statement of thought-provoking insight. To paraphrase it, Paul is saying, "If by God causing Israel to have partial blindness and hardness of the heart, the rest of the world received the good news of salvation in Jesus Christ, just imagine how good it will be when Israel returns to God — it will be like a loved one returning from death to life.

The casting away of Israel has had a profound impact upon the spread of the gospel. It was through the Jewish race that our Savior was born, from which Paul was called as an apostle to the Gentiles, and to whose nation Jesus will bodily return in glory. And although they are, at this present time, a despised people, the day is coming that their restoration with God will be complete. It is then that they shall be brought from relative obscurity and pain to a place of divine prominence: "But ye shall be named the priests of Jehovah; men shall call you the ministers of God" (Isaiah 61:6).

Verse sixteen gives us an unusual picture to help us understand Israel's continued favor with God. "Firstfruit" represents Abraham as the father of all Israel. ,God by sovereign elective grace chose Abraham, and His faithfulness to Abraham is the same faithfulness which will be manifested in the "lump," which is Israel. Probably Paul was thinking of the heave-offering in Numbers 15:19-21. In that passage, the obedient Jew would take a portion of her dough and cast it into an oven, suggesting by that action that as this "first-fruit" was well-baked, so also would the remainder of the dough. Clearly, if God did not fail Abraham those many centuries ago as the Firstfruit, He will not fail the Jew now as the lump.

Another way of saying the same thing is used in this verse. "Root" is representative of Abraham while "branches" represents Israel. Either analogy may be used as evidence of God's trustworthiness in keeping His covenant promises.

Verse seventeen refutes some pretty bad theology. We often hear of a "Gentile church" that came into existence because all Israel rejected Christ. How wrong such teaching is! First, all Israel did not reject Christ; as we have previously seen, there has always been a remnant. Second, since there are multitudes of Jews who have Jesus as their Lord and Savior, the church is God's "called-out ones" which cannot be limited to any racial or ethnic or national group.

To explain what I have just said, please note that verse seventeen says that "some of the branches were broken off." Not all the branches were broken. In other words, not all Jews were forsaken by the Lord. Not all Jews rejected Jesus. I cite as an example such Jews as Peter and Paul. These two men who were a small part of a faithful Jewish remnant, produced much fruit in the lives of both Jew and Gentile. Had it not been for such fruit being borne by this remnant, the Gentile world would have been hopelessly lost.

This verse also shares the supernatural aspect of the gospel's deliverance to the Gentile world. Botanical grafting is done by taking a wild root and grafting a good branch to it. By using this method, the good branch will receive the necessary nourishment from the wild root, but will produce the fruit normally associated with the plant from which the good branch was cut. Not so in this verse. The reverse takes place to show that this grafting process is indeed the work of God. The wild branch of Gentiles is grafted to the good root of Israel but the fruit that is produced is that of the root instead of the branch.

You see that in the phrase, "partaker with them of the root." We have already established that the root is Abraham, so that means that when a man is saved he receives certain of the benefits that were granted him. Principally, we receive "the fatness of the olive tree" which is a symbol of righteousness. The saved Gentile, therefore, is grafted into the righteousness of Abraham which is by faith.

Verse eighteen warns the Gentile believer to avoid assuming a stance of superiority over the Jew. After all, the Jew was not attached to the Gentile; the Gentile was attached to the Jew. The only possible person who would have any human reason for boasting would be the Jewish Christian. But if his heart is right with God, he will be the very first to admit that he would rather glory in the cross.

Verse nineteen shows how ridiculous the thinking of some Gentiles can be. And it is true, just as this verse states, that there are some who believe that the branches of faithless Jews were broken off so that believing Gentiles might be added. That is not the case at all. Verse twenty explains verse nineteen. Israel had sinned as a nation. As noted before, there was always a remnant within the nation that loved and followed God. But the majority of Jews refused His loving-kindness. As a result, they were broken off. That breaking-off was not God's way of providing room for the Gentile. The breaking-off was God's punishment of sin — nothing more and nothing less.

When the vacancy occurred because of that punishment, the Gentile was introduced to the root by grafting. But that introduction did not mean that he was better than the Jew who had just been eliminated. We must always remind ourselves that whenever God blesses any of us, it is by an act of His wondrous grace. It is not because of our superior merit in comparison with others, because we have all come short of His glory.

Verse twenty-one completes the warning of verse twenty. God hates sin and stubborn pride in whomever He finds it. This verse explicitly states that if God would not spare His chosen ones of Israel, He will not spare the engrafted Gentile who commits the same sins. "Spared" is an interesting word. In the original language, it means "tenderly forbear." Dear reader, never allow yourself to believe that God will deal with you in a less stringent manner than He has others. He will not deal tenderly with the Gentile in transgression anymore than He did the Jew in transgression.

Verse twenty-two grants us a contrasting view at the two opposite extremes of God's dealings with man. First, we see His "goodness," which is better translated "gentleness" or "generosity." Second, we see His "severity," which means "to be destroyed as one falling from a high cliff."

God is patient. He is long-suffering. He waits and waits and waits for His children to quit their sins and return to Him. His goodness is extended toward us when we deserve it the least. Many of the Jews took His goodness for granted and paid dearly for it. They were broken off in severity like people cast to their destruction from a high cliff. In this verse, Paul is advising the Gentile believers in Rome that they would do well to heed the warning of the casting away of these Jews. He admonishes these believers to remember that although they are presently enjoying God's goodness, they could quickly be severed and discarded.

Verse twenty-three provides another of many biblical prophecies concerning the restoration of Israel. "Shall be grafted in . . . " is in the future indicative passive in the Greek, which means that the nation's future is as bright as the promises of God. Just because God broke them off does not mean that He cannot graft them in again; and indeed, this verse says that He will!

Verse twenty-four is a resounding voice of assurance for the Jew that has been cut off. By comparison, Paul speaks of the Jew as a "good olive tree." He speaks of the Gentile as a "wild olive tree." The good olive tree is, even in these modern times, extremely useful as a source of wood for beautiful carved pieces of furniture and ornaments, as well as for its oil that supplies a base for foods, medicines, and cosmetics. The wild olive tree is virtually useless, producing a very crude oil that only the poorest of the poor dare use. So, Paul suggests, since the Gentiles were taken from such sorry circumstances and grafted into a good tree, does it not make sense that the branches which were removed from a good tree could once again be restored to that same tree?

Our next section in this chapter deals with the restoration of Israel that we have just discussed:

25 For I would not, brethren, that ye should be ignorant of this mystery, lest ye should be wise in your own conceits; that blindness in part is happened to Israel, until the fullness of the Gentiles be come in.
26 And so all Israel shall be saved: as it is written, There shall come out of Zion the Deliverer, and shall turn away ungodliness from Jacob:
27 For this is my covenant unto them, when I shall take away their sins.
28 As concerning the gospel, they are enemies for your sakes: but as touching the election, they are beloved for the fathers' sakes.
29 For the gifts and calling of God are without repentance.
30 For as ye in times past have not believed God, yet have now obtained mercy through their unbelief:
31 Even so have these also now not believed, that through your mercy they also may obtain mercy.
32 For God hath concluded them all in unbelief, that he might have mercy upon all.
33 O the depth of the riches both of the wisdom and knowledge of God! how unsearchable are his judgments, and his ways past finding out!

Verse twenty-five is one of the most important verses in all the Scriptures concerning the restoration of Israel. Quite often, I hear good men of the Bible interpret this verse to mean that when the final Gentile is saved, that "the fullness of the Gentiles" will come in, the rapture of the church will occur, and the seven years of great tribulation will then follow, during which God will deal with Israel again. That is almost, but not exactly, right. Be very careful in your interpretation of this verse that you not describe the church as exclusively a Gentile institution by speaking of the "final Gentile" who will be saved before the rapture. Remember, the church has Jew and Gentile alike within its ranks. Instead, this reference to the "fullness of the Gentiles" is better understood to mean that period of God's prophetic plan that will end when the last convert, Jew or Gentile, comes in during this church age. This phrase, "fullness of the Gentiles," in my estimation, means the same thing as "times of the Gentiles," found in Luke 21:24. While many outstanding and worthy commentators try to make a difference, I sincerely believe there is none. This end of the "fullness of the Gentiles" will mark God's restoring full sight to a partially blinded Israel and the resumption of Daniel's seventy weeks. For detailed clarification, see my commentary on Daniel, chapter nine.

Verse twenty-six informs us that when this restoration of their sight has taken place, "... all Israel shall be saved." Please do not erroneously interpret this to mean that every individual Jew will be saved. It does not mean that! Neither does it mean that the Jews will be given a second chance at salvation! What it does mean is that Israel, as a nation, will again be brought into fellowship with God. This passage has to do with "national" restoration, not "individual" salvation.

In this verse, Paul quotes Isaiah 59:20. But Isaiah 59:19 prophesies a time when the enemy "shall come in like a flood." Because of Paul's quotation in this verse that is taken from Isaiah 59:20 and describes the Redeemer returning to Zion, we can feel confident that this conflict depicts the coming Battle of Armageddon. So, verse twenty-six, is a wonderful reference to the second coming of Christ in glory!

Verse twenty-seven may have been quoted by Paul from either Isaiah 27:9 or Jeremiah 31:34. Whichever is the actual source makes no difference. The truth is the same; God is one day going to forgive national Israel of her sins.

What is this covenant mentioned in this verse? Back in verse eight of this chapter we saw God placing Israel in a state of partial blindness. His covenant with them is that as surely as He did that, He will also one day restore their sight and grant national restoration.

Verse twenty-eight repeats a message that those of us in the Gentile world should always underscore. The Jews were, and to a great degree still are, enemies of the gospel. But if they had not been enemies, God's plan for extending salvation to the Gentile would have been thwarted. Therefore, it was for our sakes that they were enemies.

But, on the other hand, they are "beloved for the fathers' sake." This word, 'beloved," has an infinitely greater intensity attached to it than does the word, "loved." Whatever their spiritual condition as nation, they are yet the "beloved" of God because of His promises to Abraham and David, among others. These ancient covenant promises were made in complete accord with God's foreknowledge. And what God has determined in eternity can never be changed in time!

Verse twenty-nine is a statement of finality that reflects God's attribute of changelessness. The phrase, "not repented of," is more accurately translated, "not subject to change or modification." The promises God made to the patriarchs and prophets of the Old Testament concerning national Israel are just as binding today as they were the day that He uttered them! God does not equivocate! He is not whimsical!

Verse thirty is a reminder to any saved Gentile that he was once as disobedient to God as any Jew in the House of Israel. All you need to do to understand that statement is to read again Romans 1:24-32 and review the degradation of the Gentile world. A casual glancing about in America wills how that we have only grown worse. No sane Gentile, saved or unsaved, should ever sense himself as better than his Jewish counterpart.

However, once again Paul declares that our salvation became possible through the continued disobedience of national Israel. If for no other reason, we ought to pray earnestly for the multitudes in that dear land.

Verse thirty-one is another declaration of warning for the Gentile, especially when considered with verse thirty-two. In this verse, we are confronted again with the universal nature of sin and God's reaction to it. As a result of Israel's sin, the gospel was taken to the Gentiles. And because God has extended mercy to the Gentiles, which means the gospel message can be moved in full cycle back to the Jew.

Verse thirty-two expresses the full intent of God toward the Jew and Gentile alike. Since both have been weighed in the measure of God's requirement for holiness, and have fallen short, God has been able to display His grace toward everyone. We are all sinners. This is an echo of Paul's opening essay concerning the doctrine of condemnation that we studied early in this book.

Verse thirty-three shouts a veritable amen chorus from the heart of Paull This whole discussion of God's sovereignty and elective purpose in these last three chapters has left Paul breathless with excitement. God is so wise! G0d's knowledge is so limitless! His judgments are so unsearchable! "Unsearchable" literally means "beyond the ability to see or possibly understand." Another way of saying the same thing is also in this verse — "no way of finding out." Even the most brilliant of minds pales into an empty vacuum when trying to discern the intricacies of God's doing.

Our final three verses in this chapter extol the Almighty God:
34 For who hath known the mind of the Lord? or who hath been his counsellor?
35 Or who hath first given to him, and it shall be recompensed unto him again?
36 For of him, and through him, and to him, are all things: to whom be glory forever. Amen.

Verse thirty-four is a quote of Isaiah 40:13. It is a verse of glorious praise in honor of the Most High God. The two words, "hath known," in the Greek, carries the idea of timelessness in grammatical usage. No man has ever known or shall ever know the mind of the Lord.

Certainly no man can be God's "counsellor." Occasionally there will emerge a religious leader who conducts himself as though he is indispensable and as though God could not possibly get along without him. How absurd!

Verse thirty-five is taken from Job 41:11. It is a continuation of adoration of the Lord. Man is the recipient of everything that is worth anything from the hand of God. It is not within man's puny power to give God something that He could not already have had, simply by choosing to have it. After all, God is omnipotent.

Verse thirty-six proclaims the position of the Almighty. Three things are said of God. "Of him . . . " means that God created all things. "Through him . . . " means that God regulates all things! "Unto him . . . " means that ultimately all things conclude with God! Based on these three fundamental truths, can we do less than join with Paul in saying, "To him be glory forever!"

Chapter Twelve
The Perfect Will of God
How to Determine His Will

The opening verses of the twelfth chapter may well be the most crucial verses in the entire Word of God for the believer who is sinking in a morass of indecision and uncertainty about the future. How the black clouds of despair seem to roll over the life of the poor saint who sees himself as continually making wrong choices. His present situation is bad enough, but the contemplation of his future days getting no better gives him a sinking feeling of "so what's the use in trying." It is to that frustrated follower of Jesus that Romans 12:1-2 are addressed:

1 I beseech you therefore, brethren, by the mercies of God, that ye present your bodies a living sacrifice, holy, acceptable unto God, which is your reasonable service.
2 And be not conformed to this world: but be ye transformed by the renewing of your mind, that ye may prove what is that good, and acceptable, and perfect, will of God.

To begin our discussion of the will of God, we must first recognize the three ways that His will is demonstrated in the lives of men. You will uncover these three manifestations when you examine the Scriptures as His:

PERFECT WILL: This is the blessed position in which the favor of God especially shines on an individual. Here is the man who is Spirit-controlled, directed exclusively by the Word of God for his life. It is that special will of our Lord about which Paul speaks in these two verses. Since this is the preferred state for the saint, we will look, in concrete fashion, at the steps one must take to attain that state.

(2) PERMISSIVE WILL: Of the three aspects of our Lord's will, this is decidedly the least desirable. Sometimes God allows a man to do or to have certain conditions because of that man's stubborn persistence in wanting those conditions. One good example is in the twenty-second chapter of Numbers. Balaam, the prophet, repeatedly came to God pleading with the

Lord to place a curse upon Israel. There is no question that the nation deserved harsh discipline from the Lord because of their continual pride and gross wickedness, but Balaam wanted the curse because of a bribe that had been offered to him by a pagan king. Finally, God relented and by His permissive will did as Balaam requested. From that very day, this greedy prophet's name became a title of scorn and shame. For example, Jude ll says of false teachers: "Woe unto them! For they have gone in the way of Cain, and ran greedily after THE ERROR OF BALAAM, for reward, and perished in the gainsaying of Korah."

`Another example of the exercise of God's permissive will can be found in the eleventh chapter of Numbers. The children of Israel had been delivered from Egypt, and were miraculously fed the manna from heaven. But in spite of God's graciousness, they began to complain: "And the mixed multitude that was among them fell to lusting, and the children of Israel also wept again, and said, who shall give us flesh to eat? We remember the fish which we did eat in Egypt freely; the cucumbers, and the melons, and the leeks, and the onions, and the garlic. But now our soul is dried away; there is nothing at all, besides this manna, before our eyes" (Numbers 11:4-6). What was God's answer to this ungrateful cry of these people? His answer was in the form of His permissive will as He spoke with Moses: "And say unto the people, sanctify yourselves for tomorrow, and ye shall out flesh; for ye have wept in the ears of the Lord, saying, who shall give us flesh to eat? For it was well with us in Egypt; therefore the Lord will give you flesh, and ye shall eat. Ye shall not eat one day, not two days, not five days, nor twenty days; but even a whole month, until it come out at your nostrils, and it be loathsome unto you; because ye have wept before him, saying, why came we forth out of Egypt?"(Numbers 11:18-20).

These two examples of God's permissive will brought pain to those who complained until God gave them their desire. And when they got what they wanted, they did not want what they got! It has always been so. I call this trying of the Lord's patience, "the curse of answered prayer." How often I have heard the sorrowful account of a woman who married the wrong man! The story is forever the same! She just knew that this man was her Prince Charming. Wise Christians tried to dissuade her, but to no avail. As a sweet and sincere young Christian herself, she prayed about her marriage, but was aware that God did not want her to join herself in marriage to this particular man. But she persisted. Finally, God allowed her, by His permissive will, to do that which she had already determined in her heart to do. Now, with the passage of years, she has wished countless times that God had turned a deaf ear to her stupid pleas. On the other hand, there are multitudes of women who thank God every day that they listened for His perfect will in the choice of their mates.

(3) ULTIMATE WILL: God has an eternal plan for all the nations and the individuals of the world. This, His ultimate will, is to be accomplished nationally with the final re-gathering of Israel and individually with each redeemed person becoming just like Jesus: "For whom he did foreknow, he also did predestinate to be conformed to the image of his Son, that he might be the firstborn among many brethren" (Romans 8:29).

From what we have now seen in the perfect will, permissive will, and ultimate will, it is rather obvious that man receives the greater benefit by living in the realm of the perfect will until the ultimate will is accomplished in his life. Since that is so, how may a believer determine that will?

We must first reject the popular notion that we "find" God's will for our lives. There is absolutely nothing in the Scriptures that teaches the "finding" of God's will. Instead, our Heavenly Father longs for us to operate on a daily basis in the smooth channel of His divine guidance. If we do no enjoy such bountiful direction, it is because of our own doing, not His! It is the height of absurdity to believe that a loving Father would tease us by playing some sort of hide-and-seek with His perfect will for us.

We must recognize God's formula for the revelation of His will as presented by Paul in the first two verses of this twelfth chapter. That formula is P+T=W (presentation plus transformation equals will). By the unrestrained presentation of our bodies and the continual transformation of our minds, we are brought to an awareness of the perfect will of our Lord.

The Old Testament system of sacrifices exists no more. God is not interested in the dead body of a lamb or bull. He wants every believer to be a living sacrifice, a vigorous testimony, of His grace.

That kind of sacrificial offering of oneself to God demands discipline. Just as the Old Testament altar had fleshhooks to prevent the animal from sliding from the place of sacrifice, we are to be willing to be "tied down" to the responsibilities that are assigned by the Lord. Being "tied down" means that we place highest priority on the tasks that are uniquely ours to perform, such as teaching a Sunday School class, singing in the choir, visiting prospects on the church outreach night, etc. The presentation of one's body as a "living sacrifice" means that the pleasures and whims of this world will not dictate where we go and what we do.

Indeed, closely behind presentation of our bodies comes transformation of our minds. We are exhorted to " . . . be not conformed to this world: but be ye transformed by the renewing of your mind . . . " Every believer is in a condition of conforming or transforming, whether he recognizes it or not.

Conformity means that he is blending in with his world; to be transformed means that what he is within himself is allowed to show outwardly with no restraint. Conformity is like the camouflage uniform of the military that renders its wearer indistinguishable from his surroundings of leaves, earth, and grass. Transformation comes from the same word in the Greek as "metamorphosis," which is also the same word from which springs "transfiguration/" When a caterpillar is metamorphosized or changed into a butterfly, it is becoming outwardly what it has been inwardly. When Jesus was transfigured, the God nature of His inner man was gloriously radiated to those men assembled there. We are to do the same. By the exercise of our conscious will, we are to choose for the new man within us to be seen and heard by those with whom we associate.

How can this transformation be accomplished? We are told by Paul that it is through the renewing of our minds. How do we renew our minds? Very simply, we are to examine carefully the things, both seen and heard, that we allow to enter our minds. We are daily bombarded by a veritable barrage of material from the commercial and entertainment world that is unfit for mental consumption by the believer. We would do well to heed Paul's words in Philippians 4:8: "Finally, brethren, whatsoever things are true, whatsoever things are honest, whatsoever things are just, whatsoever things are pure, whatsoever things are lovely, whatsoever things are of good report, if there be any virtue, and if there be any praise, THINK ON THESE THINGS."

As we present our bodies to the Lord for His free use and as we transform our minds, the daily will of God for us will slowly become a reality. And please take note that verse two is a command, not a simple request. Verse one is unmistakably clear that all of the above is not beyond the call of duty, but rather is to be considered as "reasonable." Jesus said the same in Luke 17:10: "So likewise ye, when ye shall have done all those things which are commanded of you, say, we are unprofitable servants: we have done that which was our duty to do." In other words, whatever is required of us by the Lord in order for us to operate in His perfect will is not to be viewed as undue hardship. All things commanded are reasonable.

The One Body

An ideal church would be one in which all of the members are cooperating in the sphere of God's perfect will. In order for a physical body to function at peak performance, each of its parts must operate to the highest limit of its special capabilities. When even a little toe hurts, the entire physique of a superbly-conditioned body will hurt and demand appropriate attention. Likewise, in a well-balanced New Testament church, the most minor member receives due compassion from the others in the fellowship whenever a need arises. No member should place himself in a position of greater prominence than another. We are where we are because of God's choosing, not our own:

3 For I say, through the grace given unto me, to every man that is among you, not to think of himself more highly than he ought to think; but to think soberly, according as God hath dealt to every man the measure of faith.
4 For as we have many members in one body, and all members have not the same office:
5 So we, being many, are one body in Christ, and every one, members one of another.

Included in verse three is an interesting little phrase, " . . . according as God hath dealt to every man the measure of faith." Within the local church

God has placed the members of the body into the tasks that fit their positions in faith. Obviously, He will not select a recently-saved ten-year old boy to teach an older men's Bible class. His growth in the experiences of faith and the Word of God have not yet brought him to the level of skillful maturity which is necessary for success. The importance of this growth cannot be overestimated. It is vital.

We may liken it to an automobile trip at night from Jacksonville to Atlanta. The journey could not be made if the driver refused to leave until the entire stretch of highway was illuminated at one time. That would be an impossible request! As you know, the headlamps of an automobile shine some two hundred feet forward. When that two hundred feet is traveled, another two hundred feet can be seen. So it goes through the night until the distance is covered and the trip ends in Atlanta.

How stupid it is for so-called believers to demand that their road of faith be illuminated at one time all the way from their salvation to heaven! That is impossible! Rather, we are to move forward each day by the sure and steady guidance of the Holy Ghost. As the days go by, we are granted more responsibility and greater opportunity by virtue of the ever-increasing strength of our faith as we more and more learn to rely upon Him. That is the very reason that although Billy Graham could not always preach to thousands in a crusade, he can now! Simply, the measure of his faith is now sufficient to meet the challenge of today's commands.

The Gifts of The Spirit

As we continue through the chapter, it is apparent that the transformation that takes place, and subsequently strengthens the whole body, manifests itself outwardly in the demonstration of several spiritual gifts. These gifts should be studied in terms of their usefulness to the work of the kingdom through the church. The gifts enumerated by Paul in this passage should be studied in connection with I Corinthians 12:1-11 and Ephesians 4:11-12. Here, the gifts listed can be noted in Romans 12:6-8:
6 Having then gifts differing according to the grace that is given to us, whether prophecy, let us prophesy according to the proportion of faith;
7 Or ministry, let us wait on our ministering: or he that teacheth, on teaching;

8 Or he that exhorteth, on exhortation: he that giveth, let him do it with simplicity; he that ruleth, with diligence; he that sheweth mercy, with cheerfulness.

Seven spiritual gifts are presented in these verses. The word for "gifts" is "charismata," which literally means that these are "grace" gifts. You will note immediately that all of these gifts are "service gifts." They are for our employment, not for our enjoyment. Each one is to be used in ministry. Verse six uses this phrase, "Having then gifts differing . . . " This clearly establishes that we are not all to have the same gifts as some would suggest.

Because these particular gifts are essential to the productivity of the church, let me earnestly suggest that you prayerfully search the mind of God in relation to one of these seven:

(l) PROPHECY: This gift does not pertain to the ability of FORETELLING; no, it is FORTHTELLING. Forthtelling is the taking of God's Word and sharing it to the edification, exhortation, and comfort of the hearers, and when that is done by someone, that person has exercised his gift of prophecy. 'How do we know that is so? Read the definition of this spiritual gift as given in I Corinthians 14:3: "But he that prophesieth; speaketh unto men to edification,and exhortation, and comfort." Edification is "to build up."

Good Bible teachers do this regularly as they dig the mines of scriptural principles and share those ageless nuggets of truth with their classes, thereby giving them something to build homes and lives upon. Exhortation is "to fire up." Good evangelists possess this unique, God-given trait of motivating people to act upon what they have heard. Comfort is "to hold up." Those who compassionately counsel, either in an office or a sickroom, have this special, divinely-bestowed quality. So you see, this gift of prophecy is very beneficial to the church and quite unlike that which is ordinarily defined as prophecy.

MINISTRY: This word comes from "diakonia," from which we get our word, "deacon." It means "serviceable labor for others." Ministry has become too closely aligned with the pulpit, when actually, in the biblical context, it has more meaning when associated with manual labor. The men who were chosen to assist the apostles in the sixth chapter of Acts "waited on tables." Taking lunch to an invalid, sweeping the floor of the church sanctuary, or driving children to a Sunday School social are just a few of the countless ways that the gift of ministry may be used.

TEACHING: The gift of teaching differs from the gift of preaching in that teaching is
aimed at the head while preaching is aimed at the heart. Systematic Bible study is essential for victory against the subtle enemies of this world. The believer who possesses this gift has special insights and interpretive abilities through which he is able to make the Word come alive.

(4) EXHORTATION: This gift is a part of the greater gift of prophecy, mentioned already.

(5) GIVING: Very few sermons about spiritual gifts have very much to say about giving, yet it is an important gift. God has prospered some believers financially. They are placed in a position of being especially helpful in providing the church with monies above their regular tithes and offerings.

(6) RULING: This gift is necessary for those who are in leadership positions. The utilization of this gift gives the one who possesses it a tender heart but a tough exterior. Otherwise, because of the cruel treatment that comes with a leadership role, the absence of this gift will result in an embittered heart or a feeble effort of leading.

(7) MERCY: Mercy in its most common definition means to refuse to deal with people as they deserve to be treated. I believe that nursery workers have the gift of mercy. Crying preschoolers and messy diapers do not deter them from being extraordinarily kind and compassionate. How can a believer know which gift is his? First, he should re-study this passage and its companion passages in I Corinthians 12:1-ll and Ephesians 4:11-12. Second, he should ask himself these three questions about any gift that he may feel could possibly be his:

(1) Do I feel comfortable exercising this gift? A hand feels comfortable doing

the work that is normally associated with a hand. It would not feel comfortable trying to do the work of a foot. Can I satisfactorily do the work that is normally associated with this gift?

(2) Do others recognize this gift in me? If a hand is displayed, everybody readily recognizes it as a hand. An effective use of a spiritual gift will likewise be readily appreciated by observers.

(3) Do I get results normally associated with this gift? There is no doubt that Billy Graham has the gift of evangelism because of the multiplied thousands who continue to respond to his crusade invitations. The right use of a particular gift brings the desired ends for the use of it.

Christian Behavior Toward Others

The final thirteen verses of chapter twelve contain explicit commands for the believer to follow in his dealings with those who are not saved as well as the ones who are. Paul recognizes that although everything that he has already shared in this chapter should make these following statements unnecessary, most saints need some straight-forward instructions to keep them on track. Too, it is important to note that verses one through eight are more directly concerned with the believer's relationship to God while verses nine through twenty-one are more concerned with man's relationship to man.

(1) Unfeigned Love

9 Let love be without dissimulation. Abhor that which is evil; cleave to that which is good.

That word, "dissimulation," means "to feign" or "to act." How often we see someone trying to "butter-up" or flatter someone. Remember, flattery is like perfume; it smells good but don't swallow it. Our love should always ring true. That is only possible when we " . . . cleave to that which is good" in the other person. I believe this confirms very well the old ditty:
"There is so much good in the worst of us,
And so much bad in the best of us,
That it hardly behooves any of us,
To speak ill of the rest of us."

(2) Affectionate Love
10 Be kindly affectioned one to another with brotherly love; in honour preferring one another;

Some very pious folk will profess their love for others, but they refuse to demonstrate it in positive works. It is not enough for us to have unfeigned love; we are to get involved in the lives of others with acts of genuine affection. And, in those times when our personalities are drawn into more intimate relationships with some than others, we are still commanded to treat those others with genuine respect.

(3) Business Integrity
11 Not slothful in business; fervent in spirit; serving the Lord.

No greater discredit comes to the cause of Christ than is brought by the shoddy ways that many churches, and saints, pursue their organizational and business dealings. Many individuals who are red-hot for God are no more than barely lukewarm in the conducting of their personal affairs. The word, "fervent," is the same word that is used for "fever." It means internal heat. Our motivation toward excellence in business matters should come from an intense desire within the heart of the saint. We ought not divide life, as we are prone to do, into that which is religious and that which is secular. Every endeavor of the believer's life should be done with the primary drive that this is another way of "serving the Lord."

(4) Peace Under Pressure
12 Rejoicing in hope; patient in tribulation; continuing instant in prayer.

The word, "hope," means more in the Scriptures than it does in the way that we use the term today. We use it when we are speaking of wishful anticipation; the Bible uses it in reference to "holy certainty." That is the reason we have for rejoicing. Regardless of the pain of this life, there is a day just ahead when our blessed Lord Jesus will come for us! And even if we die before He comes, we will be "absent from the body, present with the Lord."

It naturally and logically falls in line that we will endure tribulation when we reject Satan's seductive offers and begin to follow the Lord. The crushing of tribulation experiences are best encountered with a tough temperament of inner patience. A resolute dependency upon God to work a way through the severest of difficulties pays high spiritual dividends, but that is only possible by a daily walk with God in prayer, continually praying for His divine leadership.

(5) Charity To Others
13 Distributing to the necessity of saints; given to hospitality.-

Ours is not the life of an "easy touch" for every freeloader who passes our way. Two words stand out in this verse, "necessity" and "saints." We have a responsibility to those who are saved in terms of financial aid, not to those of the world. But the limitations of that responsibility are drawn tight along the line of the saints' needs, not their wants and desires. Paul indicates that we should be watchful for ways to lend aid; we should be "given to hospitality." Another, and better, translation of "given" is "pursuing." We are to pursue hospitality. A spirit of selflessness rather than selfishness is the heartbeat of the caring saint.

(6) Kindness When Attacked
14 Bless them which persecute you: bless, and curse not.

A person who persecutes another is not just a person who injures; he is a person who follows someone trying to find fault. The Pharisees persecuted Jesus by trying to embarrass Him publicly, asking trick questions that had been designed to make it appear that He was a lawbreaker.
In this verse, Paul teaches that we are to bless the one who persecutes us. What does it mean to bless? It is "to speak well of" another. When attacked, our flesh recoils in preparation to deliver a blow in return. However, we are to speak well of the persecutor.

(7) Spirit of Empathy
15 Rejoice with them that do rejoice, and weep with them that weep.

Empathy is more than mere sympathy. Empathy is the ability to put oneself in the shoes of another. When our brothers and sisters in the church hurt, if we are empathetic, we will hurt with them; if they are glad, we will be glad. In this matter of empathy, we can identify with others.

(8) Humble
16 Be of the same mind one toward another. Mind not high things, but condescend to men of low estate. Be not wise in your own conceits.

It is an inclination of the flesh to look for associations with people in the prestigious positions of wealth and authority. Most of the time, these are people who are able to use their influence to our advantage. But God prefers that we follow His example and look downward toward those that we can help. That may not be wise in the eyes of the world; but it is definitely wise in the eyes of God. The Bible is a book of paradoxes. The way to live is to die, to get is to give, to move upward is to go downward.

(9) Not Vindictive

17 Recompense to no man evil for evil. Provide things honest in the sight of all men.

How often we hear some saint say, "I don't care what people think!" Perhaps you have said that yourself. Realistically, we do care, and sometimes an intended deed by someone to do evil against us can evoke an urge to retaliate. Is it not better to reach that level of Christian development in which we can absorb the slings and arrows of premeditated insult and still maintain a godly demeanor before men? The world is always watching the saint to see if he really lives in stressful situations according to the commands of God.

(10) Peace-loving

18 If it be possible, as much as lieth in you, live peaceably with all men.

This does not say that we are under an absolute command to live peaceably with all men. We may as well face it! Some people are so thoroughly obnoxious that it is impossible to please them. When you have done all that you can do to rectify a poor relationship, withdraw yourself to others who will be thrilled with friendship.

(11) Not Given To Revenge

19 Dearly beloved, avenge not yourselves, but rather give place unto wrath: for it is written, Vengeance is mine; I will repay, saith the Lord.

We are in a most enviable position as children of God. We do not have to worry about "getting even" with those who do us wrong. This must have been a frequent topic among the Roman believers who were under the constant threat of Rome's harassment, torture, and death. The phrase" . . . give place unto wrath . . . " is speaking of God's wrath, not ours. The Lord is fully aware of the suffering of His children at the hands of ungodly men. We can take some degree of satisfaction in knowing that God has made an emphatic declaration that He will repay, with His own stern hand of justice, those who cause His anointed ones pain.

(12) Love of Enemy

20 Therefore if thine enemy hunger, feed him; if he thirst, give him drink: for in so doing thou shalt heap coals of fire on his head.

How much better it is if we can destroy our enemies with love! The measure of our spirituality is not in the performance of church.-related activities that we enjoy. It is in the area of unpleasantries that pinpoints how much we have grown in grace and just how far we have yet to go.

(13) Live Above Evil

21 Be not overcome of evil, but overcome evil with good.

Ours is an exciting life of triumph over challenges innumerable! Because the Spirit of God indwells us, we have the necessary power to overcome every evil obstacle in our Christian walk. The choice is made by the exercise of the believer's will. We must not only allow the Spirit to reside within us; He must also preside within us. By looking for good ways to counter-attack evil situations, we can live victoriously. For example, if you are tempted to complain about some occurrence in your life, look for some other occurrence that gives you reason to rejoice. Then praise Him, and in so doing, you will overcome evil with good.

Chapter Thirteen

The Christian and Civil Government

During the past two decades in the United States, there has arisen an interesting phenomenon. Preachers have left their pulpits in increasing numbers to lead acts of rebellion against governmental decisions on a variety of issues, particularly the ones pertaining to civil rights. Those who have chosen to stay in the pulpit have often done so in an irreverent attempt to use that sacred desk as a stage from which to blast the civil authorities rather than bless the saints. Civil disobedience has emerged as a banner under which many churchmen march.

This social doctrine has been justified by these religious leaders with such frail arguments as, "If you do not feel a particular law is fair or that it pertains to you, then you have no moral or religious obligation to abide by it." That sounds so good, so noble, but God does teach against it. Even in the Old Testament, a sad state of anarchy, of social confusion, is found: "In those days there was no king in Israel; every man did that which was right in his own eyes" (Joshua 21:25). But now, in the church age, which began during the era of Rome's severe domination and torture of the new movement of Christianity, Paul warns that every saint of God is to place himself in subjection to the laws of the state:

1 Let every soul be subject unto the higher powers. For there is no power but of God: the powers that be are ordained of God.
2 Whosoever therefore resisteth the power, resisteth the ordinance of God: and they that resist shall receive to themselves damnation.
3 For rulers are not a terror to good works, but to the evil. Wilt thou then not be afraid of the power? do that which is good, and thou shalt have praise of the same:
4 For he is the minister of God to thee for good. But if thou do that which is evil, be afraid; for he beareth not the sword in vain: for he is the minister of God, a revenger to execute wrath upon him that doeth evil.
5 Wherefore ye must needs be subject, not only for wrath, but also for conscience sake.
6 For this cause pay ye tribute also: for they are God's minister, attending

continually upon this very thing.
7 Render therefore to all their dues: tribute to whom tribute is due; custom to whom custom; fear to whom fear; honour to whom honour.

If ever there lived a generation that felt the cruel, unjust heel of governmental policies toward it, it was this generation of Christians and Jews of the first century. A.D. 70 saw the ravaging of Jerusalem by the Roman iron legions. Pregnant Jewish women were ripped open. Young girls repeatedly assaulted. Boys were butchered; old men humiliated and killed. Later in that same century, it was common for the Christians to suffer unbelievable persecution, like being hung from treetops in private Roman gardens, covered with oil, and set ablaze.

But in spite of such horrible treatment, some of which existed during Christ's days on earth, we do not hear one single word from His dear lips or read one single word in the entire New Testament that would urge us into a revolt against the state. One of the truly great Christian couples in the Scriptures was Aquila and Priscilla, and these two dear people left their home because of the orders of a ruler: "After these things Paul departed from Athens, and came to Corinth, and found a certain Jew, named Aquila, born in Pontus, lately come from Italy, with his wife Priscilla (because Claudius had commanded all Jews to depart fromRome), and came unto them" (Acts 18:1-2).

Verse two should be remembered by those social changers who espouse civil disobedience. When a man places himself against the powers of this world, he is automatically setting himself against the powers of God Himself. If translated literally from the Greek, we actually find this verse saying, "So that the one who is resisting the power has opposed the ordinance of God." To be right with God, a person must be obedient to the laws of both heaven and earth. This is exactly what Jesus meant when He said, "Render therefore unto Caesar the things that are Caesar's; and unto God the things that are God's" (Matthew 22:21). Compared with our complicated judicial systems in America that are designed to protect the rights of the individual, the Jews dwelling in Rome during the first century were virtually without help, living in a social and governmental system that was extremely alienated against them. Yet, in spite of such cruel atrocities committed against them by heads of state, they no less chose to obey God in all things.

Verse three reminds us that most of the laws of the government are not written onto the legal books as an attack against God or against God's people. Therefore, whenever possible, and that is the vast majority of the time, the believer can readily obey the laws of man. In fact, praise results from your willingness to obey the laws of the land. That praise will come from within yourself, will come from God, and will come from others who are looking to you for an example of genuine influence. Every community loves to honor and recognize the man or woman who is living a lifestyle of harmony and joy.

Verse four describes the governmental leader as a "minister of God." The word, "minister," is better translated, "deacon." "Deacon," of course, is actually, "servant." Does this mean that a wicked ruler is also a minister of God? Yes, a wicked ruler is a minister of God, and God will judge him for those ways that he may abuse his privileges.

You will also note in this verse that the government official " . . . beareth not the sword in vain." This verse is conclusive evidence that the state has the right of imposing the death penalty. God has instituted a chain of authority. One of the reasons that He did so was that evil doers would have someone to whom they must answer. In the Old Testament, there was an avenger of evil whose responsibility was the execution of appropriate penalties upon those who had done wrong. In this period of the Church Age, the agency by which God displays His holiness against the criminal element in our society is the government. Therefore, by virtue of this verse, found not in the law of the Old Testament but in the epistles of the New Testament, it is confirmed that the use of capital punishment is 11 God-given privilege to the state.

Verse five teaches us that the believer is to obey the law, not out of fear, but because he knows that such obedience is the will of God for him. This reminds me of a true story that an old gentleman once gave me. He said that when he was a young man, he had worked for a large bakery whose principal product was the kind of sandwich bread than is normally sold in loaves in grocery stores. In order to institute cleanliness, the company management had posted at rule throughout the plant that no cigarette smoking', snuffing, dipping, or tobacco-chewing would any longer he allowed in the baking areas. One man used a wooden oar-like device to gently stir the dough in the huge vats; he also enjoyed his chewing-tobacco. It was only when he saw a foreman approaching his work area that he would dispose of the tobacco—into the vat where he would mix it into the dough! That is precisely the subject of this verse. Here was a man who was obeying the rules of his company only when he was forced into participation by fear of rebuke. How much better it would have been for him to obey for the sake of being able to know down deep inside of himself that he had pleased God.

Verse six is an admonition for us to support these legitimate public officials and the duties they discharge with the tribute that we are expected to pay. No one particularly enjoys paying taxes, but it is by that method that a great nation like the United States, can continue to exist. This provides for them to" . . .attend continually . . ." How much better it is to elect and financially support these men and women who attain public office so that they will not be tempted to yield to the bribery attempts of the criminal.

Verse seven makes a summary statement of our attitudes in relationships. Ours is not to be a community of Christians that is characterized by griping and complaining. We are to submit readily, without pride, to the positions of authority that have been placed over us. Those authoritative positions may be parents, church officials, school officials, law enforcement officials, or elected officials. Whoever they are, and whatever position they hold, we still owe them honor and respect regardless of personal disagreements.

Now we move to our second section of chapter thirteen:
8 Owe no man anything, but to love one another: for he that loveth another hath fulfilled the law.
9 For this, Thou shalt not commit adultery, Thou shalt not kill, Thou shalt not steal, Thou shalt not bear false witness, Thou shalt not covet; and if there be any other commandment, it is briefly comprehended in this saying, namely, Thou shalt love thy neighbour as thyself.
10 Love worketh no ill to his neighbor: therefore love is the fulfilling of the law.
11 And that, knowing the time, that now it is high time to awake out of sleep: for

now is our salvation nearer than when we believed.
12 The night is far spent, the day is at hand: let us therefore cast off the works of darkness, and let us put on the armour of light.
13 Let us walk honestly, as in the day; not in rioting and drunkenness, not in chambering and wantonness, not in strife and envying.
14 But put ye on the Lord Jesus Christ, and make not provision for the flesh, to fulfil the lusts thereof.

Verse eight may appear out of date in this modern day of easy credit. Its injunction is clear! As believers, we are to pay off everyone we owe. We are to get out of debt so that we are not in financial bondage to anyone. The only debt we are to owe anyone is our love for them.

As you know, in the Greek there are various words with different meanings which we translate in the English, "love." The particular Greek word for love in this verse is "agapan." This word represents God's love. When we love our fellow man, it is not to be with normal, brotherly love. It is to be a love that comes through us from God to others.

Verse nine lets us know that believers are not exempted from keeping the righteous aspects of the Mosaic law. In this verse, we have those parts of the Ten Commandments that specifically deal with our relationships with others. Although we are not bound by the law, we must always remember that the moral codes built into the law are the highest standard of conduct ever given to mankind.

However, there is another dimension, a dimension of love and not of human logic. That is why we are told to love one another as we love ourselves. As perfect in design as was the law, love moves our concern for the plight of others to a nobler and more sacrificial plane. Such love has no bounds. It will transcend all racial and socio-economic barriers to say, "I love you." Verse ten completes the thought begun in verse nine. The word, "worketh," expresses a never-ending attitude. We are to love our neighbor without ceasing. The man who plans some sort of ill against his neighbor is a man that is out of fellowship with God.

Verse eleven, when seen in the original language, does not mean by its use of the word, "season," that there is a particular time being denoted. It actually can refer to any time when certain circumstances exist. As we view the world-scene in light of scriptural prophecies, there is no doubt whatever that we are living during a time when it is needful for us to be fully awake spiritually.

Paul believed that the return of the Lord could be at any moment. He speaks in this verse of our salvation being nearer than when we believed. Always remember that salvation is in three tenses. We were saved from the penalty of sin, we are day-by-day being saved from the power of sin, and one day we shall be saved from the very presence of sin. It is that latter phase of which Paul is speaking here.

Oh, Dear Reader, if the coming of Jesus could be so near in those ancient days, how much nearer must His coming be today? Most assuredly, we are not faced with the same wretched conditions in America as were those long-dead believers in Rome. Nevertheless, the mental anguish and spiritual wars of the modern saint compel him to cry, "Oh, come, Lord Jesus, come!" It seems to me that we are facing one of three realities in the near future. We will have either a revival, we will be ruined, or we will witness the return of Chris t. I am thoroughly convinced that Jesus will come very soon! While I would never be an unscriptural date-setter, I would still suggest that I believe that Jesus will come before the year 2000 has arrived, and in that conviction I rejoice.

Verse twelve uses a figure of speech, "the night is far spent." Two things are implied by Paul in this verse. First, the bright day of Christ's return is very near because the night is almost over. Second, the darkest hours of the night are just before the dawn; Hold on, dear reader, we are almost there; joy comes in the morning!

What is the "day" that is at hand? I believe that this is an allusion by Paul to the rapture of the church when we shall be removed from this wicked world. Previews of the Great Tribulation are everywhere. The spirit of the anti-Christ can be sensed in the proliferation of identification techniques; the computer age has made personal privacy a luxury of the past. But, thank God, we will all be gone!

Therefore, Paul advises us to "... cast off the works of darkness." We cannot be neutral. We must separate ourselves from the dark and seamy things of this life. Continually bathing in the water of God's Word can keep us clean before God. Upon entering the corridors of reading that wind through the various books of the Bible, a believer soon finds that each verse becomes an oasis that is full of the sweet waters of eternity. Both by drinking from the fountains of the Word and washing briskly in it, the believer is made spotless before God as an acceptable vessel of service.

What is this "armor of light?" This special armor is truth. Truth always can withstand Satan. Remember, Jesus is the way, the truth, and the life. Let Him protect and lead; He is Truth and Light!

Verse thirteen warns us to walk as in the day. The Bible tells us that men love darkness rather than light because their deeds are evil. Wherever we are and whatever we do, our words and actions should be as pure as they would be in the brilliance of the noonday before God and the whole world.

Paul lists six sins that the believer must avoid:
(1) Rioting: merry-making that is usually associated with high levels of alcohol consumption;
(2) Drunkenness: occasional or frequent drinking of alcoholic beverages;
(3) Chambering: sexual promiscuity;
(4) Wantonness: lust, lewdness, and sexual perversion;
(5) Strife: sowing discord among friends and brethren;
(6) Envying: being a rival or encouraging rivalries.

Verse fourteen gives us the secret for overcoming the sins just mentioned. Since the believer is saved and indwelt by the Spirit of Christ (Romans 8:9), putting on Christ does not refer to salvation. Instead, it is the outward display of an inward reality. The only way that is possible is to avoid "making provision for the flesh." Here is an example. If you are a chain smoker, the only way to quit, if that is your desire, is get rid of your cigarettes. That means not saving an extra pack in the cabinet "just in case." If you do that, you are "making provision" for the flesh, and you are not putting on Christ!

Chapter Fourteen

Consecration Introduced

It seems almost needless that we should require any instruction in the way that we are to treat our fellow believers, especially those who have not matured in the faith by virtue of their recent conversion. Yet, Paul, by the inspiration of God, pens this chapter in direct response to that problem. I wish that it were not so, but we are often impatient with the person who is stumbling along in his first steps of his new-found faith. With that in mind, let us consider these opening verses:

1 Him that is weak in the faith receive ye, but not to doubtful disputations.
2 For one believeth that he may eat all things: another, who is weak, eateth herbs.
3 Let not him that eateth despise him that eateth not; and let not him which eateth not judge him thateateth: for God hath received him.
4 Who art thou that judgest another man's servant? to his own master he standeth or falleth. Yea, he shall be holden up: for God is able to make him stand.
5 One man esteemeth one day above another: another esteemeth every day alike. Let every man be fully persuaded in his own mind.
6 He that regardeth the day, regardeth it unto the Lord; and he that regardeth not the day, to the Lord he doth not regard it. He that eateth, eateth to the Lord, for he giveth God thanks; and he that eateth not, to the Lord he eateth not, and giveth God thanks.
7 For none of us liveth to himself, and no man dieth to himself.

Verse one speaks of newborn Christians as being "weak in the faith." This phrase, "weak in the faith," should not be taken as a criticism of the new Christian. He is weak in the same way that a newborn baby is weak. It is not a willing or volitional weakness resulting from personal failure; it is merely a weakness that is natural because of a lack of experience in learning to trust God. He has not matured. Especially does he have spiritual difficulty if he is a recent convert from a pagan religion or from Judaism.

We need to be very careful in the church concerning how we use such a person. It is unwise to put him in a place of authority before he has had ample opportunity to mature. That is the meaning of " . . . not to doubtful disputations." In the original language, this means that he lacks the necessary discernment to rightly distinguish in issues that involve wisdom and foolishness, truth and error. Most often, the new believer is so excited about the fact that his sins have been washed away in the blood of Jesus that he has a tendency to overlook the guidelines of the fundamental doctrines of our faith. Such zeal, while admirable, and in most cases too soon ended, can be disruptive to the fellowship of the church and injurious to the spiritual growth of the new convert unless channeled properly.

Verse two shares an example of a situation of relatively minor importance that can be blown out of proportion by the young believer. The mature saint understands the Word of God concerning the proper diet for the believer. He has taken note that Peter on the rooftop at Joppa had been shocked at the Lord's invitation for him to kill and eat animals that had been labeled "unclean" under the law (Acts 10:13). In this dispensation of the church age, it is acceptable before the Lord for us to eat anything.

However, the immature convert, especially if he has come from a background that forbids the eating of meats, may insist on eating herbs (vegetables) only. A very prominent group in our day that has a gross misunderstanding on this subject is the denomination known as the Seventh-Day Adventist Church. This church is composed of many wonderful people but they stumble because of their inability to understand the correct relationship between law and grace. Paul's commentary in this verse is that the person who holds the doctrine of vegetarianism as definite scriptural teaching is definitely weak in the faith.

Verse three continues this illustration of diet as viewed by mature and immature believers. The basic thrust of this verse is that our various feelings about the "rightness" or "wrongness" of what we eat should never be a test of fellowship. How often this is so! Some pastors will have nothing to do with other pastors who do not embrace the same view of prophecy as they espouse. I have known religious leaders who have refused to participate in city-wide evangelistic crusades because of the presence of some "liberal" churches on the list of sponsoring churches. It is my conviction that we need to be very careful how we apply the terms "liberal" or "conservative." Sometimes, these terms are more relative than accurate. To some observers, I am liberal; to others, I am conservative.

This brings an interesting question. Is there a test of fellowship? I think so. I determine my fellowship based on three criteria. Does this person believe that salvation is in the shed blood of Jesus Christ and in His shed blood alone? Does this person believe every word of the Bible to be the literal Word of God? Does this person believe that the Spirit of God indwells the believer, giving him power to live victoriously in this present world? If he believes these three things, I can have fellowship with him. While we may differ on interpretations of other biblical teachings, we can have joy together in what Jesus has done for us.

Verse four describes the "gray" areas of personal experiences. There are some activities we do in our daily lives that are not discussed at all in the Scriptures. They are not listed as godly, and they are not listed as ungodly. Obviously, if the Bible makes a clear statement, such as, "Thou shalt not covet," the issue is settled. Here, in this verse, however, we are addressing the multitude of "gray" situations, and in these areas, God may lead one believer to do one thing that He will not allow another believer to do.

This verse asks an important question. Who has the right to go into a man's home and criticise the way his host's maid serves the meal? The answer is obvious. No one has that right. If the maid does not perform as she ought, she is answerable to her employer. If she performs well, she is answerable to her employer.

The phrase, "...to his own lord he standeth or falleth..." clarifies that point. That maid, to use my simple analogy, will do everything she does at that dinner with her primary desire being to please the one who hired her. Her desire to please the dinner guest is secondary to that primary desire. In a sense, if she does well, her boss will pay her well and use her again; he will make her to "stand." If she does a poor job, he will probably not ever call for her services again; he will make her to "fall."

Dear reader, we are all servants in the household of faith. God may call you to a place of service that He will never call me. He may call me to a place of service that He will never call you. Here is the good news! Whatever position we are given in the household of faith, God "is able to make us stand." Every saved person, weak or strong, is given a job to do. And he need not fail God is able to give him power to do the task and to do it right, and nobody but God has the right to judge anybody else in God's family.

Verse five uses another picture. The Old Testament law was saturated with holy days and feast days. livery Jew had to conform exactly to the commands surrounding each of these days. But we must understand--the law has two aspects. It has a righteous aspect which has to do with the inward mall, and it has a ceremonial aspect which has to do with the outer man. The righteous aspect is still binding upon the believer, but the ceremonial is not. Colossians 2:16 confirms this truth by saying, "Let no man, therefore, judge you in meat, or in drink, or in respect of an holy day, or of the sabbath day."

I think that it is important at this point that you understand that there is no such thing as a "Christian Sabbath." Saturday is the Sabbath; it always has been and always will be. Sunday is the "Lord's Day." After the resurrection of Christ, the Lord's Day became the appropriate time for public worship and was thus practiced by the church in the Book of Acts. In Acts 20:6-7 are these words: "And we sailed away from Philippi after the days of unleavened bread, and came unto them to Troas in five days, where we abode seven days. And upon the first day of the week, when the disciples came together to break bread, Paul preached unto them, ready to depart on the morrow, and continued his speech until midnight."

According to these verses, Paul and his party abode in Troas for a full week-- seven days. Obviously, they could have chosen any day to worship. Which day did they choose? They chose to worship on the first day of the week, the Lord's Day, not the seventh day, the Sabbath. Therefore, it is clear that we are to join in public worship on the Lord's Day whenever possible.

However, sometimes it may not be possible. In the modern nation of Israel, for example, the church constitutes a very small minority of the total population. While in America, we are accustomed to businesses being opened on Saturday and closed on Sunday, the reverse is true in Israel. Therefore, most churches, out of necessity, worship on Saturday, the Sabbath. Does this break their fellowship with God? Not at all. The day of worship is an important outward observance, but the inward appropriation of Christ's shed blood is that part of man about which God is concerned.

Verse six is best understood by the prominence given to the Lord in it. Whatever day is the day that a believer worships God, God is honored. But if a man is not truly worshipping God, whatever day he chooses is to no avail because the Lord will not be honored. The condition of the heart is of greater importance than the day on the calendar.

As far as eating is concerned, the particular diet we choose will not make us more spiritual or less spiritual. In I Corinthians 8:8 are these words: "But meat commendeth us not to God; for either, if we eat, are we the better; neither, if we eat not, are we the worse."

Verse seven summarizes the relationship between the believer and all other of his brethren. We cannot isolate ourselves from the influence of others. On the other hand, we will influence others. We are a family. In life, though there may be differences of secondary doctrinal importance, we can enjoy sweet fellowship. In death, we can sorrow for fallen brethren and challenge our own survivors to live nobler lives.

We must now turn our attention to the next section of verses in chapter fourteen that deal with our personal accountability to the Lord:
8 For whether we live, we live unto the Lord; and whether we die, we die unto the Lord; whether we live, therefore, or die, we are the Lord's.
9 For to this end Christ both died, and rose, and revived, that he might be Lord both of the dead and living.
10 But why dost thou judge thy brother? Or why doest thou set at naught thy brother? For we shall all stand
before the judgement seat of Christ.
11 For it is written, as I live, saith the Lord, every knee shall bow to me, and every tongue shall confess to God.
12 So then, every one of us shall give account of himself to God."

Verse eight expands the seventh verse we have just seen. Indeed, for the believer, this is one of the Bible's greatest promises. Whether we live or whether we die, God is always aware of our needs. On the human level, we see death as the end of life, but that is not the message of this verse. This verse expressly teaches that life moves into the dimension of death without a break or a barrier and that God never fails to claim us as His own. Thank God that we do not have to fear the uncertain tomorrows of our lives!

Verse nine explains in succinct fashion why there is no dread of death for the believer. Jesus entered both realms. As incarnate God, our Lord Jesus willingly laid down His life to identify with those who physically die. By His bodily resurrection, He showed the world that death can be overcome. therefore, Christ and Christ alone can claim lordship over life and death. That being so, it behooves us to recognize Him as Lord for the eternal welfare of our own selves.

Verse ten asks a question that is desperately needed for today's church member to hear. Most modern churches are filled with murmuring, slander, and backbiting. Harsh and unfair attitudes of judgmentalism tear away at the effectiveness of the average church.

A very personal statement is made, and then it is repeated. Twice we are bluntly challenged with, "Why dost thou?" You can almost hear the righteous indignation boiling in the breast of Paul as he looks directly at each of us. We are without excuse if we think there is justification for destroying the character of another.

The most spineless and hypocritical people I know are those who slink around, having secret meetings, and viciously trying to destroy a servant of God. We are urged by Paul to remember that we must all stand before the judgment bar. Each person has enough with which to contend in himself without trying to measure the spirituality of his brother, when, in fact, he does not have all the facts.

Verse eleven quotes Isaiah 45:23. In Isaiah, this statement looks forward to the millennial reign of Jesus. Its application is just as meaningful for the Christian. The certainty of the statement is bound up in the words, "As I live." Just as surely as Jesus lives and reigns at the right hand of the

Father is just as surely that every person will one day forget his own pettiness and the flaws of his neighbor so that he will fall on his knees before Christ and honor Him!

Verse twelve states the final conclusion. We will each stand before God. At that time, we will answer for the activities of no other person but ourselves. That ought to sober our thinking and modify our attitudes toward those around us.

The following section of verses is especially written for our consideration of the importance of our influence for good or bad upon our neighbor:

13 Let us not, therefore, judge one another any more; but judge this, rather: that no man put a stumbling block or an occasion to fall in his brother's way.
14 I know, and am persuaded by the Lord Jesus, that there is nothing unclean of itself; but to him that esteemeth anything to be unclean, to him it is unclean.
15 But if thy brother be grieved with thy meat, now walkest thou not charitably. Destroy not him with thy meat, for whom Christ died.
16 Let not then your good be evil spoken of;
17 For the kingdom of God is not meat and drink, but righteousness, and peace, and joy in the Holy Ghost
18 For he that in these things serueth Christ is acceptable to God, and approved of men.
19 Let us, therefore, follow after the things which make for peace, and things with which one may edify another.
20 For meat destroy not the work of God. All things are indeed pure; but it is evil for that man who eateth with offense.
21 It is good neither to eat flesh, nor to drink wine, nor anything by which thy brother stumbleth, or is offended, or is made weak.

Verse thirteen quickly admonishes us to quit judging others "any more," suggesting that if we are participants in such negative activities, we should immediately put an end to it. In light of the opening verse of this chapter being addressed to the stronger Christian, we may safely apply this verse to the attitude of judgmentalism that may exist between the stronger believer and the younger believer. The only kind of judging that is honored by the Lord is the judgment of oneself. Especially if we find ourselves in a position of influence with the less mature, we would do well to examine the way we appear before them, lest we cause them to stumble in the faith. The phrase, "occasion for falling," is better translated from the Greek to give the idea of "setting a trap." Oh, how sad that so many who are weak in the faith come to some churches looking for fellowship that will help them to grow in the faith, but instead they find themselves beginning to deteriorate spiritually because of caustic attitudes and judgmental pettiness.

Verse fourteen is too often used as artillery for the liberal believer who wants to live and do as he chooses. Frequently this verse is quoted by religious supporters of social drinking. However, this should never be read as a blanket statement in allowing a man to live as he pleases. Remember, this chapter is not discussing the sins that are clearly delineated in the Word of God. It is directed toward the "gray" areas that a careful study of the Bible will yield no statement or principle concerning. It is a distortion of the Scriptures to try to make this verse applicable to all human conduct. I must emphasize again that Paul is speaking of a person's privilege to determine a thing as clean or unclean in those areas that are not addressed either directly or indirectly in God's Word. It is a statement of "liberty,' not license.

Verse fifteen provides a quality, or attribute, of Christ that we would do well to emulate. He loved us so much that He sacrificed His very life for us. Surely, we can inconvenience ourselves in terms of diet or some habit so that a weaker brother will not stumble.

Do not be confused by the use of the word "meat." This word is an old word that may be used as a general term foray kind of food—meat, fruit, vegetables, etc. The verse is quite clear. Even if you enjoy meat of any kind, whether it is actual meat or some other kind of food, if you are with a weaker brother who sincerely believes that the eating of such food is a sin, then you are not to offend him by eating it in his presence. This verse does not at all mean that you are to cease forever from eating that food. Neither does it mean, as the Seventh Day Adventist suggests, that you are never again to allow meat as a part of your diet, and that you are to become a strict vegetarian. The Seventh Day Adventist inaccurately translates "meat" as used here, to mean only meat and no other kind of food. That is a gross error in translation.

We have great liberty in Christ, but we should never abuse that liberty at the expense of hurting a brother's growth 'in the Lord. Our stubborn refusal to give up temporarily something that we do not perceive as wrong, but he does, may "destroy" him. Does this mean that we may cause him to lose his salvation? Of course not! We have already seen in the study of this book that absolutely nothing can separate us from the love of Jesus. However, we may destroy the weaker believer's confidence, his assurance, his steadfastness in the work of God. Please remember this. The man who asserts, "I'll do what I please because I know my rights, is a very unspiritual man, because when a man is saved, he loses all his rights to Jesus Christ. That being so we should readily consider in every situation the good of our weaker brother and the glory of our Lord. Personal preferences should be laid aside in order that our brother may grow in grace.

Verse sixteen is a command! I believe that it has two applications for the believer and both are accurate. First, and primarily, the context in which we find this verse reminds us that the good that we have done for Christ can be tarnished by a lack of consideration for the weaker areas in a brother's life. Let me give you an example. On a Sunday morning, a visiting preacher thunders home the great truths of God's Word with many people responding to his invitation for salvation at the end of his message. On the way to the home of one of the church members for his noon lunch, he asks the member to stop at a shopping center. The member, a new convert, informs the preacher that he believes that it is wrong to do shopping of any kind on the Lord's Day. In spite of his protest, the preacher forces him to pull into the parking lot and wait while he purchases a few items. What do you think that member's attitude will be at the evening worship hour? It will be impossible for him to respect the man of God as he had in the morning service. The preacher's "good" (his preaching) will be "evil spoken of"(not held in its deserved esteem) because of the afternoon incident.

Second, whether we are mature or immature in the faith, no one has the right to judge the good that we do with unfair criticism. We are commanded to defend our good works for God!

Verse seventeen uses an interesting term, "the kingdom of God."

There is another similar term that is often confused with this one. The term is "the kingdom of heaven." To correctly understand this verse, we need to differentiate between these two terms.

"The kingdom of heaven" is anywhere in God's creation in which men live outwardly by the laws of God. Of course, in heaven the saints who are already there live in "the kingdom of heaven." The same is true of angels. On earth, the redeemed children of God live in the "kingdom of heaven." But also included are the moral, upright, inhabitants of this planet who have never known God. Remember, on the outside, these people live by the very highest standards set forth in God's Word although they are not saved. It is possible, therefore, for a man to live in "the kingdom of heaven" without actually going to heaven.

"The kingdom of God" is occupied only by those who are saved. Being moral and upright will never provide access to this special sphere. Whenever this term is used, it is expressly indicative of the saints and the saints alone.

Now return to verse seventeen. By understanding the meaning of "the kingdom ' of God," we can better understand the verse. Dietary restrictions have to do with the outer man and is a throw-back to the ceremonial laws of the Old Testament. The entire thrust of why Jesus came was to show us the way to inward righteousness, joy and peace. He did not come to reinforce the dead ritualism of outward acts. Whether we are vegetarian or not does not determine our spirituality.

Verse eighteen shows the blessed state of the man who is truly a man of grace and faith. We have two relationships with which we must concern ourselves. There is our vertical relationship with God, and there is our horizontal relationship with our fellow man. No man can genuinely be right with the one unless he is also right with the other. The word, "approved," as used here, means from the Greek, "to fully honor after close examination." This is a skeptical world in its view of the Christian community. In fact, the world will often more carefully scrutinize the lifestyles of the believer than will his brethren in the church. So, when the world says that a man is "for real," it says much about the believer and brings honor to his Savior.

Verse nineteen contains two wonderful conditions that ought to exist by the introduction of a group of Christians into a society in the throes of confusion. There is no other person on the face of this earth, besides the believer, who can bring peace to this old world. That peculiar trait among the household of faith has resulted in church-founded orphanages,' colleges, and a multitude of charitable organizations. Thousands are daily looking to legal and illegal drugs for peace. They buy lavish homes and pour fortunes into a variety of recreations. But peace, real peace, is a gift of God, to be found only in the believer. By a faithful witness to the troubled, we can communicate God's peace from our hearts to theirs. In so doing, we "edify" them; that is, we build them up.

Verse twenty should cause every believer to pause for sincere reflection. A good paraphrase for the opening word sof this verse might be, "Do not tear down the building of God in a fuss over food!" What does this mean? Dear reader, some things in the work of God are of far greater importance than a heated Bible argument over whether we should be vegetarians or not. Now, while there may be some significance that should be attached to such a discussion, when compared with the great commandment to be a soul-winner, we must admit that quibbling over what we eat is somewhat silly.

Further, this verse indicates that for a more mature believer to suddenly develop a head strong spirit and stubbornly trample over the protests of a weaker believer is to sin. This produces divisions between brethren in the church. Therefore, God's great work suffers. Chain reactions, of a hostile nature, can have their beginnings in such a trivial way. We need to be very careful that we are not found being the cause of uncountable harm.

Verse twenty-one concludes this whole matter. We are not "to do anything" that may cause our brother to stumble. If you will read I Corinthians 6:19-20, you will find that the believer is not his own. He has been bought with a price. If we compare the puny sacrifices that we are sometimes asked to make on behalf of a lesser brother with the ultimate sacrifice that Christ made for us at Calvary, it becomes crystal clear that the little we do is not worthy to be measured. Our weaker brother must not suffer.

Now, we come to two verses that I have used often in my daily life and in my conversations with others. Throughout this chapter, our attentions have been focused upon the relationship between the stronger believer and the weaker believer. Here, we will -apply what we have learned:

22 Hast thou faith? have it to thyself before God. Happy is he that condemneth not himself in that thing which he alloweth.
23 And he that doubteth is damned if he eat, because he eateth not of faith: for whatsoever is not of faith is sin.

Verse twenty-two reminds us to avoid any appearance of self-boasting. I must not strut my "superior spirituality" because I am not convicted by the Spirit about matters that may cause conviction in another. If I am not convicted, I should graciously express my gratitude before the Lord. We can be happy that we are not judged. But the implication seems to be that even in those areas in which we may feel perfectly comfortable to participate, God expects us to honor the feelings of others who may sincerely disagree or else we sin.

Verse twenty-three should have a gold star placed by it. Paul is teaching us that whatever we do must be done with the one hundred percent assurance that what we do has the approval of God. Often, young people will ask me if it is all right to smoke cigarettes or go to the prom. My stock answer is always the same. I quote this verse and then tell them that the fact that there is a question in their minds confirms that they do not have a total assurance of faith about it.

Everything we do can have God's power if we are sure of His endorsement before participating. If there is the slightest doubt about the rightness or wrongness of an endeavor, it is wrong to do it.

Chapter Fifteen

Consecration Continued

      This wonderful chapter is a continuation, especially in its opening verses, of the bond that exists between brothers in the Lord. Our first section shows that:

1 We then that are strong ought to bear the infirmities of the weak, and not to please ourselves.
2 Let every one of us please his neighbour for his good to edification.
3 For even Christ pleased not himself; but, as it is written, The reproaches of them that reproached thee fell on me.
4 For whatsoever things were written aforetime were written for our learning, that we through patience and comfort of the scriptures might have hope.
5 Now the God of patience and consolation grant you to be like-minded one toward another according to Christ Jesus:
6 That ye may with one mind and one mouth glorify God, even the Father of our Lord Jesus Christ.
7 Wherefore receive ye one another, as Christ also received us to the glory of God.
8 Now I say that Jesus Christ was a minister of the circumcision for the truth of God, to confirm the promises made unto the fathers:
9 And that the Gentiles might glorify God for his mercy; as it is written, For this cause I will confess to thee among the Gentiles, and sing unto thy name.
10 And again he saith, Rejoice, ye Gentiles; with his people.
11 And again, Praise the Lord, all ye Gentiles; and laud him, all ye people.
12 And again, Isaiah saith, There shall be a root of Jesse, and he that shall rise to reign over the Gentiles; in him shall the Gentiles trust.
13 Now the God of hope fill you with all joy and peace in believing, that ye may abound in hope, through the power of the Holy Ghost.

      Verse one may be more accurately translated from the Greek as, "We who are fully grounded in the faith have an obligation to bear and to keep on bearing the infirmities of the babes in Christ." The word, "strong," should not be used in reference to physical strength. Oh no! It refers to those who are morally and spiritually strong.

We do not have to look very far to find the unfortunate who are in need. Some are sick. Some are destitute of even the basic requirements for living. Some are lonely. And some are lost. Our world is in a convulsion of tears, sobbing for someone to care.

Ours is a mandate from heaven that we not just live "to please ourselves." The life of Christ is a life that challenges us to care for that person with a hurting heart. This old world needs Jesus. And, as the old proverb says, "The only Jesus that some people will ever see is you." The measure of a Spirit-controlled life is the active involvement of the saint in the hurts of the less fortunate.

Verse two sets the boundary line of our activity with our needy brother or neighbor. That line is drawn by the use of the word, "good." In the English language, "good" is attached to a variety of objects or conditions. For example, we may have a good time, a good car, a good meal, or converse with a good person. But in the Greek, the specific word that is translated "good" actually means "noble" or "virtuous." How does this relate to this verse? Whatever we do for or with our neighbor should be tested by this question, "Will this make him nobler or more virtuous?" All other activities should be avoided under the biblical principle of separation.

Verse three hearkens back to verse one and advises us to think of the good of others before thinking of ways that we may be benefited. It is also a quote from Psalm 69:9. I think this verse expresses a beautiful thought. Christ bore our reproaches, so we should just as willingly bear the reproaches of our fellow man. When our neighbor is scorned and ridiculed and slandered because of his stand for things that are right, we ought to be the first in line to stand with him, regardless of the abuse we suffer in doing so.

We must all certainly agree that one of the most outstanding attributes of our Lord was His willingness to be selfless, not selfish, in His care for all mankind. He suffered as no man has ever suffered so that we could be saved. That kind of sacrificial compassion for an undeserving world is the kind that we should readily share as a lifestyle.

Verse four should be read with gratitude to our wonderful God. One of the mainstays in my ministry has been my insistence that the Bible is the verbally inspired Word of God. By verbally inspired, I mean that the Bible is word-by-word the Word of God! Each word is exactly the word that God chose to be penned through the instrumentality of a human writer. The Word of God is inerrant; it is infallible! We can depend on any of it! We can depend on all of it!

Dear reader, "whatsoever things were written" means that the entire Bible is the object of the blessed promise in this verse. And what is the promise? The Bible has been written to instruct us so that we may have hope. In the original language, the word that is used for "hope" in this verse actually is better translated as "certain expectation or anticipation." Only in the words of the Scriptures can we find the assurance we need to look forward to all the tomorrows of our lives. Indeed, there is comfort in the Scriptures!

Verse five reveals two characteristics of Almighty God that we ordinarily regard as human qualities. Those characteristics are "patience" and "comfort." The admonition of this verse is that we be in harmony with each other; that is, we should have the mind of Christ. I think it is interesting that the implication of the verse is that if we have patience in our dealings with our fellow man and if we take the time to comfort him, we will then be in harmony with him. Patience requires us to take plenty of time before jumping to conclusions. Comfort is a trait that acts with all due haste even when inconvenienced. We must always live in our interpersonal relationships by the words of John 15:12, "This is my commandment, that ye love one another, even as I have loved you."

Verse six is more correctly translated, "that ye may with one mind and one mouth glorify and keep on glorifying God." How desperately we need unity in the church! Unity is different from union. Many churches have union; only a few have unity. Union can result from bodies sitting together in a building, but unity can only come about by a common spirit. Fellowship is not the result of people belonging to the same church. It is a family condition resulting from the experience of the new birth. Difficulties in local churches would be very nearly eliminated with this unity of purpose, heart, and mind. I believe that the great need of the church of the Lord Jesus Christ is for harmony among its members.

Verse seven twice uses a form of the verb, "receive." In the Greek, it conveys the meaning of receiving without ever ceasing to receive. It is to receive as Christ received. His love for us drives Him to continue to receive us to Himself during the times that we are unlovely as well as the times that we are lovely. Remember the words of Christ and mark them well when He said in John 6:37, ". . . him that cometh to me I will in no wise cast out" (John 6:37). Regardless of our faithfulness or faithlessness, Christ has promised that He will always love and honor us, and never reject us.

Please note that we are told to " . . . receive ye one another . . . " Let there be no question about it! When we meet someone who has been born again, that person is to be accepted by us without reservation. There is absolutely no justification for any kind of prejudice that makes the household of faith off-limits for anyone because of race, nationality, etc. The sole qualification is that of atonement through the blood of Jesus Christ.

Verse eight speaks of the "circumcision." The circumcision refers to Israel. Christ was born, lived, and died in accordance with the prophecies of His life that had been made by the prophets in the Old Testament. Jesus was God's statement of His own faithfulness in performing to the most incidental of details the promises He had made. As God's method of keeping His word, Jesus became a "minister." Had Jesus not fulfilled these prophecies, a huge, uncrossable gap would have occurred in the Bible. Salvation would have been impossible for the human family. But as God's minister of truth, Jesus fulfilled the requirements of the Old Testament so that He could become the Savior of the New Testament.

Verse nine continues this theme. Paul is attempting to show that the gospel message is for everyone. At first glance, it may seem that God loved only the Jew. But as we proceed through the Old Testament, it becomes obvious that God was developing His own master plan for saving the entire world. It is interesting to note that verse eight shows that the Jews can praise God because of truth, but the Gentile can praise God because of mercy. The Jew was blessed by the truth of the law that was given to them through

Moses. The Gentile was not given the law. There was no element of written truth toward which the Gentile could look for spiritual guidance. Therefore, truly it can be said that the Gentile is saved through the mercies of God.

We also have in verse nine a quote that can be found in two places, Psalm 18:49 and II Samuel 22:50. The phrase, "it is written," is more accurately translated from the Greek, "as it has been written." In other words, by the mood expressed in the Greek grammatical structure of this phrase, the fact of God's praise among the Gentiles has already taken place. Paul is the person who is doing the quoting here, and he is doing it in relation to his missionary work among the Gentiles. But remember that this quotation from two Old Testament references indicates that even during the period of the law, prior to Calvary, God had extended mercy to certain ones in the Gentile world and received praise for it. I cite as an example the mercy granted to Rahab the harlot just before the conquest of Jericho.

Verse ten should be read by us who are Gentiles as a command to praise the Lord. This verse quotes Deuteronomy 32:43, which is a cry by the Israelites for the Gentiles to sing with them the song of deliverance. This same feeling is expressed again in Psalm 117:1. I think that we can all recognize that Jews and Gentiles have never really joined in one world-wide effort to praise the Lord. The full completion of this command to praise God, therefore, will not find its completion until the sweeping revival of the great tribulation.

Verse eleven may be viewed as a repetition of verse ten. It must be seen as a prophetic statement for future days. Immediately following the revival of the tribulation, the millennial kingdom of our Lord will begin. Universal praise will rise in jubilant worship to the Lord Jesus Christ who will rule from the throne of David in Jerusalem.

Verse twelve quotes Isaiah 11:10, which is an obvious prophecy of the Messiah. Please note that the Messiah must be of "the root of Jesse." Of course, Jesus fulfills this qualification. An examination of the genealogy of Jesus in the third chapter of Luke will provide sufficient evidence that Christ was a descendant of David, the son of Jesse, through Mary. Jesus is "the root of Jesse."

I think it is important to identify a gigantic problem facing the Jew. He is looking for the coming of the Messiah, having rejected Jesus. But this verse says that the Messiah must be in the line of David as one of his descendants. Historically, we know that the Roman general, Titus, destroyed all Jewish family records when he overthrew Jerusalem in 70 A.D. That being true, there is absolutely no way to trace the bloodline of any Jew living today back to David. So, as Paul affirms here, our hope must be in Jesus Christ. He will gloriously rule over all nations one wonderful day.

Verse thirteen reminds us that our God is "the God of hope." And He wants us to abound in hope. I think that is wonderful! We need not ever be in despair. The God of hope will supply us with hope — abundantly! Four words of encouragement are in this verse: joy, peace, power, and of course, hope. The joy and peace result from believing. When we can finally arrive at the point in our spiritual maturity that we can simply believe God in every situation, we will experience the wonder of inward joy and peace, despite the external turbulence that may surround us. The power of the Holy Spirit is better seen and appreciated by the believer who has learned the sweetness of joy and the security of peace through belief in God's Word.

Now let us move to our next section of verses in this chapter. In it, Paul elaborates on the various aspects of his ministry.

14 And I myself also am persuaded of you, my brethren, that ye also are full of goodness, filled with all knowledge, able also to admonish one another.
15 Nevertheless, brethren, I have written the more boldly unto you in some sort, as putting you in mind, because of the grace that is given to me of God,
16 That I should be the minister of Jesus Christ to the Gentiles, ministering the gospel of God, that the offering up of the Gentiles might be acceptable, being sanctified by the Holy Ghost.
17 I have therefore whereof I may glory through Jesus Christ in those things which pertain to God.
18 For I will not dare to speak of any of those things which Christ hath not wrought by me, to make the Gentiles obedient, by word and deed,
19 Through many signs and wonders, by the power of the Spirit of God; so that from Jerusalem, and round about unto Illyrieum, I have fully preached the gospel of Christ.

20 Yea, so have I strived to preach the gospel, not where Christ was named, lest I should build upon another man's foundation:
21 But as it is written, To whom he was notspoken of, they shall see: and they that have not heard shall understand.

Verse fourteen seems to make it clear that the many things that Paul has said about human relationships in chapters thirteen, fourteen, and fifteen were not specifically addressed to the Roman believers. He says that they are "full of goodness, filled with all knowledge, able to admonish one another." These are great words of compliment. If this church is so mature, as he suggests, then why does he so strongly warn them about the ways they are to treat each other as he has done so many times in the immediately preceding chapters? The answer to that question is obvious. Whenever things are running smoothly in our church relationships, we ought to remind ourselves that such a sweet and precious family spirit must be guarded and never taken for granted.

Verse fifteen completes Paul's advice that was begun in verse fourteen. Here, he justifies his reasons for speaking so boldly to the believers in Rome. He says that it was "because of the grace that is given to me of God." For a man to be a spokesman for the Lord, he must speak from the point of God's authority, not his own. That authority always is built upon the grace of God. For Paul', as for all true men of God, grace for authoritative teaching and preaching is manifested in two aspects. First, there is the grace of salvation that is by the common faith in the atonement and is shared by all believers. Second is the grace of being chosen by God to preach His Word. No man can preach as boldly as he ought unless he knows that he has been saved and that he has been called to preach the unsearchable riches of Christ.

Verse sixteen can be better understood by comparing "minister" as it is used in this verse with the same word's usage in Romans 13:6. From this comparison, a needed definition for today's church emerges. A minister, in the governmental sense, has the authority to oversee all the various situations that have been delegated to him by the law of the land. Similarly, a minister of the gospel in the role of pastor, is the authoritative voice in the church. In spite of the mistaken notion, that is so prevalent today, that-the deacons are to be the church's administrative officers, there is no such teaching to be found in the Bible.

"Ministering the gospel" is better translated as "sacrificing the gospel." This does not seem to be in harmony with the Scriptures. Closer examination shows the clear meaning of the phrase, however. Paul is attempting to identify his role as a minister of the gospel to the Gentiles. He likens that role to that of the Old Testament priest who presented and proclaimed the blood of animals as a covering for sins. As a preacher of the gospel, Paul is holding before all the world the blood of Jesus Christ as the "once-for-all" sacrifice for the cleansing of sin.

When that presentation of the gospel was made by Paul to the Gentile world, it provided an access to the Father by which they were "acceptable." It must be plainly understood that acceptability by God is a result of sanctification by the Spirit which results from justification by Jesus. The entire trinity of the Godhead is involved in the process of mans reconciliation. That is the real beauty of verse sixteen. The role of the minister and the messages he bears are both contained in it.

Verse seventeen is another example of Paul's constant refusal to take pride in any of his personal achievements. He fully recognized that anything good that he did must be laid at the feet of Jesus. I believe that nothing could have nauseated the Apostle Paul more than to hear someone applaud his accomplishments as a messenger of God. It is a sad commentary in our day that the modern pastor has established for himself the same criteria for a measure of professional success as that of the world. If a pastor has more "nickels and noses" this year than last, he is a success; if not, he is a failure. How foolish! God does not ask us to be successful; He asks us to be faithful.

Verse eighteen continues that same train of thought. He absolutely refuses to accept any praise for anything that he has done in either word or deed. Paul was one of the most talented and capable men ever to preach the gospel. Yet, his phenomenal work was the result of his availability rather than his ability. Paul found no greater thrill than magnifying Jesus.

Verse nineteen has the phrase, "through the power of signs and wonders," that should more accurately be translated, "by the power of signs and wonders. You will notice that the next phrase is "by the power of the Holy Spirit." Paul lays no claim to the merits of his ministry. As far as he is concerned, his work revolved around the manifestation of signs and wonders which were, in turn, the work of the Spirit in him. We must always remind ourselves, especially if we are preachers of the gospel, that what we do, if it has any eternal value, is the work of God in us.

You can also see in this verse the fervency of Paul in carrying the message of Christ. He preached it with all of his might in the major city of Jerusalem that already appreciated Jehovah God. But just as intensely, Paul preached the gospel to a small, totally pagan town like Illyricum, a small Roman village across the Adriatic Sea. In other words, we ought to preach the gospel everywhere with all the strength that we can muster. God grant it to be so!

Verse twenty provides a glimpse of Paul's method in choosing routes for his missionary journeys. He loved to visit places that had never been exposed to the gospel message. His heart was in the founding of churches. There may be a reason, that is not so obvious, for his refusal to build upon another man's foundation. It is so difficult to build a dynamic church upon the foundation of a previous pastor who was not evangelistic. I think it is far easier to "start from scratch" and install the kind of principles and policies that need to be used from the very first.

Verse twenty-one is a quote of Isaiah 52:15, which is a Messianic prophecy that will be fulfilled when Jesus sits on the throne of David in the millennial kingdom. The partial blindness of the Jew will have been completely removed. The kingdom will have been restored. It reminds me of the song by Jim Hill that says,

"What a day that will be, When my Jesus I shall see, And I look upon His face The One who saved me by His grace."

In a broader sense, this verse is an expression of joyful praise. Jesus is coming! He really is coming!

We have now reached the final section of verses in this chapter. In these verses, we hear Paul share his desire to visit Rome:

22 For which cause also I have been much hindered from coming to you.
23 But now having no more place in these parts, and
having a great desire these many years to come unto you;
24 Whensoever I take my journey into Spain, I will come to you: for I trust to see you in my journey, and to be brought on my way thitherward by you, if first I be somewhat filled with your company.
25 But now I go unto Jerusalem to minister unto the saints.
26 For it hath pleased them of Macedonia and Achaia to make a certain contribution for the poor saints which are at Jerusalem.
27 It hath pleased them verily; and their debtors they are. For if the Gentiles have been made partakers of their spiritual things, their duty is also to minister unto them in carnal things.
28 When therefore I have performed this, and have sealed to them this fruit, I will come by you into Spain.
29 And I am sure that, when I come unto you, I shall come in the fullness of the blessing of the gospel of Christ.
30 Now I beseech you, brethren, for the Lord Jesus Christ's sake, and for the love of the Spirit, that ye strive together with me in your prayers to God for me;
31 That I may be delivered from them that do not believe in Judea; and that my service which I have for Jerusalem may be accepted of the saints;
32 That I may come unto you with joy by the will of God, and may with you be refreshed.
33 Now the God of peace be with you all. Amen.

    Verse twenty-two is Paul's explanation of why he has not already been to Rome. He had been hindered several times. Obviously, the fact that he had met obstacles indicates that he had often made an attempt to start for Rome. In chapters nineteen, twenty-three, and twenty-eight of the Book of Acts can be found references to those hindrances.

    Verse twenty-three finally brings Paul to the place that he can head for the place of his longing -- Rome. Again and again Paul had preached in virtually all the areas of Asia Minor. He had been faithful in every respect. Therefore, having completed his work by saturating these areas with the gospel, Paul can now turn his attention to Rome. How I pray that whenever I leave a place of service that I will always be able to say that I have done all that I could have done.

Verse twenty-four poses a question of minor importance. Paul is saying that on his way to Spain he will stop at Rome to visit with them for awhile. Did he ever get to Spain? No one knows for sure. It is my conviction that he did not. Nevertheless, he did go to Rome. But he did not arrive there as a preacher of the gospel, free and on his own time and will. He came in shackles as a prisoner of the state. But nevertheless, to Rome he came.

Verse twenty-five shows that Paul had one more job to do before heading for Rome. He had first to minister to the saints at Jerusalem. The word, "minister," means more than to preach the gospel. It conveys the idea of doing whatever needs to be done to help someone. I believe that this particular mission by Paul is for the purpose of taking to them the offering that he had been gathering from other churches to relieve the poverty of the saints at Jerusalem. For example, he urged the church at Corinth to give cheerfully toward this particular need (See I Corinthians 16).

Verse twenty-six is a report by Paul concerning the generosity of other churches. This verse is a wonderful commentary on the saints of Macedonia and Achaia. We know that the saints at Jerusalem were poor, many of them undoubtedly so because they had lost their worldly goods because of their uncompromising stand for Christ. But we must also remember that Macedonia was a very poor church in terms of finances. In II Corinthians 8:1-2 are these words: "Moreover, brethren, we do 'you to wit of the grace of God bestowed on the churches of Macedonia; How that in a great trial of affliction the abundance of their joy and their deep poverty abounded unto the riches of their liberality."

Why do you suppose that a church in "deep poverty" like Macedonia would contribute to another church that is poor? Other than the fact that they were people who listened to God in matters of sacrificial giving, I believe that the Macedonians saw themselves as debtors to the church at Jerusalem, because it is to the Jerusalem church that we all owe our gratitude for standing faithful in those crucial early days of the church. In like manner, we ought not ever forget the rich heritage that our forefathers have provided for us.

Verse twenty-seven continues the theme of why the Gentile churches, including Macedonia, gave so willingly to the offering for the poor at Jerusalem. However little the Macedonians had in material goods, they still were blessed with more "carnal things" than were the saints in Jerusalem. And since the believers in Jerusalem had been the source of bountiful spiritual blessings for them, it only made sense for them to return the favor in money.

Verse twenty-eight reveals Paul's determination to care for the poor saints back home. He does not trust anyone else with the project. It must be "performed." He uses the term, "sealed," which means in this usage "to certify or complete a legal document." Paul was the kind of man who could not be satisfied with jobs only half done.

Verse twenty-nine shows the confidence in the Lord that was locked in the heart of this grand apostle of grace. He was convinced that he would soon be in Rome, and he knew that his arrival would be with the full authority and blessings of Christ. Everything in Paul's life, good or bad, was for the furtherance of the gospel: "But I would ye should understand, brethren, that the things which happened to me have fallen out rather unto the furtherance of the gospel" (Philippians 1:12).

Even though some terrible adversities faced Paul in Rome, he was never intimidated by the circumstances of life. He marched forward undaunted. Pain was nothing more than a drumbeat by which he measured the impact of his witness. Whether he was loved or whether he was hated, he never quit. And more than that, because he was always careful to proceed in the center of God's will, he knew that Christ's fullness of blessing would always be his to enjoy.

Verse thirty opens with the same phrase as can be seen in Romans 12:1. It is a plea for the saints to pray for him. As you read this verse, you see that the entire trinity of the Godhead is involved in this request. Paul was headed back into Jerusalem, a place that was the home of some of his bitterest enemies. And while Paul was a totally committed man of God, he was still a human being who could suffer pain and anguish. So, he turned to the saints for intercessory prayer on his behalf.

You will note that Paul speaks here to these believers of Rome that they will "strive together" with him in prayer. This phrase, in the original language, means "to fight alongside of." Whenever a poor saint is beset by enemies and plagued by Satan, is it not wonderful when friends will encircle him with prayer support and "fight alongside" of him?

Verse thirty-one expresses Paul's fear of his enemies. The phrase, "I may be delivered," literally means, "I may be dragged out of danger." Two things were in his heart as he asked for prayer. First, he wanted victory over his foes. Second, he wanted his offering that he had collected from the churches to be satisfactory for the poor saints in Jerusalem.

Verses thirty-two and thirty-three are Paul's parting words of inward joy for the saints at Rome. He longs to enjoy the refreshment, the rest, that he believes will be his when he can finally be with them. Toward that glad day of his delicious anticipation, Paul extends his prayer for them that the "God of. peace" will be with them, especially until he is there himself.

Chapter Sixteen

Paul's Benediction

The first sixteen verses of this final chapter of the Book of Romans contain the names of many dear saints who were loved by Paul because of their faithfulness. For the most part, their lives are of obscure note, if not altogether forgotten. However, their inclusion in this passage is significant because it testifies that each had to make a decision about his personal salvation. Second, each one is now in eternity, regardless of the length or brevity of his life here. Third, each one is still known and remembered by God, though forgotten by men, and will one day receive a reward according to his works. But with all due respect to the names listed here, it is not the intent of this study to establish the identities of those who have nothing more than their names given by Paul. I will comment on those about whom he comments, and leave further outside research to the initiative of the reader:

1 I commend unto you Phebe our sister, which is a servant of the church which is at Cenchrea:
2 That ye receive her in the Lord, as becometh saints, and that ye assist her in whatsoever business she hath need of you: forshe hath been a succourer of many, and of myself also.
3 Greet Priscilla and Aquila my helpers in Christ Jesus:
4 Who have for my life laid down their own necks: unto whom not only I give thanks, but also all the churches of the Gentiles.
5 Likewise greet the church that is in their house. Salute my well beloved Epaenetus, who is the firstfruits of Achaia unto Christ.
6 Greet Mary, who bestowed much labour on us.
7 Salute Andronicus and Junia, my kinsmen, and my Fellow prisoners, who are of note among the apostles, who also were in Christ before me.

Verse one has provided faulty fuel for some churches that have an office within their structure by the name of "deaconess." This term has no basis for being compared to the office of deacon. It more aptly should be used as a description of some noble woman, such as Phoebe, who faithfully gave herself to work in the church. Although the word, "servant," has the same root as "deacon" in the original language, we err in interpretation if we try to make Phoebe into something she was not. By a study of I Timothy 3:8-13, it is clear why this is true. The diaconate is described in masculine terms (such as "he") in these verses, and never in the feminine.

Verse two has been used often by me in the funeral services of sweet women of the Lord. Here was a woman who was a "helper." It would be interesting to know why Phoebe was coming to Rome. Perhaps because of her aid to hated men of God like Paul in the early church she was having to flee to the refuge of other saints in the same way that many had fled to her. Perhaps she had heard of the hardships of the church at Rome and felt she could be of assistance. We just do not know. What we do know is that she was a stalwart saint in Cenchrea, the harbor area along the coast from Corinth, and she served God well.

Verses three to six are a commendation of one of the most outstanding couples in the entire Word of God, Aquila and Priscilla. More about them can be found in the eighteenth chapter of Acts. In that chapter, you will find that Aquila, a Jew, had been forced to leave Italy because of the command by Claudius in 49A.D. that all Jews must leave. According to the best ancient records of the time, there were 20,000 Jews living in Rome, not counting the rest of Italy. Claudius, the emperor, had both fear and hatred for them, so he ordered them all out of the country. One historian, Suetonius, said that the royal edict resulted from the fact that many Jews were intensely loyal to "Chrestus," or Christ.

This dear couple not only provided a home for the establishment of a church, but they also laid themselves open for harsh persecution by providing protection for God's men. Too, they were well-versed in the doctrines of our faith. This is evidenced by their private tutoring of Apollos (Acts 18) who knew only about the baptism preached by John. Recognizing him to be a person of unusual oratorical and persuasive ability, they instructed him in the truth of Jesus Christ.

This Mary, in verse six, I believe was the Mary who is listed in Acts 12:12 as the mother of John, whose surname was Mark. It was at her house that a prayer meeting was being held the night that Peter was delivered from prison by an angel. How wonderful to see such noble characteristics of godliness in a woman's life during a time when society placed little value on womanhood.

Verse seven speaks of two men of God who had been saved before Paul came to know the Lord. By the use of "kinsmen," I believe Paul is identifying them as Jews, not as literal kinsmen as we ordinarily use the term in our day. Even though they had been followers of Christ for quite some time, they still were faithful in the ministry God had given them. That is the reason Paul can say that they are "fellow-prisoners" and "of note." Time had not diminished their commitment.

Verses eight to sixteen are filled with the names of obscure believers from long ago. Not much is known of them, other than the brief comments by Paul found here:
8 Greet Amplias my beloved in the Lord.
9 Salute Urbane, our helper in Christ, and Stachys my beloved.
10 Salute Apelles approved in Christ. Salute them which are of Aristobulus' household.
11 Salute Herodion my kinsman. Greet them that be of the household of Narcissus, which are in the Lord.
12 Salute Tryphena and Tryphosa, who labour in the Lord. Salute the beloved Persis, which laboured much in the Lord.
13 Salute Rufus chosen in the Lord, and his mother and mine.
14 Salute Asyncritus, Phlegon, Hermas, Patrobas, Hermes, and the brethren which are with them.
15 Salute Philologus, and Julia, Nereus, and his sister, and Olympas, and all the saints which are with them.
16 Salute one another with an holy kiss. The churches of Christ salute you.

These dear saints of God are relatively unknown today. But they are well-known before the Lord. He has not forgotten them. Somewhere in heaven, they are still "settling in" to their eternal rest. Dear reader, you may not be recognized outside the church where you worship or the place of your employment, but God knows you by name. And it is infinitely more important that He knows you.

I think that it is another mark-of Paul's personality that he was not a "name dropper." He could have easily inserted the names of "great" Christian leaders like Peter, James or John, but instead, he salutes the "little" Christians. I do not believe that it ever occurred to Paul that anyone ought to be impressed with the people he knew. Far more important was the Blessed One that everyone must know.

Our next section, verses seventeen to twenty-four, provide a final warning about those who would cause discord, as well as a few final remembrances for certain of Paul's brethren in the Lord:

17 Now I beseech you, brethren, mark them which cause divisions and offences contrary to the doctrine which ye have learned; and avoid them.
18 For they that are such serve not our Lord Jesus Christ, but their own belly; and by good words and fair speeches deceive the hearts of the simple.
19 For your obedience is come abroad unto all men. I am glad therefore on your behalf: but yet I would have you wise unto that which is good, and simple - concerning evil.
20 And the God of peace shall bruise Satan under your feet shortly. The grace of our Lord Jesus Christ be with you. Amen.
21 Timotheus my workfellow, and Lucius, and Jason, and Sosipater, my kinsmen, salute you.
22 I Tertius, who wrote this epistle, salute you in the Lord.
23 Gaius mine host, and of the whole church, saluteth you. Erastus the chamberlain of the city saluteth you, and Quartus a brother.
24 The grace of our Lord Jesus Christ be with you all. Amen.

Verse seventeen is a stern warning that should be heeded in every church. Too often, we allow disruptions within the fellowship because we lack the courage to stand against members who are undermining the ministry. Because these treacherous people have been members for years and years, and never miss a service, we somehow attribute a respect and a level of spirituality to them that they do not deserve. Service in the work of the church does not necessarily mean spiritual maturity. I have never seen a church split caused by the people who come only to the Easter services. Church splits are the products of men and women who are "there every time the doors are open," but have no love for Jesus. Instead, they have a love for the tradition or organization of "their" church. Eventually and inevitably, such people will rebel against the leadership of a pastor who is attempting to lead the people into an ever-deepening love for the person of the Lord Jesus Christ.

To some it may seem unchristlike, but Paul is saying in this verse that we are to identify such sinister members and stay away from them! They are not to be respected or honored in any way! Innumerable ministries have been destroyed by tolerance for such people of evil intent.

I was once invited by the pastor selection committee of an historic church in a major city to come and accept their pastorate. Knowing the excellent reputation of the church, I journeyed to that city and drove my automobile along the boulevard approaching the church facility. It was a magnificent edifice that I beheld — a huge, colonial structure situated upon a gently sloping and well-manicured hill.

This great church sanctuary comfortably seats 1750 people, and there was a time that it had been full with seats regularly placed in the aisles. Entering, there seemed a deadness everywhere. A custodian told me that fewer than 200 people gathered for worship on Sundays anymore.

As I later met with the committee, I heard the sad story of how vicious critics had been tolerated in their attacks upon the pastor some thirty years in the past. That man of God finally suffered a nervous breakdown and later died with a heart attack. It soon became clear that God's glory departed that place. The Lord had written "Ichabod" over their door. How sad! And all because a few vindictive members were allowed to continue their evil work against the authority of the man of God.

Verse eighteen condemns these sowers of discord as people who serve their "own belly," not Jesus Christ. They are not satisfied unless they have the positions of prominence. Whatever work in the church is done by them is done because of their hunger for ego-satisfaction. Many a pastor has learned that the ones he first thought were his most spiritually-mature members were actually his most immature.

These lieutenants of Satan are deacons, Bible teachers, and staff members. They smile and pray and witness. They sing and teach and counsel.

But when the time arises that the pastor feels led in a direction that is contrary to them, these stubborn messengers of hell begin their behind-the-scenes attacks of slander, innuendoes, and lies. They will visit the homes of the simple or call them by telephone. Because these blasphemers of good have been so active in the church, their words and accusations have a ring of genuine sincerity. The gullible are bewitched, and before the pastor knows that anything is happening, an outright war is on his hands. Paul says that these people must not be allowed the privilege of continuing in the church. They are to be refuted. They are to be ostracized. They must be plainly expelled from the fellowship.

Verse nineteen provides the Roman believer with both a compliment and a wise counsel. Paul brags on their widespread reputation for being submissive. We must remember that a believer in Rome was forced to live in constant anxiety about the physical well-being of his family and of himself. To be obedient in such uncertain circumstances was certainly commendable.

But he urges them to a higher dimension of spiritual awareness. The word, "simple," as used in this verse, means "unmixed." Paul desires that they be unmixed with those things that are morally bad. This is familiar advice from the lips of the Apostle. For example, he says in Philippians 2:15-16: "That ye may be blameless and harmless, the sons of God, without rebuke, in the midst of a crooked and perverse nation, among whom ye shine as lights in the world; Holding forth the word of life; that I may rejoice in the day of Christ, that I have not run in vain, neither laboured in vain."

Verse twenty is such a blessed comfort! We have not "a" God of peace; we have "the" God of peace! In other words, our position of sublime rest is beyond the powers of this world to shake. Our Lord is always near in the most turbulent of times to give us all that we need in Christ Jesus.

The fact that Paul exclaims that God will soon "bruise Satan" is conclusive evidence that he believed that the opening chapters of the Book of Genesis are to be believed and received by the reader as literal truth. His statement here hearkens back to the first prophecy in the Bible concerning the Messiah (Jesus Christ) which is found in Genesis 3:15: "And I will put enmity between thee and the woman, and between thy seed and her seed; it shall bruise thy head, and thou shalt bruise his heel." This bruising of Satan's head was realized at Calvary. Paul's promise in Romans 16:20 that the God of peace "shall bruise Satan under your feet shortly "simply means that the full victory over Satan's menacing presence, as well as his awful power, will soon be complete because of our removal from the world at the rapture.

Verse twenty-one is a recognition of Timothy's steadfastness in standing near his father in the ministry during a time of personal danger. The same is suggested of Lucius, Jason, and Sosipater. As kinsmen of Paul, they could easily have come under the same sentence of death, but still remained with him.

Verse twenty-two provides an interesting bit of Bible trivia. It was not actually Paul who authored Romans. It was Tertius, probably because of Paul's poor eyesight.

Verse twenty-three mentions three other believers. Apparently, they are men of prominence who accepted Christ through the witness of Paul. In I Corinthians 1:14, Paul speaks of baptizing a man by the name of Gaius. Most students of the Bible believe that he is the same as the one listed here. There is an Erastus in Acts 19:22. He is probably the same man as found in II Timothy 4:20 and the same also here.

We now have arrived at the final section of verses in this remarkable book:
25 Now to him that is of power to stablish you according to my gospel, and the preaching of Jesus Christ, according to the revelation of the mystery, which was kept secret since the world began,
26 But now is made manifest, and by the scriptures of the prophets, according to the commandment of the everlasting God, made known to all nations for the obedience of faith:
27 To God only wise, be glory through Jesus Christ for ever. Amen.

Verse twenty-five says that there is a person who has power to establish the believer according
to the gospel. Who is that person? It must be the Holy Spirit who lives within us.

There is no other way that an individual can rightly discern the Scriptures than by His wondrous aid. This work of the Spirit of God is just as important and just as powerful todayas it ever was. His work is continual in bringing the gospel to greater light in the life of the saint. Indeed, this verse summarizes Paul's theme for the entire book. It is to make the believer secure in the faith; that is, to establish or "set" him so that the cunning ways of Satan will not entice him away.

What is the mystery that has been revealed in this book? It is the mystery of how God seemed to choose the Jews to the exclusion of the Gentiles while, in actuality, He was using the Jews to include the Gentiles. The gospel of Jesus Christ was a shadowy thing to the Old Testament Jew, although the prophets tried hard to describe it to Israel. Its full revelation exploded upon them on the day of Pentecost and continues until this very day.

Verse twenty-six confirms that to be so. God has commanded that the gospel of salvation be taken to the whole world. Not by the sacrifice of an animal are we saved.

We are saved by the "obedience of faith." This is the only way of salvation, universally applicable to every individual in "all nations."

Verse twenty-seven glorifies Jesus Christ who is the object of Paul s adoration. We must give glory to Him, and to Him alone.

Our study has come to its conclusion, but I must advise you that the truths of this book by Paul are unfathomable. No one commentator can fairly and fully deal with this epistle. I will consider it a compliment if you use my feeble efforts as an elementary spring-board to a deeper study of Romans. If you do so, you will find as I have found, that Jesus IS wonderful!

HAROLD F. HUNTER

www.ingramcontent.com/pod-product-compliance
Lightning Source LLC
Chambersburg PA
CBHW050859160426
43194CB00011B/2216